A Cinema Near You

EAST
MIDLANDS
ARTS

ASHLEY FRANKLIN

A Cinema Near You

100 years of going to the Pictures in Derbyshire

The Breedon Books
Publishing Company
Derby

First published in Great Britain by
The Breedon Books Publishing Company Limited
Breedon House, 44 Friar Gate, Derby, DE1 1DA.
1996

In memory of my father
David Malcolm Franklin
(1929-1995)
who took me to see *Ben Hur* as a ninth birthday treat
(great chariot race, Dad!)

with a special dedication to
my uncle, Derek Hughes, who first took me to the pictures

and to
Lorraine Atkin, my first cinema 'date'

Fade In …

For a few pennies you could feel like royalty.
There weren't even the costs of transport...
there was always a cinema near you.

Adrian Skollin, Heanor resident.

ISBN 1 85983 057 9

Printed and bound by Butler & Tanner Ltd, Selwood Printing Works, Caxton Road, Frome, Somerset.

Colour separations by Colour Services, Wigston, Leicester.

Jackets printed by Lawrence-Allen, Weston-super-Mare, Avon.

Contents

Foreword

by Rod Woodruff

IT WAS 1967, and I was nine, when I first stepped into my Cinema Paradise... the Alvaston Rex, two streets from my Nanny's. We were king of the world at football, and though I never understood why my brother and Dad cried and Alf Ramsey seemed so sad, there he was on the giant screen before me, his wispy hair dancing back. I was always Bobby Charlton.

Two more visits spring to mind: *Zulu*, a colour and fight that ran riot with my imagination – and the first time with my mates. I remember something of those strange, local 1970s ads, and a torch that told us to keep quiet. But I remember everything of *The Battle of Britain*: the baddie Germans, and the one landing in the corn field surrounded by Home Guard – "Good afternoon my bloody arse!" – and a pitchfork that made us laugh. Spectacle and colour and dog-fights in early stereo. I'd sit as the audience all left, wondering at that enormous list of names and what they all did.

Something was born here long ago, before I knew my mother was an usherette and my uncle the projectionist. A couple of bob, whatever it was, a strange subconscious investment for the future by my dad.

Thirty years on I return to the UCI, a modern multi-complex of new age cinema. A dichotomy of emotions: this place seemed so abstract, so alien and yet I felt as if I had come home. The Premiere played. An audience laughed and cried where I'd once had blank paper. I left the auditorium, my credit for the birds. I had another picture to make.

A Cinema Near You has revived and evoked further compassionate memory for me. A frame burning up, an angry audience; turning from the front seat to see where the magic came from; the first stereo sound; the light; the colour; the stories; the characters; the journey into emotions; the magic, the magic, the magic.

This is Ashley's book. A book that breaks new ground in its informative nature as it cleverly orchestrates an education through the entertainment (an aspiration found difficult by many film makers of today).

A Cinema Near You is more than a slice of the social history of cinema in Derbyshire. Its highly humorous, anecdotal format gives the book a greater sense of travel than even its writer is probably aware. It holds a particular poignancy, of intrigue and memory lanes for its Derbyshire readers, and also a cinema paradise all of its own. A book that everyone and anyone who is captivated by the art format of cinematography can enjoy.

There is also a wonderful sense of struggle in the historic creativity of these picture houses and the individuals that made them happen. Nothing of any worth comes without real struggle, real commitment and a love for one's subject matter in the creation of art – the latter, a clear prerequisite of the writer. Like all the great movies we flick to record as classics; an emotion, a line, a scene, a flicker of light, a memorable tracking shot; we want to share with the dream makers a small piece of what Ashley Franklin has now added... a piece of magic.

Rod Woodruff was born at Alvaston in 1958 and has worked as a film and TV stunt co-ordinator since 1986. His film work includes *Robin Hood – Prince of Thieves*, *Patriot Games* and *Indiana Jones & The Temple of Doom*.
His first film as a screenwriter was *Clockwork Mice*, which received its Midlands Premiere at the Derby UCI in 1995 and his next film (as both director and writer), *Kathy's Lion*, is scheduled for release in 1997.

The First Time
My Uncle Derek started me off on all this...

1958: Derek Hughes of Cwmbran, South Wales, married but still awaiting his first child, decided it was time for his niece and nephew to taste the same thrill that he had experienced in his 1930s youth: a visit to the local picture palace.

His niece, Lynette Franklin, was four. Nephew Ashley was only three. Their mother, Vera, was only too glad to be relieved of her toilsome maternal duties for a few hours on a Saturday morning.

Uncle Derek adored us. He loved children. He should have had nine kids, at least. Only a few weeks after we started going to the weekly Pictures, he did have nine kids... every Saturday morning. Once word got out that Uncle Derek was taking Lynette and me to the cinema, the whole neighbourhood wanted to go. He remembers taking my best friend Steven Osborne (who, as far as we knew, was the only black kid to ever come and live in Monmouthshire), then Mr and Mrs Griffiths asked if their Sharon could come, and THEY must have told Mr and Mrs Burdette, because soon after that, their Kerry and Gary were in the party. Three other children were to join us, but they must have been very quiet and undemonstrative, because we can't remember who they were.

Uncle Derek didn't just have a car; he had a great stonking Vauxhall Wyvern. It was described as 'roomy', and it wasn't the biggest Vauxhall you could buy, but when you were only four years old, it was a stretch limousine. It was a funny grass-green colour, and was swathed in chrome.

Such was the treat of a car ride for a youngster in the 1950s that even before we reached Cwmbran village, we had had the time of our lives. We insisted on being driven three times around the local roundabout. Dizzy but exhilarated, we eventually reached the picture house.

The Olympia was run by the Davies brothers. A common sight in Cwmbran was the day's takings draped over the handlebars of their bikes as they cycled to the bank. Nobody could understand why they didn't own a Vauxhall Wyvern each, because it was reckoned the Davies brothers did very nicely out of running the local picture house.

They were certainly glad of Uncle Derek's custom, although the normal shilling charge for the red plush tip-up seats was reduced to tuppence for the children's matinee, and it was only a penny if you could put up with the neck-stiffening discomfort of the front bench seats.

As soon as the nine of us poured out of Uncle Derek's car, we ran to the back of the queue, which sometimes stretched all the way back to Mrs Tremeer's fish and chip shop. If we got there early, there was a twin gate in front of the cinema entrance that we used to clamber on to. Great fun, but never a good idea, as one of the Davies' brothers would suddenly appear from nowhere and thrust open the gate while we kiddies were still attached to it like limpets to a rock. Herds of less-deserving children would then throng into the picture house to grab the best seats while we were still extricating ourselves from the gate frame.

The Cwmbran Olympia was a dingy, undistinguished one-floor 'picture palace', with a steep rake. I am assuming it was steep: Uncle Derek tells me that because the outside toilet was considered dark and unseemly (and a visit there also meant missing sacred seconds of screen action), some badly brought-up children would relieve themselves in their respective rows, knowing that their outpourings would run all the way down to the front benches. Naturally, Uncle Derek's charges would never contemplate performing such a disgusting act: before we came in, he made us tinkle on the wall outside.

I have a vague memory of a great deal of noise. Uncle Derek vividly remembers a cacophony of bawling, shouting and stamping of feet, with a particularly vociferous cheer invariably reserved for the sight of the sheriff in the ever-present western.

There was much booing, too... the film used to snap on a regular basis, and was always greeted with a chorus of catcalls and a shower of objects aimed at the screen.

Children don't vocalise at Saturday morning matinées to anything like the extent we did. It's not that today's children are better behaved; it was the fact that the cinema (even in the late 1950s) was a much more exciting new experience. Children today grow up with a moving screen in their sitting room (and some have a TV set in their own bedroom). As media guru Marshall McLuhan was to reveal to me at college, television is a 'cool' medium that 'does not excite, agitate or arouse'.

On the other hand, the cinema provides a hot 'high definition' medium. And, still largely untouched by TV, we children were confronted with a genuinely novel, electrifying medium. But by the time contemporary children are taken to the cinema for the first time, the sensation of the communal big screen experience has been dulled by exposure to TV. I don't wish to get into a heavy, heated debate here about the effects of television on our young; I just wanted to explain why we were so rowdy.

If I can't recall yelling my delight at the sight of the sheriff (and I must have because I do remember being him in the playground every break-time, and never a baddie or Red Indian) I can certainly visualise the lithe, lanky figure of Tarzan swinging with acrobatic grace through a tangled tree-thick jungle. Uncle Derek tells me this was Johnny Weissmuller. His famous holler still rings in some inner recess of my brain.

I can also remember a special excitement being reserved for Popeye. Every child's fear of the bogeyman was even more pronounced for me, because I knew what he looked like – he was Bluto, my hero's arch adversary. Although Popeye pops up on TV today, the one we saw at the matinées was from the Max Fleischer shorts that Leslie Halliwell remembers for having more 'vulgar panache' than the made-for-tele-

vision cartoons. I vividly recall asking my mum to buy me some spinach. Popeye grew strong on it, and it just had to taste good. I hated it. It was one of my life's earliest disappointments.

As well as Popeye and Tarzan, we were treated to Roy Rogers, The Lone Ranger, Flash Gordon, Mickey Mouse, and Laurel and Hardy. My Mum claims I would have had a particularly exciting morning if I'd seen Old Mother Riley. I must have been a strange boy.

As for Uncle Derek, he simply enjoyed seeing us relive his own excitement as a child of the cinema. A good job, too, because he was always out of pocket after he'd unloaded the car. All of our parents paid for the admission, with a little extra for ice-cream and sweets, but that little extra was never enough. Half the time he spent more than he needed to, because he could never fully memorise the garbled requests of nine excitable children, so Steven or Sharon would end up with lollipops, which were dearer than the ice-cream wafers they had ordered in the first place.

This Saturday morning treat lasted until 1961, when we moved to the East Midlands. Not long after, Uncle Derek was confronted by one of the Davies brothers in a local pub. He was clearly agitated.

"Derek, what did we do to upset you?"

"What do you mean?"

"You stopped bringing all those children to our cinema. Did we do something wrong?"

Uncle Derek explained. One caring cinema proprietor was mightily relieved that day.

Davies 'the Pictures' kept the Cwmbran Olympia open until the late 1960s. It's now boarded up. So at least it hasn't suffered the fate of so many old cinemas, namely demolition. Uncle Derek says he'll take me to see it next time I come down. I'll make sure it's on a Saturday morning, too. Maybe Steven Osborne is still around, and can come as well. Mind you, where are we going to get a grass-green Vauxhall Wyvern from?

Ashley Franklin
Derby
June 1996

Acknowledgements

My very special thanks go out, above all, to Sam Winfield, David Roddis, Duncan Cross, Graham Nutt and Colin Wardle who helped me so much with information, photographs and such boundless enthusiasm!

My wife Francine, the world's nicest and finest librarian, obtained all manner of books and articles to aid my research, and constantly encouraged me. My daughters Claire and Helena have been an inspiration, just for being there.

I'd like to thank my Mum for letting Uncle Derek take me to the pictures, and to my Auntie Audrey for marrying him.

Warm thanks to Rod Woodruff for his kind words. I am still blushing!

Thanks are also due to Jan Beardsley for her irrepressible encouragement (and flattery!) when I wondered if I would ever see this through!

Thanks to friends and colleagues on the Guild of Regional Film Writers, particularly Hilary Oliver, Ian Barclay and Romilly Paradine.

Thanks to Jon Osborn and Julia Peck for their outstanding photographic print work.

The following people gave me a particular lift with their wonderful reminiscences: John Avery, Len Brown, Eddie Burnham, Peter Dakin, Peter Davies, Bill Doyle, David Harrison, Dennis Howells, James Fryer, Marjorie Severn, Alec Turner, Patricia Turner, Len Waller.

Other people helped me with valuable information, assistance and guidance: the Staff of Libraries at Alfreton, Ashbourne, Derby Local Studies, Heanor, Ilkeston, Matlock, Ripley and Swadlincote; my photography team of Bill Attenborough, Dave Barraclough, Alan Booth, Peter Cheetham, Gill Dishart, Peter Dishart, Marshall Grey, Terry Hawkesworth, Geoff Hood, Jon Osborn, Julia Peck, Bob Pickering, Andy Wilson; and Wendy Ashworth, Belper Conservative Club, Tony Bowler and the *Derby Express*, John Bowman, Jackie Brumwell, *Derby Evening Telegraph*, Des Caffrey, Roy Christian, Maxwell Craven, Geoffrey Dearle, Con Docherty, Carol Frost of the *Ashbourne News Telegraph*, Anne Guisti of National Amusements, Peter Good, Don Hale of the *Matlock Mercury*, Caroline Haywood of the British Film Institute Stills Library, Doug Hodges, Brian Hornsey, Jeff Humphries of the *Derby Trader*, John Lilley of the Local Studies Library at Chesterfield, Paul Mackenzie, Cyril Maskery, Caroline Pick of East Midlands Arts, Anton Rippon, John Shaw, Paul Southall, Cyril Sprenger, Sue Spurrier, Mervyn Stockbridge-Gould of the Mercia Cinema Society, John Taylor, Kenneth Roy Taylor, Joe and Hazel Vowles, Rick Wakeman, Phil Walkley of Cinema 100, Hilda Webb, Tony Whitehead of the Derby Metro, Mark Whitty and the staff at the Derby UCI, Jennie Wilcox, Jo Wingate of the Derby Metro, Maurice Woodcock.

Thanks to all the other people who provided reminiscences, information and photographs. Some illustrations are reproduced by kind permission of Sound Associates, London.

The author gratefully acknowledges the financial assistance of East Midlands Arts.

Things To Come

I consider that the greatest mission of the motion picture is first to make people happy... to bring more joy and cheer and the wholesome good will into this world of ours. And God knows we need it.

Thomas A.Edison

"THE greatest sensation and invention ever placed before an audience."

This was how moving pictures were described when they first came to Derbyshire in 1896, although as we moved into this century, still only a portion of the population had experienced the projection of animated photographs on to a screen. Ask a Belper millworker or Melbourne market gardener of the time to describe a 'penny gaff' or 'bioscope', and you would more than likely be met with a perplexed gaze.

In 1896, the word 'cinema' meant next to nothing. Derbyshire's first purpose-built cinema didn't appear until 1910. Yet by 1916, annual attendances at the nation's picture houses had topped 350 million. It is estimated that some 3,000 British cinemas were built in the next ten years. By 1940, Derby itself had 17 'dream palaces' (11 of them with a seating capacity of over 1,000), with over 60 cinemas in the rest of the county. Annual cinema attendances in Britain had begun to top one billion.

Before we were midway through the century, cinemas were to be found everywhere across the world, from Durban to Derby, Crich to Christchurch and from Rio to Riddings.

After that, it is well known that the cinema suffered a sad, demoralising decline in the face of competition from TV. No other entertainment this century has experienced so rapid a rise and so steep a fall.

Yet British cinemas began 1996 by celebrating the highest-grossing weekend in its box office history, with customers paying a record £7,240,821. These takings have stunned an industry which had become used to a quiet January, with the added significance of the previous record being set in July 1993 when *Jurassic Park* opened nationwide.

Britain's largest cinema chain, UCI, saw takings improve a staggering 73 per cent on the same period the year before. According to Steve Knibbs, UCI managing director: "These record-breaking figures show that the British public still holds cinema close to its heart."

In the context of cinema's 100-year history, this is a somewhat fanciful statement. Have you noticed how convenient it has been for the industry to publish box office figures ever since admissions began to dip but admission prices soar? Let's look at actual 'bums on seats': a pie chart made-up of five-yearly blocks of cinema attendances this century would reveal a giant slice for both halves of the 1940s, a generous helping for the late 1930s and early 1950s, but only a sliver for the first half of the 1990s. In fact, in the cinema-going peak of 1946 (annual admissions totalled 1,650 million), it was estimated that 73 per cent of the population were cinemagoers, with nearly half of them going once a week or more.

However, we must be fair to Steve Knibbs of the UCI. For him, the cinema is booming. Furthermore, his lifetime has been one of a cinema in the doldrums rising to reclaim a position closer to our hearts.

Had this not been the case, I doubt whether I would have been galvanised into writing this book. At the end of 1988, Derby became the first city in the UK to house two multiplex cinemas. A year later, it was revealed that more than a million people had come back to the Pictures in Derby. Through my urging, BBC Radio Derby recognised the need to respond to this resurgence: I introduced an arts show, *Sound and Vision*, on BBC Radio Derby – a direct consequence of this astonishing cinema revival.

My increasing involvement in the local movie scene inexorably led to the feeling that I ought to reflect cinema's centenary in this area, with a radio documentary series. The invitation by Jeff Humphries, editor of the *Derby Trader*, to write a fortnightly cinema column was a decided incentive in writing a book to accompany the Radio Derby series. A further incentive was the formation of the organisation Cinema 100, with thanks to Phil Walkley, in particular, for his enthusiasm at regional meetings. My membership of the Guild of Regional Film Writers has also helped instil in me the belief that I could be a respected and effective voice out in 'the sticks'.

This book spans the rich, rapid progress of cinema from the 'penny gaffs' of the turn of the 1900s, the

Beatrice Guest (93), a former cashier at the Alexandra and now Derby's oldest surviving former cinema employee, pictured with Wyn Barker (84), the oldest surviving former employee of the Picture House (formerly the Midland Electric Theatre) at the unveiling of a Cinema 100 plaque at the site of Derby's first purpose-built cinema in Babington Lane.

'tuppeny rushes' of the silent screen era, to the picture palaces of the 1930s and 1940s through to the multi-cinema complexes of the 1990s. More specifically, *A Cinema Near You* charts a social history that, considering its considerable impact on our lives, has been ill-served by publications in the past. Audrey Field's *Picture Palace* documented the social history of British cinema in general up to the 1960s, albeit in a somewhat lofty, stilted style; Leslie Halliwell wrote an entertainingly nostalgic account of his upbringing as a picture-goer in Bolton in *Seats In All Parts*; and recently the Museum of The Moving Image provided the impetus for a collection of South London cinema memories from the 1920s to the 1960s entitled *Enter The Dreamhouse*.

Locally, there have been three worthy books about

cinema. The first to appear, in 1992, was *Tuppeny Rush* by Graham Nutt, subtitled *The Arrival of Cinemas and Film-Making in Swadlincote*, which fascinatingly reveals the 'pioneers of cinema' in the area, including Messrs Raynor, Bridgewater and Lawrence who made their own silent films for showing in the town's picture houses. A year later came *The Thrill Of It All – The Story of the Cinema in Ilkeston and the Erewash Valley* by David Roddis, a labour of love by a genuine cinema enthusiast. A similar publication in 1995 at last provided a paean to the picture houses of Derby – *Dream Palaces of Derby* by Sam Winfield. All three books exhibit extensive research and are heavily laden with information, with the latter two lavishing particular attention on the facts and figures surrounding the cinema buildings themselves.

This book is less concerned with facts and figures, more interested in the actual experience of cinema, from the point of view of those people who both frequented their local picture palace, and worked as a part of it. Although the aforementioned books include interesting reminiscences, I have tried to reach further to not only include a wider wealth of personal recollections but also place them in a more complete historical context. I have also had the advantage of widening my area of research to the whole county, which has enabled me to make appeals in most Derbyshire newspapers, not forgetting the considerable benefit the local broadcasting medium has offered me.

Whilst seeking out reminiscences countywide, I have discovered not only that few lives have remained untouched by the cinema but also that most people carry a fond memory of their picture-going experience. Some lives have variously been affected, influenced, or briefly but memorably lit up by the cinema. A few lives have been more than lit up by the cinema: they've been positively led by it. When Duncan Cross wasn't projecting films at work, he was going out – to the Pictures. To be a weekly visitor to a multiplex is a proud achievement, but less noteworthy in comparison to the cinema-going of the 1940s, when four visits in one week was not uncommon.

I have sat and listened to innumerable local folk steeped in fond reminiscence. Many people's recollections have been accompanied by the comment: 'They don't make 'em like they used to', or 'It's not as good as it was in my day'. However, I am not aiming to set one generation against another as to which enjoyed the 'better' cinema era. This book is intended as a celebration of cinema, whatever the period in history.

In mining this rich seam of memory, I have had my

sense of history enlightened. Frankly, I used to be someone who almost shared Henry Ford's denouncement that 'history is bunk'. What use does history serve? It deals in the past, and that was that. But now, a year or so on from my delvings into the area's bounteous cinema past, history has served me with a mixture of appreciation and envy. I am not only deeply appreciative of the sense of occasion, thrill and wonder that distinguished a cinema visit, but also highly envious of the fact that I never shared in it. My early cinema-going days were in picture houses that had long gone to seed and were on a crash course with Mr Sledgehammer.

Nowadays, of course, I am privileged to have the plush multiplexes, with perfect picture clarity and state-of-the-art sound. I also personally prefer the sophisticated production values and more heightened realism of today's films. But however vociferously my generation may applaud multiplex mod cons, this particular generation member will harbour a dream unfulfilled. I sat many times in a still beautifully-appointed Derby Gaumont auditorium in its final days as a Cannon concern. But how much more enhanced the enchantment would have been for families of domestically-modest means in the 1930s and 1940s, to taste the tingling thrill of thronging into a floodlit, pristine picture palace like the Gaumont, whose marble steps, walnut walls, decorative ceiling and chandelier-like lights brought an immediate and sumptuous escape from an austere, rationed world. Not only that, one could then settle back in a double-seat embrace whilst an illuminated organ rose from the floor, before the plush, tasselled curtains drew back and drifted you and over 2,000 others into a dream-filled world.

Although the Derby Gaumont still stands in some splendour (with the news that the Derby Metro is seriously looking at taking over the site, and that a recently-formed group called Trocadero Project 2000 is aiming for a complete restoration of the building), virtually all the other cinemas that were built in this county have vanished. Out of over 80 picture houses that came into being up to 1940, only three remain in business – the Ilkeston Scala, Screen Long Eaton and Matlock Ritz. Equally as tragic, only a handful of the original sites remain. Handsome cinemas like the Derby Cavendish, Coliseum and Alexandra, the Chaddesden Majestic, Alfreton Odeon and Ilkeston Kings have been bulldozed out of sight. The tragedy is that most of these cinemas closed at a time when little heed was paid to phrases like 'historical preservation'. If these cinemas had hung on into the late 1960s, they might have been saved from defacement or demolition. The more enlightened view we now take of protecting historical landmarks came too late to rescue our cinema heritage. Consider, for example, Derbyshire's first purpose-built cinema – the Derby Midland Electric Theatre – which became well known and well loved as the Picture House. Not one trace remains of it. In what was once a palace that sold dreams is now a store that sells sofas.

At least there is now a permanent reminder of that cinema in the form of a commemorative Cinema 100 plaque which I successfully applied for. For middle-aged and elderly passers-by, it will at least refresh a few memories. Here is a book that will revive some more memories and hopefully inform and entertain those who missed out on the days when cinema-going was the great social habit. Contained within these pages are numerous mementos of sights, sounds, sensations and stories connected with the cinema. Many are amusing, amazing, profound or poignant. They range from the convivial to the dramatic, the trivial to the tragic.

Lord Attenborough declared cinema to be 'the art form of the century'. *A Cinema Near You* should also show that it has been the most well loved.

Empire Of The Senses
Mr Morritt comes to Derby

'The reproduction of scenes in motion as in every day life is really a startling scientific achievement and it has proved quite a sensational 'turn' at the Empire'
extract from the *Derby Express*, 22 September 1896

THERE is a perfect irony in the fact that when Charles Morritt first came to Derby, in 1895, he put someone in a trance. He was a hypnotist. Less than a year later, when he opened Morritt's Empire, it was probable that several hundred people entered a dream-like state, but Charlie didn't need to flex his mind and fix his eye. All he had to do this time was crank up a machine.

Derbyshire's cinema history began on the evening of Monday, 21 September 1896. In Britain, it began earlier that year, in London (nothing has changed in one hundred years). As he was evidently a busy variety theatre turn, it's unlikely that Londoner Charles Morritt would have had the time or intellectual inclination to attend the inaugural showing of something known as the Cinematograph at the Royal Polytechnic Institute on 20 February, presented by the patent owners Louis and Auguste Lumière.

The French brothers had presented the same public show in Paris on 28 December 1895. That day, down in a dingy basement of the Grand Café sat a small cloth screen in front of 33 people, who had paid one franc. It was reckoned that no one from the press had bothered to turn up. The audience itself knew little or nothing of what was to come. Perhaps some people were anticipating visual trickery of the kind presented by professional conjuror and magician Georges Méliès, as he was there amongst them, on a special invitation.

Méliès is credited in cinema's history as the first person to create 'trick films' incorporating dissolves and double exposures (he created that memorable image of a rocket lodged in the eye of a tear-stricken moon). It is likely he decided to devote his life to the medium after witnessing the following 20-minute programme. Nothing unusual occurred at first: on to the screen was projected an image of a Lyons square, which seemed to be alive with people, horses and carriages. Within a few seconds, the audience saw it really was alive, as a horse was seen pulling a cart towards them.

After ten short films of this astounding 'moving' experience, those 33 audience members became very animated themselves. Some fled their seats in fright at the sight of a train seemingly set to spill out into the room. The early spectators at these shows must have spread the word like wildfire. Audiences swelled to 2,000. Cinema was born.

Some cinema historians still argue over the birth. Ever since the 17th century, luminous images had been projected by the magic lantern. By the 1830s, a succession of separate images could give the impression of motion. The science of optics, spurred on by the public's fascination for illusionary effects produced, arguably, the first forerunner of the cinema: the Diorama (a refinement of the 18th-century Panorama). The Diorama presented large paintings and pictorial views combined with changing scenic and optical effects produced by magic lanterns and translucent colours (the invention of another Frenchman, Louis Daguerre). As Roy Christian points out in the book *Yesterday's Town: Derby*, there is a record of a Diorama presentation of The Holy Land in the city's Lecture Hall on the Wardwick in 1862. There were probably several other presentations in town and county around this period.

In the 1870s, the development of photographic cameras led to all kinds of inventions with intimidating names – the Praxinoscope, Thaumotrope, Phototachygraph – all merging movement with pictures. Many Derbyshire youngsters from well-off families would have had a Zoetrope. Produced as a toy, the Zoetrope allowed a child to observe moving figures through the slits of a small revolving drum.

British photographer Eadweard J.Muybridge made a notable breakthrough in 1877 when he photographed a running horse using 24 timed cameras attached to a trip wire. This experiment was reportedly instigated by the settling of a bet as to whether a champion horse ever had all four feet off the ground at once (it turned out it did).

At the same time, a French physicist Etienne

MORRIT'S EMPIRE, DERBY.—MONDAY, SEPT. 21st ANE
EVERY EVENING.
SPECIAL NOTICE.—The Greatest Sensation and Inven
tion ever placed before an audience.—Mr. CHARLES
MORRIT'S latest and greatest novelty, THE LIFEOGRAPH
Moving Photographs of the following : Sandow, Grantham Rail
way Station, the Derby Fair Ground, Ladies and Gentlemen
Bathing, the Electric Tramway, American Piccanni Dancer, Derby
School with Children, Grand Theatre, Leeds, Tower, Blackpool
SISTERS GUEST and Grand Star Company.
Time and Prices as Usual.   48

Newspaper advertisement for 'moving photographs' at Morritt's Empire in Derby.

Marey developed a single gun-shaped camera to study the movement of birds in flight. The time when an assembled public could view moving pictures was not far off, and was hastened in the 1880s when George Eastman manufactured the celluloid roll film – the penultimate piece in the cinema jigsaw.

In 1891, the great American inventor Thomas Alva Edison introduced the 'peep-show' or Kinetoscope, described as 'the seed box of the motion picture'. Three years elapsed before an audience crowded into the first peep-show parlour and stared through a hole in an upright wooden box to view (via a magnifying lens) a continuous reel of film, no more than 50ft in length.

Edison's invention (actually attributed more to his assistant Dickson) soon attracted excited interest across the world. The peep shows crossed the Atlantic, and were first viewed in a Kinetoscope parlour in 70 Oxford Street, London (although the building has gone, a video store appropriately occupies the site).

Various attempts were made to turn the peep-show machine into a piece of projection apparatus. The Lumière brothers' father Antoine, a maker of photographic equipment, saw the Edison Kinetoscope in Paris. Naturally, he was to alert his sons. In London, inventor Robert Paul threw himself into experiments and successfully projected animated pictures in his Hatton Garden studio. If only he had invited an audience, he might have become as famous as the Lumières.

The fame, credit and kudos accorded to the Lumière brothers are attributable to the simple fact that Louis and Auguste not only provided a practical solution to the problem of projecting moving pictures, but also were the first to project publicly. However, both Auguste and Louis failed to attend the ground-breaking first show in Paris. In fact, their father deserves further credit for his sons' place in history, as he was the one who secured the Grand Café basement room, hired the chairs, and personally greeted the audience. What is even more ironic is that Antoine was sceptical about the future of the Cinematograph. He foresaw a restricted commercial

appeal. By all accounts, so did his sons. Auguste believed the Cinematograph could be 'exploited for a certain time as a scientific curiosity', while Louis was said to have told his colleague Méliès that the cinema was 'an invention with no future'. He definitely described it as 'a peddlar's trade'.

The showmen were the first cinema peddlars. The Cinematograph undoubtedly lit up the entrepreneurial eyes of showman Charles Morritt, as he was to show this new sensation to Derbyshire eyes just over six months after the Lumière's London show.

The first locally-recorded reference to Charles Morritt appears in the pages of the *Derby Express* on 18 November 1895. An advertisement in the Amusements column proclaimed the appearance at the Corn Exchange, Albert Street, on 25 November of 'the long-looked-for Charles Morritt who will put a man in a Trance for Six Days and Nights'.

Just prior to his Derby debut, the wording in the paper was even more acclamatory:

The Sensation of the World!
Special Engagement at an Enormous Cost of the World Renowned
and only Morritt, from the Royal Aquarium and Empire, London.

Later we read that Morritt 'once put a man in a trance for ten days. He was visited by no less than 500 doctors – they were perfectly satisfied that the man was unconscious during the whole of that time'. Charles Morritt was also credited with a performance of 'sleight-of-hand tricks'.

As the papers of the time were staid, formal news sheets, there is only one brief, unexcitable review, again in the *Derby Express*, given to Morritt's hypnotic act. It would have been fascinating for any Express reader to have read a revealing profile of this remarkable showman, because less than a month later the *Derby Express* carried a 'Special Notice' that the Empire, Derby (almost certainly the Corn Exchange) was to be opened by 'Morritt, The Renowned Wonder Worker' on Monday, 23 December, 'and will run as a first class Variety Theatre on entirely new lines. London artistes only are engaged and will appear week after week in rapid succession.'

Oddly, no further mention is made of this new entertainment spectacle, not even in advertisement form in the week of its supposed opening. Either Charles Morritt then relied on publicity through street handouts or else failed to secure the promised first-class artistes, and dropped the idea. It certainly appears that Morritt was away from Derby in the first half of 1896, because the first mention of his Empire

How the Derby Express reported the arrival of the sensational Lifeograph at Morritt's Empire.

THE EMPIRE.

Mr. Morritt has brought a remarkably strong company to the Empire this week, and on Monday and Tuesday evenings there were, as was expected, crowded houses. The principal attraction is undoubtedly the Lifeograph, which consists of the projection of a number of animated photographs on to a screen. This performance, which has created a furore in London, is a perfect novel sight in Derby, and as such is bound to attract attention. The re-production of scenes in motion as in every day life is really a startling scientific achievement, and it has proved quite a sensational "turn" at the Empire. Among the scenes reproduced are Sandow giving his renowned entertainment; Carmencita, the skirt dancer; a railway station, with porters and passengers, and train moving in and out; an electric train in motion; re-production of Derby Fair, &c., &c. A number of interesting "turns" are also given by a very strong company, chief among which may be mentioned the Sisters Guest, dashing duettists, who quite take the audience by storm. Clarke and Argyle, the "national dancers," have been seen before in Derby, and the excellency of their performance is well known; whilst the other artistes engaged—Godfrey West, character comedian, Miss Amy Victor, male impersonator, Miss Gertie Corrie, burlesque actress and dancer, and Miss Lily Iris, skirt dancer—are not lacking in ability. The company is, in fact, one of the strongest that has ever visited Derby, and it is to be hoped that the public will show their appreciation of the excellent bill of fare arranged for them.

shows that year didn't appear until 7 September, and this was not a variety theatre show, but a boxing match, starring Peter Jackson, 'Champion Boxer of the World'.

So, one can only speculate on Charles Morritt's supposed sudden withdrawal from Derby and his reappearance nine months later. What is certain is that during the first half of 1896 he was exposed to moving pictures.

It is likely that Morritt eventually saw a demonstration of moving pictures himself (Robert Paul's Animatograph was soon set up in the Empire Music Hall, Leicester Square, with a further show in the Square at the Alhambra) and that he encountered a fresh, novel entertainment medium he could exploit.

Would Derby audiences respond accordingly? Charles Morritt's absorption in the variety theatre world told him they would. The Corn Exchange, for instance, had a music hall tradition dating back to the 1870s. Furthermore, there was little else to do of an evening. A glance at the newspapers would have confirmed scant interest for the working man.

The *Derby Express*, on that momentous opening day for Morritt, contained a public notice of a lecture by the Reverend D.McDonald on Armenia, 'with Limelight Illustrations' (a magic lantern show), a dancing class at the Assembly Rooms, local tuition on 'banjo, mandolin, violi, piano and voice production', plus a report on the annual dinner of the Loyal True Benevolent Lodge of the Improved Independent Order of Oddfellows, not forgetting the annual gathering of the Primrose League.

It was even duller out in the county. According to the *Derby Express* District Notes And News, 'Belper is in a dead calm... everything and everybody is as quiet as possible... the police are quiet, and can find little to do'. Belper folk must have been cheered, though, by the concluding announcement that 'there will be a turn presently, as one or two bazaars are announced'.

It appears that most entertainment was addressed to the middle and leisured classes. For the Derby working classes, life was hard. Illness was rife, with consumption rampant. Wages were small, working hours were long. And when the working man came home, it was to a meagre, overcrowded dwelling.

One gains an impression of a bored working class seeking solace in the plentiful ale-houses. At that time, Derby had one pub for every 125 people, in marked contrast to the 1930s, when the figure was one for every 530. It comes as no surprise to see that in the same week as Charles Morritt's animated pictures, the Grand Theatre on Babington Lane was presenting 'the great moral temperance play *Drink*'. The local newspapers of the time included innumerable reports of drunkenness which had come to court. By 1896, the Victorian adage about gin: 'drunk for a penny, dead drunk for twopence' was out of date. A measure of gin was now threepence, and that is all it cost to seek out 'Mr Charles Morritt's latest and greatest novelty, THE LIFEOGRAPH'.

No documentation exists of the Lifeograph, but British Film Institute Archivist Luke McErnan believes it was a projection apparatus manufactured by Robert Paul, and sold to many people involved in the magic trade, a fact that lends considerable weight to Luke's belief knowing, as we do, of Charles Morritt's profession.

As the *Derby Express* report tells us, there were 'as expected, crowded houses' with the Lifeograph 'the principal attraction' amongst a series of live variety acts. Considering the reaction of the crowds at the Lumière shows in Paris, the stiff, temperate nature of provincial British journalism of the time probably holds back on the true excitement felt by those crowded Morritt's Empire houses:

'This performance, which has created quite a furore in London, is a perfect novel sight in Derby, and as such is bound to attract attention.'

The nearest the unnamed reviewer gets to recounting audience response is to report that the projection of animated photographs on to a screen 'proved quite a sensational turn'. It is more likely that the Derby townsfolk, like the Lumière show spectators, felt a mixture of astonishment, disbelief and elation. Here was an audience of largely working-class people who might have barely clapped eyes on a still photograph before, never mind an animated one.

Furthermore, the Morritt's Empire crowd would have seen moving pictures of local scenes. The opening week's programme included two short films entitled *Derby Fair Ground* and *Derby School with Children*. In the course of my conversation with British Film Institute Archivist Luke McErnan, mention of these films astonished him: although many local scenes were shot in these early years, these two would be considered extremely early examples, in being made within seven months of the first Lumière shows in London. It is almost certain that Charles Morritt would have sought out film makers and despatched them to Derby in order to provide an extra attraction for the town's first sensation of moving pictures, a clear example of this showman's astute enterprise

In view of a recent remarkable discovery, there is a chance, albeit extremely slender, that these two films of Derby scenes are lying in storage somewhere. In 1995, a Devon radio collector called Ray Henville contacted the television show *Schofield's Quest* following a British Film Institute appeal for early films. Four years earlier, Ray attended a local auction and purchased an old radio as part of a 'job lot' comprising a TV set, deep fat fryer, sandwich toaster, baking tins... and a box of old nitrate films. He responded to the BFI call on 1 November, four days before he was due to throw the films on to a bonfire. The Film Institute archivists must have turned delirious with delight: amongst the 18 films contained in Mr Henville's box was one containing scenes from the Derby, of 1895, filmed by one of the great early pioneers Birt Acres. The excited BFI historians were watching the earliest known film made in Britain.

Never mind the Epsom Derby, what of these films about Derby the town? They were more than likely destroyed: thousands of short films were produced in these rampant first few years of motion pictures, but the early nitrate celluloid would have produced a crude visual image even on the first showing of a film. The quality would have deteriorated over subsequent screenings, and thus it was that so many of these retrospectively historic films would have been discarded. But if you occupy a Victorian house once owned by a Morritt, it might just be worth a check in the attic.

Two films shown to the audiences at Morritt's Empire still exist, both originally filmed by Thomas Edison: *Sandow*, a film depicting a legendary German boxer, and *American Picanni Dancer*. However, numerous copies would have been made of these films, hardly likely in the case of the *Derby Fair Ground* and *Derby School with Children*.

The Morritt's Empire shows – always a mix of moving pictures and variety acts – continued for only a month, despite being hailed in the second week as a 'glorious success'. A 'grand new programme' included footage of the 1896 Derby 'with Persimmon winning by a neck', the Coronation of the Czar at Moscow, and '12 other splendid pictures'.

Once again the *Derby Express* gave due attention to the show, no doubt owing to the fact that 'the house was crowded'. A review in the third week stated that 'this marvellous development of photography appears to have lost none of its novelty', with the fourth and final week even producing glimmerings of film criticism: 'Each week Mr Morritt arranges for a fresh set of scenes, many of which are excruciatingly funny' (many of the early films contained slapstick humour).

However funny those films might have proved, the eager townsfolk keen to see more were apparently abandoned. There is no mention of decreasing audiences at the Empire, yet there are no more newspaper notices of further Lifeograph shows, nor indeed of Charles Morritt's name. Why did he leave Derby? Had this 'long-looked-for' artist been found by a theatre prepared to offer him a lucrative engagement as a trance master? Had his supply of films dried up? Did the Lifeograph lead a short-lived life and break down? Or was this a man who believed he was a pioneer of this new medium of mass entertainment and had other towns to conquer?

Only a few years later, within the same Corn Exchange walls where Derby was shown this moving slapstick, there came a variety turn, a young dancer who was to develop his own slapstick and become a true pioneer of motion pictures. Appearing in what had then become the Palace of Varieties was a teenager who was later to entertain more Derby people than anyone else in cinema history. His name was Charlie Chaplin.

On With The Show
Fairground attractions and 'Penny Gaffs'

You've seen pictures of people in books, all frozen stiff. You've never seen people come alive in pictures, moving about natural like you and me. Well, go inside and see for yourself living pictures for a penny. Then tell me if I'm a liar.

notice outside a 'Penny Gaff'

ALTHOUGH an exciting new entertainment medium had been born, she proved an errant infant and a problem child. Only when she reached teenage did she begin to assume some responsibility and attain a measure of respect. In other words, after the concept of moving film came into the world, the ways and means of showing it to the world were erratic and, in many cases, dangerous. Eventually, the 1909 Cinematograph Act forced this footloose industry to reform, at the same time enabling it to forge ahead, with the provision of proper, permanent, purpose-built cinemas.

During the years 1897 to 1910, moving pictures could be seen on a largely fitful basis, as a fairground attraction, inside an unused shop, or as part of a music hall theatre bill. How many of these early shows would have been viewed by Derbyshire folk is difficult to gauge, owing to the dearth of documentation. According to local newspaper 'Amusements' notices, no one came along to exploit Charlie Morritt's four-week foray into film entertainment at the end of 1896. Astonishingly, the next recorded announcement of a motion picture show in Derby doesn't appear until three years later. A *Derby Express* notice of December 1899 refers to an evening of *Scenes From The War* in the same Corn Exchange hall used by Morritt – now entitled the Palace Theatre of Varieties, at the corner of Albert Street and Exchange Street. It is likely these three 'scenes' (all of Boer War incidents) were the highlights of a much bigger programme of films, as each one would be no more than about 1¼ minutes long (even by 1902, no film was longer than five minutes). Two of these war films, *The Siege of Mafeking* and *Shooting A Boer Spy*, were described as Dramatic Representations of Current Events, a grandiloquent term for fakes. Although genuine pictures were taken behind the battle lines (and stimulated the development of the newsreel), it was felt that much of the real footage lacked the excitement felt by a public reading front line reports in the newspapers, so film-makers shot these Dramatic Representations in their own studios. One of these Boer War films might even have been made in nearby Loughborough.

If Derby received only second best on that occasion, let us now record what is thought to be an historical first, which occurred only two months later. Although the Derby papers contain no notices of a local film show on Wednesday, 7 February 1900, the British Film Institute owns a poster proclaiming, on that date, a Diorama show of various world scenes, along with the Great American Bioscope (another form of projection apparatus) in the 'Infant Schoolroom, Mickleover'. The proprietor Walter Fearn brought a 'one night only' show of 'War Scenes, Comic Scenes, Interesting Scenes of all sorts', all part of a 'Refined, High-class and Thrilling Entertainment'. Not only that, it was 'free from Vulgarity throughout'. It would have needed to be vulgar-free: prior to the evening presentation at 8pm, there was a 'Children's Performance'. This is the first recorded instance of a children's matinée in British cinema history, and by some way, too: Peter Dakin recalls that his grandfather John opened the **Central Hall** cinema in Carr Vale, Bolsover and advertised a 3pm matinée for children in April, 1909; and according to Derby West Ender Maurice Elliott, the first children's matinées he can remember in the town were at the Spot Cinema in 1914 (although it's possible the Derby Temperance Hall ran Saturday afternoon children-only shows even before this).

Whatever the exact date, the Bioscope performance in Mickleover is still a remarkably early one, and according to the British Film Institute, there is no record of any children's matinées prior to this. A Cinema 100 plaque has been erected to commemorate this momentous event; it can be seen on the wall of the Mickleover Community Centre, which is now the site of the Mickleover Public Elementary School.

There is no further record of other one-night performances staged in the schoolroom by Walter

When Saturday Comes

Ray Wilmot has heard his father Jack speak many times of a football team that was born at a cinema. In the early 1930s, regulars at the Derby Cosmo got together to form Cosmo Athletic, which went on to play in a local unaffiliated Saturday afternoon football league on Rykneld Recreation Ground, winning a trophy in the 1931-32 season. Their changing facilities were a touch spartan – the old laundry on Crosby Street – which offered no washing facilities and a long walk to the pitch, but the team was fortunate in being financed by the Cosmo's owner Mr France, who also allowed the players free admission to the cinema. "Unfortunately" says Ray, "one of the club officials was not as benevolent as Mr France and apparently helped himself to club finances. As a result, the team disbanded after only two seasons." It was obvious Mr France was proud of his players: on Saturday nights, he would put the Cosmo Athletic score on the cinema screen. But only if they won.

Before the war, the Brampton Coliseum kindly catered for those regular Saturday afternoon patrons interested in football. A.H.Hall remembers sitting in the audience and receiving both half-time and full-time scores. However, they weren't flashed on the screen, so at least those uninterested in the sport could continue viewing the film. They would have had trouble hearing the film, though: one of the cinema staff entered the auditorium and proceeded to deliver the soccer scores through a megaphone.

Fearn, but that same proprietor was to continue in the local cinema business, becoming the first manager of the Derby Cosy cinema in 1913. The name Walter Fearn also appears in the records of the Melbourne Empire as its proprietor from 1913 to 1931.

In the same year as that historic children's matinée, a travelling showman called Waller Jeffs revived the Morritt spirit by hiring both the Albert Hall in the Wardwick and the Drill Hall in Foreman Street. Another rare British Film Institute poster of 1900 details one of these Drill Hall shows, announced as the 'finest animated exhibition in the world', including *The Beauties of Bonnie Scotland*, *Tommy Burns v. Gunner Moir*, one of many popular actuality films of boxing matches (or 'glove contests' as they were called), and *The Police Dogs of Paris*. Riveting stuff no doubt. Patrons were advised to come early to secure a good seat for a show that had 'The Press unanimous in its Praise'. And if that wasn't enough, there was the considerable allure of Mr Waller Jeff's motto: 'TO INTEREST and to AMUSE!!!'. Films continued to be part of a larger variety theatre presentation, although it's significant that the poster is more concerned with selling the picture show (see poster illustration), indicating a possible change of emphasis in the public's entertainment needs.

Because of the sporadic occurrence of these film shows in hired halls (and the limited number of performances), there would still be many Derbyshire townspeople experiencing moving pictures for the first time, even at the turn of the century. Basic as these film programmes appeared, it is clear that audiences were fascinated and captivated by the mere movement on screen, as this press notice confirms:

'So animated and real that one sat spellbound. The views were very clear and the action represented was so realistic that in several cases the audience could scarcely restrain their wonder, and even startled surprise at the events which were flashed before their eyes.'

Showman James Williamson, reminiscing over these early days in his unpublished notebooks of 1926, remarks that 'as regards the films, so long as something moved, the subject did not matter.' As Peter Stead states in his book *Film and the Working Class*, the millions who were going to picture shows 'was very largely because the movies were not just appealing to sections of the masses but to the masses in general'. As he states further: 'The movies worked, they fascinated and they entertained. At first they were a novelty and a fad but, perhaps even to the surprise of many in the trade, they were a novelty that did not fade.'

Even so, film historians Rachael Low and Roger Manvell, writing in *The History of the British Film 1896-1906*, believe the novelty of moving pictures would have worn off had it not been for the fairground showmen:

'It is to the fairground showmen that the cinema owes its ultimate success. The new toy, a passing fancy in the music halls, became a firmly established feature of the fairgrounds. It was they who bridged the

Poster advertising the cinematic attractions on offer at the Drill Hall in Becket Street, Derby. BFI Stills, Posters and Design.

gap between the music hall days and later, more respectable, picture palaces.'

Few records of these fairground shows were kept, but even though the fairground showmen swung into action soon after the first London exhibition of animated pictures in 1896, it's unlikely one of these travelling shows would have predated Charles Morritt's presentations at the Derby Empire. But the visiting fairs would have provided most Derbyshire people with their first glimpse of moving pictures, as early as 1897, when the Nottingham Goose Fair housed two big marquee entertainments – Collin's Living Pictures and Captain T. Payne's Electric Bioscope. In later years, the Goose Fair was to feature six separate cinema shows. As the Goose Fair traditionally split up into smaller fairs in adjacent towns, it's almost certain that Derby, Ilkeston, Ripley, Chesterfield and other sizeable county towns would have been visited by these new fairground novelties.

Were it not for the fairground bioscopes, the concept of a 'picture palace' might not have been realised. Hotly competitive, these travelling showmen used to try and outdo one another with the elaborate grandeur of their canvas cinemas. The frontage was everything. The Collin's show, for example, had a gilt façade lit by 14 powerful arc-lamps and 5,000 multi-coloured electric lamps set into a large carved wooden ornament. As Dennis Sharp points out in his book *Picture Palace*, 'these shows were small electric pavilions that drew their audiences around their light source, like moths around a flame.' 'Extras' included electric signs (the forerunner of neon?), a steam organ, and a few dancing girls, known as paraders. Once drawn inside, most audiences had to stand or sit on the floor,

Mickleover School at the turn of the century, site of the first children's cinema matinée ever to be held in Britain.

although the most sophisticated shows – like Mrs Holland's Palace of Light – had upholstered seats. Some of these tents housed 1,000 people.

Captain Payne, whose Electric Bioscope would almost certainly have been seen at various Derbyshire fairs, took great pains to declare that his films offered 'steadiness and no flickering'. This would have been a typical showman talking. For the reality, it would be more prudent to heed the words of Randall Williams, who was reckoned to be the first showman to exhibit moving pictures under canvas. The projection apparatus, for example, would have been hand-cranked, noisy and crude, and as Williams himself wrote: 'it resembled a cheap sausage machine'.

As if the largely untried, untrustworthy equipment wasn't bad enough, the films would have deteriorated with every screening in being allowed to spill out over the floor of the tent. These highly inflammable films were supposed to run into a sack, basket or bucket (to be re-wound later), but invariably overflowed, resulting in altercations with the crowds who used to tread on them.

The audience had other problems: the 'usherettes' of the time would have been told to move patrons in and out with all speed to allow the operator to get through as many 30-40 minute shows as possible, with the nervous knowledge that at any given

moment, the film would snap, snag, tangle or burst into flames. Also, because the lighting system was usually powered by an acetylene generator, it was quite usual to see the marquee visitors holding handkerchiefs to their noses and mouths, and remarking on their ability to get drunk without the usual intoxicants. 'They were right,' says Randall Williams, 'it was nearly the beginning of the end of cinematography.' Williams regrets not shooting film of the facial expressions of his patrons. However, he did go on to make his own locals, including the time he filmed the town fire brigade (it was only after the firemen left that a real fire broke out, and his crew shot an even better film!). For Randall, a turning point had been reached:

'I think it was at about that time, after people saw those local pictures, that animated pictures went up and never came down again.'

Certainly, showmen like Williams went on to amass considerable wealth, with the appeal of the locals being supplanted by a wider, higher quality range of comics, topicals, trick films, and early feature films which carried a story (and by 1906 ran to an epic 15 minutes).

Another kind of travelling show was an early form of mobile cinema, in two senses: Hale's Tours was a Goose Fair attraction from 1906 to 1912 so, again, it would have been a likely sight in Derbyshire. Paying customers would board an imitation railway coach. Once the lights were off, scenic films from all round the world were projected on to a screen disguised as a window at the front of a railway coach, to give the impression they were travelling the world by train. To add to the effect, the coach rocked and swayed, and made a few train-like noises.

But as some film showmen toured the towns, others began to settle in one place, inspired by the first American cinema parlours pioneered by Thomas Edison. These Nickelodeons (named after their cheap admission fees of only one nickel) began to appear in 1902. Mainly small, narrow rooms converted from an existing shop, with serried wooden seats in front of a simple screen, the Nickelodeons were the first permanent cinemas.

As a response to the Nickelodeon, the British establishments that turned over to picture shows were often referred to as Penny Gaffs. Like many Nickelodeons, some were converted shops, but the term Penny Gaff could be applied to virtually any venue that screened films. However, to be called a Gaff was not entirely complimentary: basically, it hinted at a cheap and shallow entertainment.

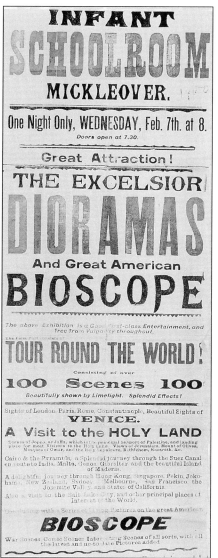

INFANT
SCHOOLROOM
MICKLEOVER.

One Night Only, WEDNESDAY, Feb. 7th. at 8.
Doors open at 7.30.

Great Attraction!

THE EXCELSIOR
DIORAMAS
And Great American
BIOSCOPE

The above Exhibition is a Good First-class Entertainment, and free from Vulgarity throughout.

TOUR ROUND THE WORLD!
Consisting of over
100 Scenes 100
Beautifully shown by Limelight. Splendid Effects!

Sights of London, Paris, Rome, Constantinople, Beautiful Sights of
VENICE.
A Visit to the HOLY LAND

Scenes of Joppa, or Jaffa, which is the principal Seaport of Palestine, and landing place for most Visitors to the Holy Land. Views of Jerusalem, Mount of Olives, Mosques of Omar, and the Holy Sepulchre, Bethlehem, Nazareth, &c.

Cairo & the Pyramids, a Splendid journey through the Suez Canal en route to India, Malta, Genoa, Gibraltar and the beautiful Island of Maderia.

A delightful journey through Hong Kong, Singapore, Pekin, Jokohama, New Zealand, Sydney, Melbourne, San Francisco, the Josemite Valley and State of California.

Also a visit to the Salt Lake City, and other principal places of Interest of the World.

Concluding with a Series of Large Pictures on the great American

BIOSCOPE

War Scenes, Comic Scenes Interesting Scenes of all sorts, with all the latest and up-to-date Pictures added

Audrey Field, author of *Picture Palace*, paints an even more fetid, uninviting picture of the 'delights' of the Penny Gaff:
'The seats were hard, the air soon became smoky and foul, the company inside was as rough and noisy as the company outside. It was not considered the place for a respectable young girl on her own, and anyone who did not want his pocket picked had to be careful.'

Derby's first regular venue for film shows appears to have been the Temperance Hall (later the Elim Church, now the Central Church) on Curzon Street, beginning as early as 1904, with a programme of pictures on a Saturday night. Fred Snelson recalls that technically, the Temperance Hall was even further down the social scale than the Penny Gaff: admission for children was only three halfpence. Fred also remembers that owing to a 'difficulty' obtaining films, two or three weeks went by without a screening.

Another Derbyshire building which served as an early cinema was the Brampton Coliseum. Although it opened in 1907 as the Central Hall (built out of a disused chapel), it was exclusively devoted to films, notwithstanding the odd classical violin solo provided in between the single-reelers by the owner's wife, Mrs Senior.

By 1908 the Derby Normanton Pavilion, a wooden structure with a corrugated tin roof, was screening many films during the winter. A totally corrugated sheet structure, known fondly as the 'Tin Truck' – Long Eaton's Palace Theatre of Pictures and Varieties – is known to have screened short films on a regular basis from 1906. Ripley, too, already exposed to the Bioscope shows at the annual Statutes Fair, enjoyed regular picture shows at the Co-operative Public Hall from 1908. A year later in the town, the Electra Theatre was built, and immediately screened films

A typical local example would be the Swadlincote Hippodrome, known in the town as Charlie Williams's Gaff. As Graham Nutt details in his excellent local study *Tuppeny Rush*, Charlie Williams ran a venue built of wood and canvas. There may well have been a tuppeny rush to the wooden benches, but richer patrons could walk unhurriedly to a cushioned bench for 4d or, if feeling flush, parted with a whole sixpence for an upholstered seat. It wasn't just the seating that was basic, as Graham points out:

'The power for the lighting was provided by a generator driven by a steam traction engine, which thumped away in the background like the heartbeat of a snoozing giant... The smell inside was a mixture of damp canvas, tobacco smoke and sawdust, and the interior was dimly lit by electric lamps.'

What wonders lay in store for these people at the fairground bioscope. **Sam Winfield Collection.**

Site of the Coliseum, Brampton. **Geoff Hood.**

along with variety acts (in 1911 it became a permanent cinema and altered its name to the Empire Palace). During this time, the inclusion of films on a variety bill was seen as highly practicable anyway, simply because two projection machines were

The Coliseum at Brampton, another Derbyshire building which served as an early cinema.

largely unheard of in theatres. So, venues like the Theatre Royal, Chesterfield would welcome vaudeville acts not only for adding variety to the evening's entertainment, but also for filling up the gaps that would have occurred whilst the reels were being changed.

The Electra Theatre in Ripley was purpose-built for 'cine-variety' in 1909. It later became the Empire.

However, there would be some theatres at this time who viewed the 'film shows' as fillers rather than the live artistes. Indeed, films were often referred to in the theatre business as chasers, in that they were used to chase customers out of the auditorium to allow fresh patrons to come in and take their place for the next performance. J.B.Priestley referred to these chasers as 'a final disregarded item in the great gaudy programmes of the music hall.' History would show J.B. that cinema was set to take over as the main mass entertainment spectacle, just as soon as the quality of films improved on the chasers, and just as soon as it found a proper, permanent home.

The film trade magazine *Kinematograph and Lantern Weekly* (now the *Kine Weekly*) reported in a 1907 edition that 'all picture shows were on the increase'. The Exhibitors Film Exchange declared that films had brought themselves within 'intimate reach of the great mass of humanity'. However, any picture show, be it in a fairground tent, converted shop or variety theatre, was unlicensed, and thus unchecked and uncontrollable. Before too long, there were calls for the cinema business to be regulated, mainly for safety's sake. One could say that for too long the industry had been playing with fire. Every time a picture house opened its doors, there was the danger of a blaze. It was common to see audiences fleeing for the picture house doors at the sudden sight of flames, invariably leaping from the projector. Basically, the cellulose-nitrate film stock was highly inflammable, particularly when old or in a state of decomposition. Sometimes films burned with a positively explosive force. Numerous fires broke out, and some fatalities occurred.

So, the Cinematograph Act was introduced in 1909. Its main purpose was to provide a separate fire-resistant projection box, along with fire-fighting appliances, such as two buckets of water, a bucket of dry sand and a damp blanket. Also, the safety measures that applied to the auditorium affected the numbers and widths of entrance doors, as well as access to them. Toilet facilities had to be provided (it was common for picture houses to reek of urine, as a result of the unwillingness of patrons to use the toilets outside, particularly as it meant dragging themselves away from the piercing images on screen).

The Cinematograph Act signalled the end of the fairground bioscope. Any picture show in 'booth, tent or structure' fell under the provisions of the Act, and thus rendered the itinerant show virtually inoperable. From 1 January 1910, when the Cinematograph Act came into operation, the cinema industry was to enter a new era.

THE "WALTURDAW" BIOSCOPE SPECIALITIES. 17

Preventive Measures.

Fires have resulted more than once from each of the foregoing causes. In the "Walturdaw" No. 3 and Power's Cameragraph No. 6 Machines, if a small piece of broken film caught fire in the gate, it would be impossible to fire the other film whilst passing through, because of the scientific construction of the letter box gate, which, when closed, makes it practically air-tight. Even if we let the film rest stationary for half a minute it will fire, but owing to the want of oxygen in the gate chamber it goes out. Everybody knows that combustion cannot take place without oxygen, and this scientific fact we have used on these machines.

As a further preventative against the possibility of a fire arising from causes outside the safety gate, and to prevent serious consequences from the ignition of the film at any point, it is only necessary to inclose both the film supply reel and the take-up reel in fire-proof chambers, and to provide valves leading into said chambers through which the film can pass freely while the film feed mechanism is in operation, but which will close instantly when the film feed mechanism ceases to operate or the tension upon the film is relaxed. If the film supply reel and take-up reel are inclosed in such fire-proof chambers or magazines, the ignition of the film at the projecting aperture is a matter of very little consequence, as the burning of the film at that point immediately causes a reduction of the tension on the film, and permits the valves through which the film passes into the magazines to close, and so prevent absolutely the passage of the flames into the magazines. Properly constructed magazines for the film supply reel and take up reel can be applied at very small cost to any moving picture machine, and if the machine is equipped with such magazines, it may even be overturned without causing any serious damage.

A New Life

The Coming of the Picture Palace

The Midland Electric Theatre Co. have now completed their beautiful palace in Babington Lane, Derby... it is certainly an interesting addition to the public buildings of the town.

Derby Daily Telegraph, 25 July 1910

THE Cinematograph Act of 1909 paved the way for the British cinema industry, clearing the squalid path populated by the Penny Gaffs. Its stringent provisions were, in effect, calling for a new era of the respectably run, permanent picture house. This it duly got. In his book *Censored* (a history of British film censorship), author Tom Dewe Matthews alludes to a conspiracy theory surrounding the introduction of the Act, arguing that the local councils of Edwardian Britain had become frustrated by their inability to exert any influence over this growth industry. He then infers that the public safety issue was a smokescreen for the authorities' main bid: to assume control of film entertainment for the masses, thus being able to ensure the content of the films was to their approval. Even if the Cinematograph Act introduced a more controlled world for those who wished to be the moral guardians of this new entertainment, it also ushered in a brighter world for those who wished to be either providers or recipients of it. Al-

Newspaper advertisement for the new Midland Electric Theatre in Babington Lane, Derby. BFI Stills, Posters and Design.

though the Act seemed to call for cinema to put its house in order, in effect it caused the industry to erect a new house, exclusively devoted to the showing of films, free from the trappings of theatre and fairground. It was a clear incentive for the building of purpose-built picture houses, borne out by the figures: in 1909, the year the Act was drawn up, there were some 2,000 cinemas in Britain. By 1911, that amount had doubled. Even before the regulations were introduced, the popularity of picture houses encouraged their owners to provide more comfort and, hopefully, a better class of clientele. According to Rachael Low in her book *The History of British Film*: 'Red plush and marble, ferns in brass pots and plenty of electric light were guaranteed to give that air of cosy refinement. The foyer must have bevelled mirrors if it was to acquire the prized bon ton which would make it a really 'high-class rendezvous'. Refinements like shaded lights, uniformed young attendants instead of the old barker, and 'tasteful plaster mouldings' to adorn the front of the up-to-date pretty picture palace became a cult... size and splendour were of less importance than good taste, elegance, and a preoccupation with daintiness. 'The preoccupation with acquiring a new respectability for cinema was seen as vital for its future. Rachael Low points to a trade 'anxious to disclaim its low birth', a point stressed by Peter Stead, author of *Film and the Working Class*, who claims the showmen were responsible for creating this mass entertainment medium but that they eventually 'clambered after respectability' in order to widen cinema's appeal beyond the working classes.

He points out that 'respectable society' at this time largely considered motion pictures as 'a mechanical novelty, a meaningless and trivial craze which might be allowed to prove a moment's distraction at a music hall or vaudeville show but which normally belonged to the amusement arcade or fairground.' Peter Stead claims that the showmen were after greater self-esteem, but that was also part of a need to build up larger audiences for the new picture houses, partic-

Site of the Midland Electric Theatre, later the Picture House and then the Ritz, in Babington Lane, Derby. **Bill Attenborough.**

The Midland Electric Theatre in Babington Lane, Derby. It was the county's first purpose-built cinema. **Derby Evening Telegraph.**

previous chapter infers, Ripley's claim that it produced Derbyshire's first cinema – the Electra Theatre – is denied by the fact that the building opened in 1909 for 'cine-variety'. Also, although **Buxton's Picture Palace** in Heanor opened sometime in 1910, possibly even before the Derby Midland Electric, and was exclusively devoted to films, the building was not purpose-built: proprietor Fred Buxton had converted Heanor Town Hall).

A few days before the opening of the Midland Electric Theatre, the *Derby Daily Telegraph* spelt out the advantages of such a venue. It offered 'continuous exhibition' so that 'visitors can step in at any time and remain as long as they like.' What visitors would also have welcomed was a steep rake, offering a 'complete view of the pictures'.

The cinema itself wasn't exactly complete at the outset, owing to a photographer named Carr. As one of the tenants of the old site, he refused to leave while his lease still permitted him to run his photographic studio. Mindful of the fact that his lease was to expire early in 1911, the cinema company gave the order for building work to proceed while an apparently bloody-minded Mr Carr vainly tried to pursue his profession. The photographer railed against Midland Electric Theatres in the local press,

ularly those that were going to go up in suburbs and small towns.

On 27 July 1910, less than seven months after the Cinematograph Act became law, Derbyshire's first picture house – the **Midland Electric Theatre** on Babington Lane in Derby – opened its doors (as the

The Derby Picture House (right) at the bottom of Babington Lane about 1920. The Grand Theatre is on the left. Kevin Wheelan.

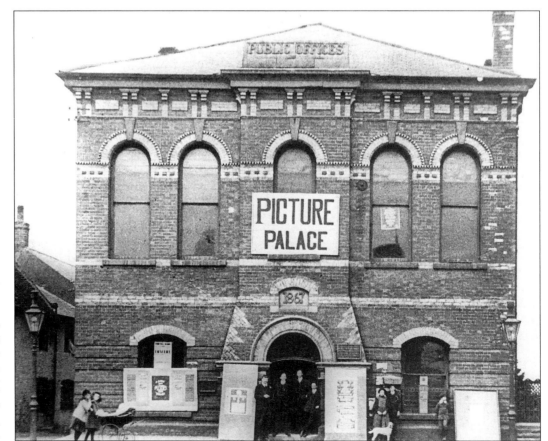

Heanor Town Hall, which became Buxton's Picture Palace, photographed about 1914. G.Eyre.

The former Picture Palace, Heanor, in 1996. Andy Wilson.

accusing the company of depriving him of a living. He had a point: the builders blocked off one of his studio doors, also causing cracks to appear in the wall. "My customers have great difficulty in getting in to my studio" complained Mr Carr. "If they DO, they see the cracks and leave. They've ruined my business."

The company tried to placate its irate tenant with a free cinema ticket at any time 'while he was being inconvenienced'. But the still image producer had no time for the moving image: "I decline the offer. I have no interest in cinematography whatsover."

When the work on the Midland Electric Theatre was finally complete, Derby architect Arthur Eaton was credited with designing 'the smartest electric theatre in the provinces' with its blue carpets and upholstered velvet tip-up seats to match 'in every part of the house'. The electric fittings were also singled out for praise, owing to their 'very elaborate nature'.

Its tall, white-arched frontage would have appealed to those with an eye for the grandiose (even if it was still dwarfed by the Grand Theatre further up the road) with the words 'Midland Electric Theatre' attractively arranged and owing its influence to the flourishing art nouveau movement. The main entrance was also illuminated by hundreds of coloured lights.

But the cinema's most handsome and talked about feature lay beyond the pay box. The foyer, once refurbished in 1913, was an appropriately grand, ostentatious touch which any learned local historian might feel was intended as a homage to Babington Hall, as it once stood on the same site now occupied by this picture palace. The family's (in)famous son Anthony Babington was executed for plotting to murder Queen Elizabeth I in order to install Mary Queen of Scots on the throne and restore Roman Catholicism in England. Mary herself stayed at the Hall for one night on her journey from Wingfield Manor to Tutbury Castle, and her complicity in the plot led to her own execution.

So, it is perfectly plausible to assume that the cinema architect was anxious to echo the stateliness of Babington Hall when he came to design the sumptuous foyer, but being bereft of any plans of the original house, turned then to the still-preserved interior of Haddon Hall, near Bakewell. As well as replicating the Minstrel's Gallery of the Hall, the baronial touch was lavished on a large carved fireplace flanked by two knights in armour, with oak panelling all around and a wide oak staircase leading up to the circle entrance. This palatial elegance was not only a giant leap from the derelict shops and canvas structures that only a few years before used to masquerade as cinemas, but also made the Midland Electric one of the first true picture palaces of the new cinema kingdom.

Later, when the Midland Electric changed to the Picture House, the balcony area became a café, with 'dainty teas' a speciality. Teas could also be served to circle seats but this proved a problem once the Talkies arrived: only then was it noticed that the rattling of spoons in the real china cups produced an irksome noise, particularly if the circle clientele took more sugar than was good for them.

Countless regulars to the cinema, particularly in its heyday as the Picture House, carry inexpressibly fond remembrances of the eye-gladdening delight of the foyer. If, in particular, they walked in from the winter's cold to be greeted by the warmth and colour of the roaring log fire and a delectable, scrumptious smell of toasted tea-cakes wafting from the balcony, then this truly was nirvana. For employees like Wyn Barker, working in such surroundings was a joy. In 1926, at the age of 15, Wyn was taken on as an 'attendant'. "There was always a wonderful atmosphere to the place", she recalls, "I've never forgotten it."

What of the actual film entertainment? The opening programme on 27 July 1910, comprised titles which would hardly have fired the imagination – *Farm Yard Friends*, *Soap In His Eye*, *Cupid In A Motor Boat*, and *North German Lloyds Steamboats*. In spite of some seemingly dull subject matter, audiences would have been thrilled by the presentation of some of them in Kinemacolour. The Midland Electric Theatres Company secured the sole rights of this process, invented in 1906 by Charles Urban and G.Albert Smith. Basically, the projection apparatus included various coloured lenses and filters. By this time, there had already been instances of film stock tinted one colour all over e.g. blue for night, red for fire and other variations. However, judging by the reaction of the *Derby Daily Telegraph* reporter, Kinemacolour was a little more advanced, producing pictures 'in all glorious colours of nature without hand colouring or machine tinting of any kind'. This new sensation was hailed in the newspaper for depicting subjects 'in all the hues and tints of nature... the actual scenes were perfectly reproduced, and were in every respect superb in their expression of tints and tones, and it is not surprising that Kinemacolour has taken its place in the front rank of the world's successes, and solved the problem of bioscoping animated scenes and moving objects in natural colours. The results are, indeed, astonishing, and the audiences this afternoon expressed unfeigned delight at this new invention'.

What may be further surprising is that at Derby's second cinema to be opened – **The Spot** – there was another process well ahead of its time: the talking picture. However, this early experimental method of applying sound to a silent film appears to have been an even cruder gimmick than Kinemacolour. The sound was produced by a phonograph playing a cylindrical record, placed at one side of the screen. According to one 'ear' witness, each cylinder lasted a paltry six minutes before having to be changed. Paradoxically, the phonograph had to be stopped more often than this, as the pictures on the screen were constantly falling behind the sound. Add to that the primitive nature of the cylindrical disc and the absence of amplification, and it's not surprising the experiment ceased after a week and, by all accounts, did not return.

The Spot Cinema didn't last long, either. While the Midland Electric swiftly grew to a 1,100-seater, a common size for a cinema of the time, The Spot could only accommodate 200. Formerly The Spot Dance Hall, it was converted by the pork butcher next door, Joseph Woolley (apparently he was anxious to find employment for his three daughters).

In what would now be regarded as estate agent jargon, the *Derby Daily Telegraph* referred to The Spot not as small, but 'compact'. It was also described as 'comfortable' and 'elegant'. One wonders if the reporter had this description fed to him by the owner (in return for being fed with a tray of sausages?), because Avis Elliot remembers The Spot as not only 'tiny' but 'tatty'. She also recalls that the foyer was so narrow that her father couldn't pass through with her at his side, so had to carry her on his shoulders.

In spite of opening with a film mouth-wateringly entitled *A Merry Widow Takes Another Husband*, The Spot was spotless in its approach to film fare: 'the greatest care and discrimination will be used by the management in selecting films, thereby ensuring cleanliness of subject and freedom from vulgarity'. However, its limited capacity must have worked against the cinema; the 800-seater Victoria Electric opened in the town only a month after The Spot, with both the Normanton Picture Palace and the Alexandra opening in 1913, and the White Hall in 1914. The Spot closed down in the spring of 1917, and

in spite of an announced 'Grand Re-opening', it stayed shut. Ironically, in an age when the public increasingly craved the moving image, The Spot eventually re-opened as a wax museum (with an emphasis on 'freaks' apparently). The original building is long gone, the site now a part of the Eagle Centre.

Derby's true second cinema (in the sense that it was purpose-built) opened a month after The Spot, and was, according to the *Derbyshire Advertiser*, 'an indication of the prevailing taste of the public in the way of entertainment'. The report proclaimed the **Victoria Electric Theatre** as 'elaborate and beautiful', and commended the cinema for its 'entire absence of pillars'. Other features included heated radiators, and the provision of 'semi-illuminations by coloured lights so that the programmes can be read while the pictures are being thrown on the screen'. It was also announced at the cinema's opening that admission was equal to 'two pints of beer'. This was undoubtedly linked with the virtues of the first manager, William Studd, who was proudly declared 'a life-long abstainer'. He was also described as 'a ventriloquist of more than ordinary ability'. A later manager was Edgar Duckworth, a Lancashire businessman. Considering how shamefully squalid and unsightly Derby's Duckworth Square has turned out, it is small compensation to know that it retains a significant link with a first in British cinema history: not only were the Duckworths the first dynasty of cinema owners, but also Edgar's father, Joshua, retains the distinction of having opened Britain's first purpose-built cinema, in Colne, Lancashire 1907.

Maybe not even a pioneer like Joshua Duckworth could have envisaged the rapid, rampant rise in the popularity of the picture house, which the Cinematograph Act set in motion two years later. But the Act's provision of safeguards from fire was dealt an ironic blow in 1911, when Derbyshire suffered one of the greatest tragedies in cinema history. During a Christmas programme at the **Chesterfield Picture Palace**, 30 children provided stage entertainment for the audience in between the films. At some point in the dressing room on the night of 27 December, a child's dress caught fire. In the ensuing inferno, five children died. Inquests followed, where suspicions of backstage smoking were aired and never resolved, but by then the reputation and popularity of the Picture Palace had already died with the children. Although the cinema re-opened less than a fortnight after the tragedy, and was refurbished three years later with a new name, it is significant that it faded away in the mid-1920s at a time when new picture houses were springing up and existent ones were packing them in.

The Normanton Picture Palace.
Sam Winfield Collection.

Site of the Normanton Picture Palace, Derby. John Osborn.

cinema's most curious and imponderable titles – *Foolshead Between Celibacy and Matrimony*. The exterior architecture of the Picture Palace was imponderable, too (although the *Derbyshire Advertiser* described it as 'imposing'). The frontage was an odd, unlovely combination of brick, cement and windows, with an ungainly, pillared entrance jutting out into the corner of Dairyhouse Road and Princes Street, and a purely functional auditorium exterior displaying its deeply unattractive largeness down one side of Dairyhouse Road (rather than keeping it hidden as many cinema architects preferred). However, it still must have proved a palace to the area's inhabitants (and the inside, according to the *Derby Daily Express*, contained 'an artistic scheme of decoration' with tip-up seats described as 'comfortable and roomy'). Furthermore, at the cinema's opening the Mayor of Derby, Alderman Wilkins, hotly disagreed with those who thought there were too many cinemas being built, as these people 'had no idea how dull and drab were the surroundings in which most people passed their lives'.

The same proprietors of the Normanton cinema were soon to open another picture house close by. Conveniently for them, the roller-skating craze of 1908, which led to the building, a year later, of the Derby Alexandra Rink, dissipated and died. Although there was a radical conversion of the site into a cinema, the **Alexandra Electric Theatre** proved an unsatisfactory transformation for some occupants of the 1,269 seats: their vision was distorted by the obtuse angle of the screen to the right wall. Their vision upwards would have been disappointing, too: another legacy of the skating rink was a framework of hulking girders. The main film – screened at its

But the Chesterfield Picture Palace incident was but a sad footnote in an otherwise exhilarating and burgeoning chapter of the British cinema story. According to the Kine Year Book of 1913, London had over 200 cinemas, Manchester had a staggering 111, and even two smaller Lancashire towns Stockport and Bolton had nine and eight respectively. By 1914, Derby had seven. A modest number, perhaps, but by today's standards, the town could be considered well endowed: a combined capacity of just under 6,000 outstrips the aggregate seating of Derby's two multiplexes by just under 1,500 (discounting even the converted picture theatres like the Temperance Hall and the Normanton Pavilion and Gardens). Also, audience turn-outs would have been markedly higher; and, let us remember that by 1914, the cinema medium was a mere 18 years old.

What of the other four Derby cinemas that opened before World War One?

Following the Victoria Electric Theatre opening in 1910, cinema-goers in the suburbs had to wait another three years before the next picture house sprang up. The snowballing demand for cinema and the lack of provision on the outskirts of the town prompted a group of businessmen from the Normanton and Peartree area to pool their resources. The result was the third of the town's purpose-built cinemas: the **Normanton Picture Palace**, with seating for 900. One of its opening films carries one of

The Alexandra, Normanton Road, Derby, between the wars. **W.W.Winter.**

Flats now occupy the site of the Alexandra on Normanton Road, Derby. **John Osborn.**

opening on 6 October 1913 – was the unpropitiously-titled *Delivered By Death*. Even though the portents might have been ringing with the follow-up feature entitled *At Handgrips With Death*, the Alexandra proved a lively attraction, and even enjoyed a Derby première in 1926 of *Quo Vadis*. On the positive side, the tip-up seats were well-upholstered, and a powerful ventilator was installed to clear the considerable tobacco smoke every ten

A restaurant is now on the site of the Cosy on London Road, Derby. **John Osborn.**

The Cosy, pictured shortly after it was opened in December 1913 as the London Road Cinema. **Kevin Wheelan Collection.**

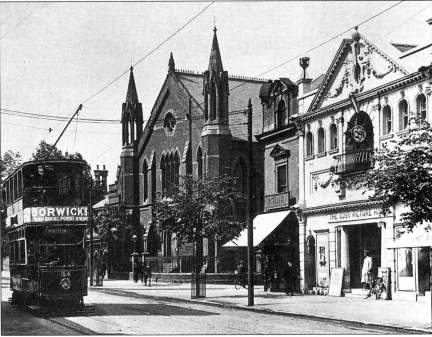

minutes. Also, although the frontage bore similarities with its sister cinema down the road, the Alexandra had a more pleasing appearance, with the decorative, glass-filled entrance resembling that of a pavilion.

Also, as the Alex and the Normanton were run by the same group (one of the directors, Peter Felix, became the proprietor of the Alex), they enjoyed the benefit of sharing the newsreels, not that it would be seen as a boon by the projection junior who had to carry the newsreels between the two cinemas by bus (an illegal practice, incidentally).

The London Road cinema which closed as the

Site of the White Hall, later the Odeon, in St Peter's Street, Derby. John Osborn.

cinema's ornate plaster work (including 'busts reminiscent of female figure heads of old sailing ships' gave the auditorium 'the atmosphere of a theatre', a feeling complemented by a horseshoe-shaped balcony extending around three walls and 'curving gracefully towards the screen'.

Yet another feature of the Cosy was indirect lighting (the first to be incorporated in a Derby cinema), noted by the *Derbyshire Advertiser* to be 'restful to the eyes'. Whatever entertainment greeted those eyes, there was sure to be an audience of rail travellers who welcomed the convenience as much as the ocular comfort of the Cosy, simply in being sited close to Derby Station. The knowledge that many passengers changed trains at Derby (and sometimes had to endure a long wait) was evidenced by a large station advertisement for the Cosy, making clear the cinema's proximity.

A year later, Derby had another cinema, although this one was intended more as a rival to the two Electric Theatres in the town centre. The **White Hall**, best remembered as The **Odeon**, opened on 14 Dec-

Cameo, and had previously borne the titles the **Picture House** and **Forum**, opened on December 18th, 1913 as the **London Road Cinema**, but soon adopted the name **Cosy**. It was thought to be appropriately named. Another feature was its decorations, described by the *Derbyshire Advertiser* as 'particularly bright and artistic'. As Sam Winfield points out in his book Dream Palaces of Derby, the

The auditorium of the White Hall, Derby, which was later renamed the Odeon. **Sam Winfield Collection.**

ember 1914, in a prime position opposite St Peter's Church. Its three-storey frontage (with 22 upper floor windows) was grand and imposing, with its prestigious look enhanced by the presence of two high-class ladies' dress shops on either side of the cinema entrance. The auditorium, although long and narrow, had a sumptuous and elegant feel (Grecian figures adorned the side walls), and the White Hall's overall air of refinement was topped off after World War One by the opening of a high-class restaurant, which became noted for its sumptuous meals and the added attraction of live music.

In later years, Pauline Cooper recalls her visits to the White Hall with relish: "the entrance to the foyer was, to say the least, dazzling. It was very wide, with a marble floor, a chandelier hung from the ceiling, and from half way up, the walls on either side were covered in smoke-coloured mirror tiles, each side reflecting the other. The reflection of the chandelier bouncing back and forth gave the impression of looking down a long corridor with dozens and dozens of chandeliers hanging from the ceiling. It was quite a sight for young eyes."

The cinemas that grew up out in the county were not quite so handsomely appointed, but they happily fulfilled the growing demand for moving pictures.

Many entrepreneurial eyes had focussed on this new medium and satisfied the public thirst by erecting a cinematographic oasis in any town previously deprived. In his book *Tuppenny Rush*, Swadlincote historian Graham Nutt reveals how several show businessmen strove to erect a cinema in the South Derbyshire town. The plans to build an Electric Theatre in 'Swad' were spearheaded in 1911 by Edwin Lawrence, who was already well-versed in moving picture entertainment, having travelled the country with a fairground bioscope show. In October 1911 Lawrence – now a resident of Swadlincote – confirmed the purchase of a site in West Street, which he duly cleared ready for refurbishment. But Edwin found that in spite of the obvious need for a cinema, there were still townsfolk factions who objected to the apparently irrepressible progress of this new entertainment. Graham Nutt believes that 'constant verbal offensive on him, both in out of court' – from religious groups and various members of the town hierarchy – caused him to abandon his project midway through 1912. According to Graham, it seems that the religious fraternity was critical not so much of cinema *per se* but of the proximity of any kind of entertainment to the local church: 'One protester's opinion was that the Devil had got his own

The Swadlincote Empire with Percy McCann on the left. The special notice carries the warning: 'Should the theatre have to close through any unforeseen circumstance created by the war, no money will be refunded. M.McCann.

The former Empire, Swadlincote. Geoff Hood and below: The Swadlincote Empire in its early days. M.McCann.

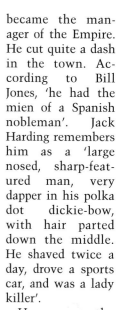

became the manager of the Empire. He cut quite a dash in the town. According to Bill Jones, 'he had the mien of a Spanish nobleman'. Jack Harding remembers him as a 'large nosed, sharp-featured man, very dapper in his polka dot dickie-bow, with hair parted down the middle. He shaved twice a day, drove a sports car, and was a lady killer'.

However, the McCann family was soon to see competition, as Edwin Lawrence's enterprise finally came to fruition. Having withdrawn his own plans to open the Empire, Lawrence – along with two other show businessmen Frank Bridgewater and Tommy Raynor – took over the ailing Alexandra Skating Rink, and converted it into a 300-seater cine-

way in allowing a Picture Palace to be built so close to a house of God'. However, within a week, a group of businessmen had renewed the campaign and, ironically, settled on a site right next to the one Lawrence had set his sights on. The protests were renewed, but on Boxing Day, 1912, the Swadlincote Entertainments Co. Ltd opened the New **Swadlincote Empire**. The cine-variety bill was a resounding success, playing to three capacity houses of 500 each.

The business group which brought a permanent picture house to Swadlincote was led by Charles Garibaldi McCann from Derby. As a result of this new venture, he sold his musical instrument shop near The Spot and set up a similar business in Swadlincote High Street. Eventually, his son Percy

variety theatre – the **Alexandra Palace of Varieties**. Frank Bridgewater proved more than a useful member of the business trio: he was an accomplished pianist, so he supplied the music for both the variety acts and the silent pictures.

How the generating equipment passed a safety inspection will remain a mystery, unless the building that housed it never actually received a visit from the authorities. As Graham Nutt recounts, the generator was a fearsome beast:

'A horizontal single cylinder diesel engine, of unknown parentage, supplied the power to propel a flywheel exceeding 10ft in diameter. A deep groove was cut into the floor of the building to accommodate the monster. A quick release handle, which did not always live up to its name, slotted into the side of the wheel. The handle allowed two people to rotate the giant, whilst another operated the decompressor on the engine.

Once it was felt the wheel was turning at a reasonable speed, one of the team would give the signal to leap clear. The decompression lever was let go, and all three would flatten themselves against the walls as the whole apparatus shook and shuddered into life.

Those who took part in, or witnessed the operation, claimed it was more frightening than anything seen on the cinema screen.'

Graham Nutt further reveals that the trio of Raynor, Bridgewater and Lawrence had bigger, more ambitious plans than the simple establishment of a picture palace. They wanted to put their own films on the screen. Edwin Lawrence knew how to make films as well as show them. By 1913, the Alexandra was advertising a film show of the Swadlincote Parade, accompanied by the alluring line: 'Come and See Yourself on the Pictures'. But the film-makers didn't stop there. They formed The Albion Film Company and went on to produce several full-length fiction films using local locations. In his book *Tuppeny Rush*, Graham Nutt lavishes fascinating detail on this sadly short-lived film-making enterprise, which mysteriously foundered within a year, even though there were plans to use the Alexandra Rink as a studio. Film-making nationwide was to be checked soon after the commencement of World War One, and there is no doubt that hostilities ended, once and for all, the plans to turn 'Swad' into a little Hollywood.

The Scala, Ilkeston, shortly after it opened in 1913. Amongst the directors pictured is the manager, Arthur Severn. R.Wilde.

The Scala at Ilkeston in 1996, looking much the same. Gill & Peter Dishart.

The war also halted the cinema building programme, but one of the most significant Derbyshire cinemas to open prior to the outbreak was the **Ilkeston Scala**. That significance might not have been felt in 1913, but it is certainly appreciated today, as the Scala still operates as a cinema (under the same name), and stands proudly in the corner of the Market Square with its comparatively petite but grand, appealing frontage virtually unchanged from the day it opened – Thursday, 4 September 1913 – with seating for 1,000. Ironically, most locals thought the Scala would be the first town cinema to close, a feeling engendered in the 1940s when its interior went to seed. More fatalistic Ilkestonians would have pointed to the Scala's erection on the site of a graveyard, yet as David Roddis points out in his book *The Thrill Of It All*, 'for all the grisly origins of the site, the Scala has never had the reputation of being haunted, a reputation some cinemas carry all their life'.

A year after the Scala, Ilkeston had its second purpose-built cinema **The Kings** (so named after a visit to the town in 1914 by King George V), swiftly followed by **The Globe**. The Kings became the leading picture house in Ilkeston, even though it had none of the noble grandeur of the Scala; as the *Ilkeston Pioneer* commented, the cinema was 'not lofty... no unnecessary decoration has been wasted on the front but it is, withal, pleasing'. However, the *Ilkeston*

Advertiser was both praiseful and utterly pretentious:

'The Star of Thespis, the founder of Drama, is in the strong ascendance in the town of Ilkeston and the present mode is to follow it to the halls where he reigns, and there worship'.

Indeed. However, The Kings' reputation as a 'picture house de luxe' would have been borne out by its large capacity – 1,374, with all but 175 of its plush seats together on one level – and embellishments such as the tapestry panels and 'a luxuriously upholstered lounge'.

As if the seating capacity at the Scala and Kings wasn't enough, 1915 saw another cinema open in Ilkeston – The Globe – accommodating 850. Once again, the *Ilkeston Advertiser* got excited, declaring that visitors to the town would have their attention 'irresistibly drawn' to a building with a 'magic' dome. The newspaper also pontificated on the cinema as a social necessity of the times, decreeing that 'variety and change are the essential antidotes to the monotonous hum-drum of the average individual'. Much more significant to any individual who managed to plough to the end of this Grub Street article was the simple, useful information that there was an uninterrupted view of the screen 'no matter what kind of headgear the occupants of the seats in front chose to wear.'

But a magic dome and a clear view were not enough to save The Globe. In 1923, the expanding Woolworth empire came bustling into town and acquired the site.

King's Picture House at Ilkeston.

Site of King's Picture House, Ilkeston. Gill & Peter Dishart.

A Fire Has Been Arranged

Swadlincote historian Graham Nutt recalls a story passed down to him by Jim Smith, who used to assist at the Alexandra, which was a popular picture house with a corrugated-iron roof. One packed night, there was a severe hailstorm. The effect of the hailstones striking the roof produced a sound strikingly akin to burning timbers. Some sport in the audience was quick to notice this and shouted 'fire!' So convincing was his cry, so pronounced was the sound of a blazing roof, that the audience sprang up and cleared the cinema. An angry manager Percy McCann was forced to close the Alex for the night, as it would have proved too consuming a job re-seating everyone, and the following day put a poster up offering a reward for the bogus fire-raiser. He was never caught.

The Palace Theatre, Long Eaton, in 1929. K.Reedman Collection.

The Screen Cinema, Long Eaton, formerly the Palace. Peter Cheetham.

Not that Ilkeston folk felt deprived, because as well as the Kings and the Scala, the Theatre Royal had also taken to screening films, and with its 2,000 seat capacity, Ilkeston could be said to be well endowed to serve its 30,000 plus population, even without The Globe.

Long Eaton should be singled out for mention, as three cinemas were in place for its 25,000 population by 1920 and, like Ilkeston, one still operates – the **Screen Cinema** in the Market Place, although its narrow, unassuming frontage conveys nothing of the splendour of the original cinema – the **Palace Theatre**. As the photograph taken in 1929 shows, this was a handsome, elegant and imposing building. Further-more, the proprietors boasted that 'whatever the weather without may be, the Palace within will be cosy, comfortable and hygienic.' Hygienic to the eyes, too: the entertainment was promised to be 'free from the faintest breath of vulgarity'.

Vint's Picturedrome, Long Eaton, eventually to become the Scala Theatre. T.Moss.

The site of Vint's Picturedrome in Long Eaton. Peter Cheetham.

Even though cinemas like the **Ashbourne Empire** (opened 1912) and the **Matlock Picture Palace** (1913) were, in later years, to gain the dubious distinction of being dubbed 'flea pits', all of the purpose-built picture houses at this time must have felt palatial in their prime, particularly to their target audiences.

So, by 1914, Derby had

The Ripley Hippodrome pictured in 1913 with its original frontage. W.Marshall.

The former Hippodrome in Ripley. Alan Booth.

Site of the Ripley Empire.
Alan Booth.

The Empire Theatre,
Ripley, rebuilt from the
Electra. G.Bailey.

two Electric Theatres, a Spot, Victoria, Alex, Normanton, Cosy and White Hall; Ashbourne, Heanor, Ripley, Swadlincote and Whittington Moor had an Empire (Whittington Moor also had a Lyceum, and Ripley also had a Hippodrome, as did Chesterfield); Belper and Matlock had a Picture Palace; Ilkeston had a Kings; both Ilkeston and Long Eaton housed a Scala; and even Swadlincote had a Premier, and Melbourne its own Electric Theatre.

Could Derbyshire support so many cinemas? For one morally-minded letter-writer to the *Derbyshire Advertiser*, there was a hidden virtue in the increase of cinemas:

'I have no patience in hearing people say that there are too many. If it's discovered that the spending power of the public is not equal to the maintenance of the picture palaces, then it must naturally be a question of the survival of the fittest, which will ensure the provision of a good, wholesome entertainment'.

However, such was the increasing and incessant desire of the Derbyshire public for film entertainment consumption, wholesome or not, that 'question of the survival of the fittest' wasn't to be broached... at least for the next four decades.

The former Picture Palace at Matlock. Terry Hawksworth.

Oh! What A Lovely War!

The growth of a social force

"I can't believe they want nothing but pictures.

Why", he continued, "they are ever so much more excited after a good turn, than after any film."

"I know they are" said Alvina, "but I don't believe they want to be excited in that way."

"In what way?" asked Mr May plaintively.

"By the things which the artistes do. I believe they're jealous."

"I can't believe it" protested Mr May, "Could they be so silly! And then why aren't they jealous of the extraordinary things which are done in the film?"

"Because they don't see the flesh-and-blood people. I'm sure that's it. The film is only pictures, like pictures in the Daily Mirror. *And pictures don't have any feelings apart from their own feelings. I mean the feelings of the people who watch them. Pictures don't have any life except the people who watch them. And that's why they like them. Because they make them feel like they are everything."*

D.H.Lawrence, from *The Lost Girl*, written 1912-13

The cinematograph has come to stay, its attractions are within reach of all, and its continual variety ensures vitality.

A spokesman for the Educational Cinematograph Association, May 1914

IN 1913, probably about ten years after his quiet, unheralded appearance as a dance turn at Derby's Palace of Varieties, Charlie Chaplin signed a contract with Keystone. A year later, with 35 short films already to his name, Chaplin signed with the Essanay company for $1250 per week, as opposed to the $250 he had been earning with Max Sennett. By 1917 he was the first screen millionaire, and his films were reaching to millions round the world. Although that magic word 'Hollywood' had yet to reach Somercotes, Swadlincote or South Normanton, the cinema had already become big business.

The attraction of motion pictures had long resided chiefly in the working classes, and it's easy to see why audiences grew as the medium established itself. According to film historian Ernest Betts, its development can be traced to the social needs of the time: "there was little amusement for the working class. The whole nation yawned with boredom during weekends and was ready to put a fortune into the hands of anyone who could relieve the tedium." Estimates show that in Edwardian Times working-class families spent six shillings a week on alcohol. Little wonder that the lure of a luxury picture palace like Derby's Midland Electric was considerable; here was a new world of easy entertainment at easy prices – from 6d in the front stalls up to 1s 3d in the circle (or 'balcony' as it was known in those days). In many other cinemas, it was even cheaper.

World War One didn't check any of the fervour for films. Although there was a temporary slump in 1914, owing to the outbreak of war itself along with the rising costs of programmes and the effects of the Amusements Tax, audiences soon returned and continued to increase. As the *Bioscope* reported in August 1914:

'The picture theatre is likely to be the last form of entertainment to suffer by the war since it is the cheapest, the most easily carried on, and under current conditions, perhaps the most attractive to the public'.

Not only did billeted soldiers seek out the local cinemas, but civilian families flocked to the films. Picture house prices were still within the means of a family deprived of its breadwinner, and as well as the usual attraction that films offered, there was the growing desire to see news films of the war.

Not all cinemas were predisposed to aiding the war effort with propaganda films. Some exhibitors believed their picture houses were places of amusement that readily provided an escape from thoughts of the war. This led to some objection: an anonymous 'neutral' sent this irate letter to *The Times* following a visit to the cinema:

'There was not one film shown to give any idea of the work of the British Army or the British Navy. The whole audience looked forward to the antics of one Charlie Chaplin'.

But even when some Derbyshire cinemas provided war films, the nature of their projection on to the screen left much to be desired. Such was the fidelity of the camera and projection equipment that real motion was never accurately reproduced. This caused consternation amongst at least one audience member who was moved to protest to his local paper about the lack of verisimilitude in the war footage. This article appeared in the *Derby Mercury* of 20 October 1916:

'HUSTLE AT THE CINEMA SHOWS'

'A cinema patron urges that pictures of war subjects should be exhibited at the pace at which they were taken. He continues: 'One sees tired troops returning at eight or nine miles an hour; a water bottle being jerked at a wounded man's mouth and jerked away again; a war ship dropping anchor with an apparent 20 knot way on her; a traction engine with a huge gun on tow and behaving like a frisky child. There is a total absence of the dignity which the subjects merit, and the way the show that I saw was hurried through, was an insult to the audiences'.

By 1916, annual cinema attendances had topped one billion (some 20 million a week), and it was estimated there were over 4,000 picture theatres in Britain. The *Bioscope* of the time summed up this new era in one succinct phrase: 'Only a few years ago a film cost a few shillings, and was shown in a shop. Now it may cost thousands of pounds, and is presented in a palace'. Not only had the industry grown and prospered with the establishment of permanent picture houses, but also the films themselves had been increasing in quality and length so that exhibitors could offer attractive, story-based 'feature' films plus the 'serial'. By 1916, for example, it was estimated that the *Exploits of Elaine* serial had been seen by ten million every week in about 40 per cent of UK cinemas.

In spite of the astonishing growth of cinema at this time, the more 'educated' classes largely stayed away. According to Rachael Low, author of *The History of the British Film 1914-18*, 'the war had the effect of the exhibitors devoting themselves quite openly after 1914 to the cultivation of the poorer people. With relief they abandoned elegance in favour of a more vulgar magnificence'.

It was reckoned the middle classes considered cinema beneath them, and preferred to crochet, play the piano, read a book, indulge in the odd card game or, if emboldened, venture out to a respectable theatre. As Bill Kirkham of Ripley remembers: "There were about five affluent families in our area, and you wouldn't find any of them going to the pictures – it was too lowly for them." However, there was recognition that something was going on. Even *The Times* of 1913 afforded this new entertainment medium some notice, albeit as a passing phase:

'Thirty years ago it was croquet, 15 years ago it was cycling, ten years ago it was roller skating...'

Ironically, the columnist's further observations actually validated the cinema as more than a mere 'fad':

'The picture palace offers immediate escape with the least possible expenditure of energy... all the work seems done for you. You never have time to be bored.'

Even though the article continued to offer the view that 'moving pictures are simpler, quicker, more direct than the best printed prose can ever hope to be', it was definitely 'not literature', nor was it 'life', 'art' or 'music'.

Historian A.J.P.Taylor recognised cinema-going as the 'essential habit' of the age, yet 'highly educated people saw in it only vulgarity and the end of Old England'. John Palmer, a virulent critic of the time, launched a scathing attack on film entertainment, contenting himself with the knowledge that it wouldn't last long:

'The picture palace has tapped a vast public looking for cheap amusement. It threatens to slay utterly the travelling show, nigger minstrels, the panorama and the circus... but we shall in a few years hear little of its competition with the theatre. Nor will those stuffy and stupefying picture palaces be able for long to maintain themselves in their hundred thousands. The limitations of this form of entertainment will soon appear, and the interest even of the threepenny public be exhausted.'

Those closely associated with the industry knew better. J.D.Best, Pathé's educational film expert declared that 'cinema is the greatest social force in existence' and that cinema 'freed man from the prison gates enclosing the mind in its narrow, monotonous circle of daily routine'.

The mood of the time was captured in similarly grandiloquent language within the pages of the *Kine Weekly* during March, 1916, describing the salutary

The original frontage of the *Somercotes Premier*. Bailey & Sons.

effects on the people who flocked to the film shows:

'Man and wife, sons and daughters, thronged the auditorium. The man, fresh from work, and the woman from the loom, sat together free from care for a couple of hours, so that the toil of the morrow could be faced with renewed courage and hope.'

The former Premier Electric Theatre, Swadlincote. Gill & Peter Dishart.

Pretentious as this may sound, it helps explain why cinemas were springing up in even the smallest of places.

Somercotes is a quiet, undistinguished Derbyshire village nestled in between Ripley and Alfreton. It grew up as a dormitory for the nearby collieries at Shady Pit, Cotes Park and Swanwick. Marjorie Severn was aged eight when the Premier picture house opened in 1912. Before the cinema came, there was a modicum of entertainment to be had, though nothing with the all-consuming novelty and appeal of the picture house. At various times of the year, Marjorie remembers Nathaniel Raynor's travelling players who used to set up a marquee in the market place to perform plays like *The Murder In The Red Barn*. Occasionally the local chapel organised entertainments. A common source of recreation was the pub. Marjorie lived opposite one: "There were always rows and fights on Friday nights," she remembers, "when the wives came to collect their husbands before they spent all of their wages." Other adults whiled away the evenings playing cards or dominoes, while the children gathered outside for marbles, hopscotch, 'Jack Jack, Shine Your Light' and other hopping, skipping and jumping games. These continued into the night under the glow of street lamps. Some of the more adventurous boys used to go out bird-nesting. The more fortunate Somercotes homes had a piano, and neighbouring families would often come together for an evening of community singing. A hardy few adults walked over to Alfreton Town Hall or the Electra Theatre, Ripley to see moving pictures.

But when the village finally got its own picture house, Somercotes was transformed. Local councillor and wine and spirits merchant George Beastall obviously saw a lucrative opportunity and opened the Somercotes Premier, Nottingham Road, on 1 January 1912, but even he was taken aback by the demand for this new entertainment, as within a short time he had to increase the auditorium capacity from 300 to 1,000, offering two houses nightly. Although the Empire was also built in 1912, as a billiard hall, that too was to change to a cinema by 1920. This meant that there were now 1,500 cinema seats for a village whose population numbered only about 5,000 (although the cinemas attracted visitors from Pinxton, Pye Bridge, Selston, Swanwick and Leabrooks).

Although George Beastall was the Premier proprie-

The Silencers

Most cinemas had problems at matinées with rowdy, disruptive or simply exuberant elements in its audience, and usually a swift word, a shine of the torch, or the mere presence of the manager, commissionaire, or a designated 'chucker-out' would be enough to quell any noise or misbehaviour. At some children's matinées, it was not uncommon to see an attendant with a stick. But Edna Millband remembers a much subtler approach at the Langwith Regal: "If we became excited and made a noise, a flashing light would come on each side of the screen, saying 'Silence Please'. It always worked, too."

Some cinema managers used to curb any unruliness by ordering the film to be stopped, and refusing to restart until the young rascals came to order. However, this would always have been both frustrating and time-consuming for the poor projectionist. Brian Gee remembers an attendant at the Pinxton Palace called Tabor who always threatened to stop the show if the young mob didn't quieten down, but he made this threat implicit in a very effective way: while the film was still showing, he would throw open the emergency doors. The result of all that harsh daylight flooding in either caused the young patrons to shield their eyes or to hinder their view of the on-screen action. Decorum was thus instantly restored, and the film show rolled on without a break.

The Somercotes Premier in the 1920s. L.Eyre.

of the area *The Thrill Of It All*: 'the centre of the proscenium arch had a crest containing the initials 'A.B.B.' which stood for Annie Bertha Beastall, the wife of the proprietor, who presided over the cash desk and struck fear into anyone who misbehaved.' Marjorie Severn remembers the fiery disciplinarian from the days she was employed by her as a chocolate seller at the Prem-

tor, there was little doubt who ran the place. As David Roddis points out in his book on the cinemas ier in 1918: "She was a bonny woman but a bit of a dragon. Us younger kids were in awe of her. If she

Pocket Money

In the days of the silent Saturday matinées at the Swadlincote Empire, most of the young cinema-goers spent their spare change on sweets. Not Len Brown: he pooled all his odd pocket money into the Bellfields toy shop opposite the Empire. For two or three pence, he could buy scrap 35mm film (presumably sold to the shop by the cinema), and the Brown household became a picture house. Young Len fed the small reel of film through a hand-cranked magic lantern-style projector, and put on a show for his pals, who were each charged a halfpenny for the privilege. They would sit in front of a stage made out of old orange boxes. Len even provided a curtain (one of mum's cast-offs), with a set of cords and pulleys so that he could automatically draw open the curtain to reveal the screen – an old bedsheet. The action on the scrap film was always a surprise, even to Len. Occasionally, there would be some football action, the simple movement of a car down a road, or a piece of slapstick comedy. Some of this spare film would only last for about 20 seconds, but if Len had spent threepence in a week when Bellfields had a good stock in, the show would last up to an epic two minutes. However, the local licensing authorities wouldn't have approved: because the illumination in the machine came from an oil lamp, and the film was highly inflammable, there was the constant danger of a blaze. Sure enough, an early show was halted when the oil lamp set fire to a film, but from there on Len learnt to be more careful, and his independent, makeshift cinema continued to screen these alternative films for a couple of years, with even the added sophistication of a record player providing suitable music.

The Big Chill

Apples and oranges were freely distributed to the children who frequented the cinema of the 1920s and 1930s. Not only was fruit regarded as a treat, but also the youngsters benefited from the Vitamin C intake (even if they did eventually hurl the apple cores and orange peel at all and sundry). Mrs Ford of Weston Underwood tells of a 1950s handout, although it's likely this was a one-off unique to the Broadway cinema in Allenton. In 1953, she and her mother visited the cinema on a snowy winter's day. On entering the cinema, every member of the audience was handed a packet of brown lozenges.

On a similar note, the Derby Cosmo, as well as providing its own soccer team, seems to have taken pity on its patrons who coughed and spluttered through performances, as it fell in with a local chemist who was obviously eager to cash in on the cinema's large clientele. In his research into Derby cinemas, Sam Winfield reveals that Fawcett & Son, 100 yards down and across the road from the Cosmo, prepared a winter formula which was sold as Cosmo Cough Cure. "It had a gingerish taste and was quite pleasant," recalls Sam. He also says it cured his cough – "or else the cough had run its course!"

turned up to look things over, signals went out and you were on your alert."

Marjorie remembers the effect the Premier had on Somercotes: "It became the focus of entertainment – the thing in the village." It was cheap, too, with seats ranging from only 2d for the wooden front seats to 6d for the velvet armchairs. Marjorie welcomed the cinema more than most: having lost her father at the age of ten, her mother had three children to support, with no pension. Securing a job at the Premier at the age of 14 provided her family with some badly-needed income. Although she also welcomed the chance of eyeing all the films for free, which "made me the envy of my friends", her pay was on a commission basis. For every shillings-worth of chocolate she sold, she earnt a penny. This was a task made more difficult by the fact that Mrs Meadows' sweet shop was right next door to the Premier, and did a roaring trade. But Marjorie usually pocketed between 2s 6d to 3s a week to help pay the rent. She worked six nights

week, and usually didn't get home until 11pm. What does Marjorie remember of the films? Mainly that they were westerns, slapstick and adventure serials, with Charlie Chaplin and Lilian Gish forever in view. "The films would be considered rather crude today" she recalls, "they were always terribly scratched – giving the impression sometimes of incessant rain – black spots commonly appeared, and they flickered continuously."

In spite of the comparatively primitive quality of both the films and their projection, the Somercotes Premier was a mirror of the way whole working communities were seduced, embraced and revolutionised by a simple yet magical new entertainment form. It was changing whole lifestyles and affecting village, town, county, nation... and world. As Charlie Chaplin was to observe only a few years later (in a statement similar to John Lennon's famous faux pas, albeit four decades early): "I am known in parts of the world that haven't heard of Jesus Christ."

Silent Witness
The Tuppeny Rush... and Tom Mix

The clamour was amazing even before the lights went down, and when the title of the film flickered uncertainly on to the screen, the noise changed to a roar of the kind that is usually associated with an 'infuriated mob'.

The Times, May 1920, describing a children's matinée.

When you weren't at the cinema, you were talking about the cinema. It was a major part of our lives.

Len Waller, matinée regular in the 1920s.

THE cinema emerged from World War One both leaner and fitter. During the conflict, some 800 cinemas had closed, but these were mainly the small, unprofitable, converted buildings. The temporary show had gone by the wayside, too. Both had become a casualty of competition from the purpose-built picture house which could offset the higher film programme costs by filling its auditorium to its more sizeable capacity.

However, for some time the overwhelming popularity of moving pictures had inevitably drawn concomitant doubts and suspicions from the establishment about the effect of this new medium on both crime and morality. Peter Stead, author of *Film and the Working Class*, believes that the cinema was initially rejected by 'respectable' society not merely because it was thought to be trivial, but also because it was regarded as corrupting and immoral:

'The whole atmosphere of the movies suggested tumult and promiscuity. It was widely assumed that motion pictures would be sexually suggestive and probably explicit, the whole tone seemed secular and irresponsible, and few doubted that children and the weak-minded were being pointed towards crime and degeneracy.'

Peter Stead also believes that respectable opinion was right, 'to a degree', as film-making had been unfettered from the outset: 'Motion pictures were free to show anything and to suggest anything.' However, even before the introduction of censorship in 1912, Peter Stead believes the showmen began to rid their picture houses of less respectable films as a consequence of their bid to win the approval of the middle classes as well as the religious, the political

and the 'serious-minded'. In 1908 the *Bioscope* recognised this drive towards greater respectability:

'The great majority of manufacturers and showmen have known all along that clean amusement is what is wanted by that section of their patrons which really matters. They have relegated the questionable film to the zone of undesirables and so, banned by the respectable frequenter of our great picture halls and uncountenanced by the bulk of manufacturers and dealers simply because they respect public opinion, and themselves recognise the evil which would most assuredly be the result of its constant exhibition, the indecent picture is gradually disappearing.'

Even so, the Press was busy printing headlines such as 'The Cinematograph and Juvenile Crime' or 'Cinematograph blamed for boy's downfall'. Even with censorship controls in place by 1912, there was still a rumbling discontent, and a call for even greater controls. On 26 May 1916, the *Derby Mercury* carried the following story:

CINEMAS and JUVENILE CRIME – DERBY MAGISTRATE'S ACTION

'Among the matters discussed at the meeting of the Derby Borough Magistrates on Tuesday was a Home Office circular in reference to the recent increase in juvenile crime. This drew particular attention to the need to further control the exhibition of Cinematograph films in view of that fact that a number of Chief Constables attributed the increase in a large measure to the showing of demoralising pictures. The letter was referred to the Improvements Committee in whose hands rest the granting of Cinematograph licences.'

In fact, the general disquiet felt amongst constab-

45

The bottom of King Street, Belper, with the Picture Palace on the right. Cyril Maskrey Collection.

Site of the Picture Palace at Belper. Terry Hawksworth.

ulary, clergy and education authorities prompted the British Board of Film Censors to invite the National Council for Public Morals to institute a committee of inquiry into the state of the cinema. There was particular concern about the effects of films on the young. Even before the moralists took their seats at the committee table, Canon Rawnsley wrote a warning letter to *The Times* about these very effects, although the poor man seemed to have been struck by a hyperbolic fit, as he described the 'horrors unimaginable' open to the 'greedy eyes' of four to fourteen-year-olds:

'Terrific massacres, horrible catastrophes, motor car smashes, public hangings, lynchings, badger-baiting, bullfights, pictures of hell fire and the tortures of the damned.'

Canon Rawsley didn't profess to having actually seen these horrific films himself, but continued in his letter to stress the appalling consequences of children's exposure to them:

'They cannot sleep at night and have been known to implore the policeman to guard them on their way home from "the horrid man with the beard".'

The minister may have had a point in expressing his alarm at the knowledge that children were tempted to sit in cinemas until 11 o'clock at night and would thus 'come weary and listless to school the following morning'.

However, Canon Rawnsley over-egged his complaint by giving the impression that these misdemeanours were more widespread than was probably the case, stating that many children had become 'petty pilferers' in order to obtain money for cinema admission, while 'others actually begin their downward course of crime by reason of the burglary and pickpocket scenes they have witnessed'.

Records show that there was no evidence of a spate of films depicting such impressionable scenes, but it was obvious the eminent clergyman wanted to make a point, as well as build up his epistle to a grand, bombastic finale:

'I dare to suggest that all who care for the moral wellbeing and education of the child will set their faces like flint against this new form of excitement.'

There were similarly condemnatory bleatings from the committee of the National Council of Public Morals, arguing that children ought to be kept out of picture palaces altogether unless they could be shown 'films about possible careers', or that they be encouraged to go to church, which was a likely eventuality as cinemas would probably die a natural death in a few years anyway.

The most temperate voice, the Chief Constable of Edinburgh, was probably the most reasoning; he stated that the admitted increase in 'juvenile

The Cosy at Heanor.
B.Hunt.

The former Cosy at Heanor, now the Cosy Market. **Andy Wilson.**

from the Council came from a probation officer called John Massey, who condemned the committee for their 'foolish' talk and lack of knowledge about 'the habits, the difficulties and the squalid lives' of the less well-off:

'Just imagine what the cinema means to tens of thousands of poor children (and their families)... for a few hours at the picture house they can find a breathing space, warmth, music (the more music the better), and the pictures, where they can have a real laugh, a cheer and sometimes a shout.'

Shout they certainly did. Poor Miss Vickers of a local Care Committee, again speaking on the National Council for Public Morals, complained that a cinema she had been to 'was very rowdy the whole time... it was like Babel'.

'Rowdy' (or 'very rowdy') is probably the most quoted phrase employed by all those I spoke with about the silent cinema era. However, I was mainly addressing those who would be of the age that witnessed the Saturday matinée. 'Vociferous' was one of the more gentle and generous epithets I heard to describe the atmosphere when hundreds of young-sters swarmed into a cinema. Perhaps more accurate words are 'chaos' and 'pandemonium.' Better still might be 'bedlam'. This was certainly how Charles Mather remembers the matinées at the Belper Picture Palace. For Maurice Elliot, who attended the early childrens' matinées at the Derby Temperance Hall, "the accumulation of noise would have made Bedlam seem like a monastery". Not surprisingly, Maurice adds that the phrase 'silent cinema' wasn't one that would come readily to mind whilst immersed in the deafening cauldron of a kids' matinée.

Not only was the noise at these 'silent' matinées at roof-raising level, but there was also a general air of unruliness. Part of the bedlam at Belper involved the ritual hurling of monkey nuts at the beleaguered orchestra. Orange peel and apple core were other handy missiles (oranges and apples were often handed to the children by the cinemas themselves, and as the fruit residue also left an appalling mess on the floor, many cinemas either discontinued with their kind gesture or else ensured the hand-outs came after the show). At the Bakewell Picture House, the tops of the orchestra's heads were always visible, and because Mr Fewkes the pianist was a bald-headed fellow with a lump on his head about the size of half an egg, he was a constant target for orange peel.

If a picture house had an upper tier, woe betide those directly underneath the balcony. Maurice Elliott refers to the Temperance Hall matinées as 'the Penny Pictures' but he says: "if you were rich, you could pay twopence to go upstairs, from where you could subject the unfortunate beneath to all kinds of

delinquency' coincided, not with the opening of the first picture palaces in 1910, but with the departure of the fathers from their homes four years later on the outbreak of the war. He backed this up with a report showing that the same pattern was recorded on the outbreak of the Boer War – a time when, of course, there were no picture palaces.

The Chief Constable also stated emphatically that the social change which coincided with the opening of the first picture palace was 'an immediate reduction in drunkenness'. Another Chief Constable was nowhere near as congratulatory. On the contrary, he stated quite simply that cinemas were 'full of germs'. Indeed, there was a terrible influenza epidemic in the years 1918-19, with cinemas blamed as one of the chief centres for disseminating the 'flu germs.

Worse still, though, according to the dissenting Chief Constable, the darkness in cinemas was the cause of numerous abuses, 'and one in particular where young women and young men attend together, not for the purpose of following the pictures but, owing to the darkness, to become spoony, and to work up passions'. In fact, one of the few agreed conclusions of the National Council of Public Morals was that there ought to be more light in cinemas. Some picture houses took heed and installed soft amber or rose-tinted lamps at low-level illumination throughout performances. This became known as 'morality lighting'. It was short-lived, forgotten soon after the National Council of Public Morals spouted its various reports.

Probably the most far-seeing and realistic comment

indignities." Len Brown also remembers the two-tier pricing system at the Swadlincote Empire matinées. You could either join in the Penny Rush or enjoy the much less frenetic path to the twopenny seats. Len paid the extra penny, and was duly dubbed a 'snob'.

Whether a Penny Rush or Tuppeny Rush, the word 'Rush' was certainly apposite. George Mellor, who attended matinées at the Heanor Cosy, confirms that the phrase Tuppeny Rush was no misnomer: "I once saw the little man who opened the door carried to the far end of the aisle!"

Another oft-used term from these times is the Chicken Run. However, this is a phrase that found its origin in the family-orientated shows. Alice Colder remembers that in order for the smaller children to see the screen (not all cinemas had a rake), they were despatched down to the front. This is probably why most picture houses installed benches on the first few rows; this would then maximise the amount of little bottoms that could be accommodated on them. However, there is little doubt that few bottoms would have found their way on to seats until the film rolled, and the resultant boisterous mêlée in the cramped, confined space in front of the screen would have resembled that of perpetually scurrying, jostling chicks in a hen house. The term Chicken Run was then generally applied to the cheaper bench seats at the front of a cinema at both family show and matinée.

However, at the matinées, the chicks would run wild all over the auditorium. Numerous are the stories of long-suffering staff pacing up and down the aisles attempting to keep order. Back to the Little Terrors of Temperance Hall, as described by Maurice Elliott: "there were those who wanted to climb on the chairs or tip someone off theirs; and those who wanted to wrestle for fun or fight for real." The clamour and combat would even continue while the films were being screened until, eventually, says Maurice, "the gentleman Magistrate would climb on to the stage to read the Riot Act, during which the attendants had a sort out, culprits were led out by one ear or collar neck, and an attempt made to get some order out of the chaos of kids and chairs. Eventually, with peace restored, the film was restarted, but was often interrupted by a repeat of the whole performance." Eventually, Maurice stopped going to the Temperance Hall, as he found himself getting involved in "a wrestling match you didn't like, a fight you didn't want, or a neckhold or earhole-handling for something you hadn't done. I decided it was too much like Russian Roulette."

However, Maurice's experience would appear to be uncommonly extreme. The matinées that other local folk recall were altogether much less riotous affairs.

'High spirits' is an oft-heard explanation for the apparently anarchic goings-on. According to Len Waller, who attended the Somercotes Empire matinées, much of the disorder was down to lack of supervision: "Imagine hundreds of kids gathered together out of school, with no teacher." Thus, this new freedom found expression in horseplay. Concerned cinema proprietors eventually began to employ a 'chucker out'. Len remembers the Empire's odd-job man George Nicholls being handed this role when Saturday came. It was rare, though, to see George actually prove true to his title and eject a child from the cinema. "We kids never did anything worse than clamber over seats" says Len. John Hassell remembers George as "a big frightening figure in a splendid red uniform, who seemed to spend most of the time trying to dodge all the apple cores and orange peel he was pelted with." However, George posed an effective threat, and helped prevent high spirits from tumbling over into wanton behaviour.

Other cinemas employed more drastic and arguably unnecessary measures. According to H.H.Hall, the Lyceum at Whittington Moor insisted on having a man parade down the aisles with an 18-foot cane. At the Swadlincote Rink, Kenneth Roy Taylor remembers his dad used to simply blow on his whistle. Other cinemas, like the Ashbourne Empire, needed only the presence of owner Mrs Stebbings to quell any disturbance. Perhaps Mrs Stebbings should have been more grateful: according to Duncan Cross, "the stamping of feet in the balcony was useful for dislodging dust."

Perhaps the most alarming case of vandalism occurred in later years at the Alvaston Rex, as recounted by Peter Flower: "Some lads used to come along with a saw and cut through just enough of the wooden forms in the front stalls so that whoever sat there next would collapse it. Eventually, the cinema had to employ a man to walk down the aisles with a long pole, and if anyone was caught misbehaving, they got a clout." Peter also remembers a much less harmful prank at the Rex, which involved the rolling of dried peas on the picture house floor – "it used to make a right din!" Most of the mayhem would occur in the minutes leading up to the start of the show. It was a different atmosphere once the first reel was running; the likes of George Nicholls would probably have returned to his odd jobs. Len Waller describes this moment with a choice simile: "You know the phrase 'pigs at a trough'?

"As soon as the farmer was seen with the buckets of slop, the pigs would start squeaking and squealing. That would be us before the programme started. But as soon as that farmer filled that trough, and those pigs got their snouts in it, there was dead silence. It was just like that when the projectionist dimmed the light."

Before we dim that light, let us consider the plight of matinée attenders like Len Brown at the Swadlincote Empire, who frequently found himself forced to perch on the front row, owing to sheer size of numbers: "the front row was least favourite because you had to hold your head back at an uncomfortable angle, and the figures always appeared elongated." But a cricked neck and a slightly dodgy view would be considered minor irritants to any viewer of the silent Saturday matinées.

A more pronounced irritant was a break in the film. The vagaries of projection equipment made this a common occurrence, and was greeted with a mixture of fun and frustration. How the operator at a matinée must have sighed as the film jammed, split or just simply stopped, knowing that it would spark a sonorous and rumbustious reception. When the show broke down at the Heanor Cosy, B.G.Ellis remembers a combination of 'stamping feet, shrill whistles and singing'.

It would have been a wholly different reaction if the projectionist had a more severe problem, namely the threat of a blaze. Edna Millband remembers a matinée at the Langwith Regal when the film caught fire, leading to a mass evacuation of the cinema. Fortunately, it was put out, no damage was done to either the projectionist or his booth, and the children were allowed back in.

There is no question of the sheer thrill felt by any youngster, in the company of his pals, at the sheer sensation of moving pictures and seeing also, as an early picture house billing would proclaim, 'A World Before Your Eyes'. For Ernest Sutton, it was fascinating enough to know that "the people we saw from other parts of the world were no different from us... even if they did walk rather jerkily across the screen."

A star who made a fortune out of 'jerky' movements was Charlie Chaplin, a particular matinée favourite. B.G.Ellis recalls that the Great Clown's early two-reel comedies would cause the young audiences to literally roll in the aisles, so convulsed with laughter would they be. "Comedies and serials were the life-blood of that cinema" adds B.G. He also cites the slapstick antics of Fatty Arbuckle, Chester Conklin, Ben Turpin, Buster Keaton... and the Keystone Cops 'racing, chasing and careering madly anywhere and everywhere'.

That life-blood would surge through young bodies at the appearance of the weekly serial, and freeze at the (sometimes literal) cliff-hanger. Popular serials at the time would include anything starring Tom Mix, William S.Hart, Eddie Polo, Pearl White (*Perils of Pauline* is a fondly-remembered favourite), William

Farnum in *The Grey Ghost*, and Elmo Lincoln (the first Tarzan) in *Elmo The Mighty*. The showing of the serial was a signal for much frenzy and exhilaration. For some children, the action was real. As Len Brown explains: "the vociferous audience were not slow in giving the hero advice when being chased by the villain, with shouts of 'look behind you!', or offering advice to the heroine tied to the railway track."

The image of the struggling female lashed to a railway line with a giant loco bearing down on her is one of the great cinema clichés. Judging by the number of times this cliffhanger scene has been mentioned to me in the course of my research interviews, it would appear that Pearl White was placed in this predicament on several occasions. Indeed, as Derby Cosy regular James Mathers writes: 'there were usually 13 episodes in these serials and Miss White would often end one episode by being tied to a railway line. The episode ended with a huge American engine thundering down only feet from our heroine'. Then would appear the exasperating announcement 'Come Next Week' or 'To Be Continued', which produced jeers, roars and angst-filled cries. As Len Brown admits: "the serials left you trembling with excitement."

So how did Pauline escape her peril? Prepare to be disappointed: James Mathers continues '...next week a pair of points would have grown into the line and the train diverted only inches from our heroine's head. Thrilling stuff'. It sounds a let down, actually, but it seems that however far-fetched the finale and however simple, contrived or corny the resolution in the following week's episode, the matinée audiences would still feel a palpable

Lilian Gish and Tom Mix, stars of the silent screen.

tension as the serial recommenced the following week.

Bill Kirkham, who attended matinées at Ripley, has a vivid memory of a 20-part serial called *The Vanishing Dagger*: "You used to beg for next Saturday to come around to see if the hero could extricate himself from his cliff-hanging fate at the end of each episode. He always did. Mind you, I once remember saying: 'he's had it this time'... I really thought he was a goner. Some Arabs locked him in a round blockhouse, where the walls were gradually closing in on him. The episode finished, and he was that close to death. Come next week, at the beginning of the episode, all he did was lean his shoulder on a giant block, and he was out!" 'And with one bound he was free', as the cliché goes. The silent screen serial must have given birth to that phrase.

There was particular affection for the western heroes. "Not many stood out" says Len Waller, "because we used to see so many of these low-budget westerns." Ken Maynard was one who did stand out, mainly for his white horse. Hoot Gibson was apparently adept at outwitting the Indians. B.G.Ellis can still recall the 'tall, lantern-jawed' William S.Hart. As James Mathers remembers: "He spoke little and seemed to be welded to his horse. He seldom appeared on foot." But whether his feet were on the ground or up in the saddle, Tom Mix was the favourite. As Jack Harding says of the Swadlincote Empire matinée days: "we used to create a storm if Tom Mix wasn't on." There could have been few Saturdays when he wasn't on: Mix made over 400 western films, and always eclipsed his cowboy counterparts by sporting spangled costumes, topped off with a white ten-gallon hat. He also brought a sense of stunt showmanship to the action (a legacy of his days as a prize-winning rodeo performer). In his hey-day, there was no one in Hollywood getting more fan mail than Tom Mix... apart from his horse, Tony. Tom Mix even came to Derby one year, putting in a personal guest appearance at the Derby Alexandra.

Tom Mix's films, along with all the other westerns, worked to a familiar and favoured formula. Frank Bacon remembers that "the hero was always clean-shaven, upstanding, never kissed a woman and always rode a clean horse." The baddie was equally as recognisable: "he had a vicious look" says Len Waller, "with an all-black outfit, and a black, scruffy horse." Frank Bacon remembers that the baddies were "always unshaven, forever chewing tobacco, drinking whisky and spitting." However, it was rare to see Tom Mix wound these villains with a gun, let alone kill them. He would normally capture the bad guys. And as Len further remembers: "the only violence I can remember in one of these films was when a cowboy got an arrow in his backside. And when people got shot, they felt no apparent pain; they just keeled over."

Len also believes that the westerns and most of the other matinée films were character building: "You came out of a good film walking tall, and feeling sort of... heroic. I don't think many modern films are good at forming character... unless you want to be a serial killer."

Len further believes that because the films were silent, one could develop one's own thoughts: "Watching a silent was like reading a play; you formed your own ideas. Alright, the films weren't very subtle, and every word and action was overstated, but it still gave your imagination great scope." The educational aspect must not be overlooked either, says Len. For him, the silent cinema was an English language aid: "It taught a lot of kids to read. When I was five, I can remember the word 'tonight' coming on the screen, and after a perplexing few seconds, the following scene was dark, and I remember saying: so that's how you spell it!"

Maurice Elliot provides further evidence of the misnomer 'silent cinema': "The film captions were read out aloud by every one of the kids including those who could read but couldn't speak properly, those who could speak but couldn't read properly, those who shouted for more time before the caption disappeared, and those who shouted: 'gerron wi' it'."

Considering the clamour and general unruliness, why did cinemas persevere with the matinées? A question John Bradford has often asked himself: "to this day I can never work out the economics of it all. At one penny a time, you had to have 240 people there to take a pound. How did they manage to employ a manager, projectionist and assistant, and three ladies to give out and check tickets, provide heating and lighting, and make a profit?"

One may well ask. Even if the cinemas were fam-ily-run with the projectionist on a part-time wage, and the rental for the films shown was recouped during the rest of the week's programme, there would have been scant returns for a picture house running a regular matinée. But it is certain that any cinema was keen to invest in its future, and even if young Tommy was a bothersome presence, climbing over the seats, throwing monkey nuts at the chucker-out, and leading the jeering when the screen went blank, he would eventually lose his high spirits, gain an education, get a job, take a wife, and become a regular attender at the evening shows... and before long, there would sit Tommy Junior, cheering on the next Tom Mix. Mind you, let's hope his generation can learn to be quieter. After all, there are rumours going round that something called the 'Talkies' is coming...

Music In The Air

The not-so-silent cinema... and its 'effects'

Some people used to flock to the Picture Palace not for the film, but to hear the orchestra!

Peter Davies, son of Alf Davies, percussionist with the Belper Picture Palace Orchestra

THE arrival of the Talkies was not just to benefit the local cinema industry, but to positively boost it. Nonetheless, there were casualties. On a wider scale, there was Charlie Chaplin, who said "films need dialogue about as much as Beethoven's symphonies need lyrics." Chaplin obviously saw his metier facing extinction. But even if Beethoven's symphonies were given lyrics, they would still require musicians to play them. However, when the silent films were swiftly supplanted by sound films, silent cinema musicians across Derbyshire saw their livelihoods erased.

Musical accompaniment to silent films would have begun in the cinema's infancy. There may even have been some kind of basic musical backdrop provided for the first ever screening of moving pictures in Derbyshire, simply because the films were shown as part of a vaudeville bill. Any variety turn taking the stage at Morritt's Empire, Derby, would have had a complement of music, so it's conceivable that the orchestra would have been instructed to play on as the lifeograph was cranked into action. But even if the flickering images were accompanied by music, it's likely it would have been sketchy, improvised and/or inappropriate. In the book *The History of British Film 1896-1906* by Rachael Low and Roger Manvell, which authoritatively chronicles the opening decade of cinema, there is no mention whatsoever of musical accompaniment to moving pictures (although in a later history, it is stated that 'the exhibition of films had always been accompanied by some form of sound'). Yet at some point, an enterprising film producer must have hit upon the bright notion of delivering his moving picture product with suggestions for suitable music, as a way of heightening the cinema patron's reception for his films. At the very least, music was a useful aid to an audience's concentration.

Orchestras were employed by the first of Derbyshire's purpose-built picture houses between 1910 and 1915, so it is evident that by this time the concept of musical scores had been developed to some organisational degree, with cue sheets being supplied to the cinemas by the 'better' renters. As Rachael Low points out in *The History of the British Film 1918-29*, renters might provide titles of particular pieces of music to be played. Apparently, romantic composers like Mascagni, Delibes, Massenet and Grieg were popular choices, with works by lesser-known contemporary British composers useful for 'lighter' stories. However, this always posed a problem for the cinema's musical director unless he had access to a large music library. Alternatively, the renter would suggest the type of music suitable for various film passages (sometimes stating exactly at which sub-title or incident the music should be placed). As Rachael Low explains:

"General instructions might suggest tragic music, flowing, sentimental, bright-lively, foxtrot, hymn, dramatic agitato, light intermezzo or very occasionally 'effect' or even 'silence'... vague instructions such as 'flowing melody' set problems for those less well-versed in music, especially as few musical directors were able to see the films in advance, although the sameness of films made their job easier."

Some musicians were clearly not up to the task: Vachel Lindsay, author of *The Art of The Moving Picture*, encountered little art in one distressing visit to a cinema:

'With fathomless imbecility, hoochey koochey strains are on the air while horses are dying.'

So, not only was appropriate music fundamental to a film, but so was the player's concentration. Furthermore, a highly proficient standard of musicianship would be required to provide differing moods for a programme of films, especially as cinemas changed their programmes at least twice a week. The job also carried with it an enormous amount of responsibility. Not only would a duff note be met with amused or embarrassed chortles from the audience but, more crucially, the patrons' enjoyment of a film could be elevated by the expertise, dexterity and even daring of an orchestra or single pianist. A point confirmed by writer Dorothy Richardson, describing the best kind

The Ripley Hippodrome Orchestra. From left to right are J.West (violin), Mr Dilks (viola), J.Oakley (piano), Mr Henshaw (cello), T.Holmes (trumpet), B.Lloyd (drums and vocalist). L.F.Wood.

of silent pianist: 'He could time a passage to culminate the break punctually on a staccato chord at a crisis. This is a crude example of his talent for spontaneous adaptation. As long as he remained with us, music and picture were one. If the film were good, he enhanced it, heightened its effect of action moving forward for the first time.'

One musician noted for raising the action was Jack Baxter, who was resident pianist in the early days of the **Heanor Cosy**. George Mellor didn't actually hear him play at the cinema, but did stumble across his talent at the turn of the 1970s when he attended a local Life Class. Jack Baxter, then a pensioner, was one of the subjects. During his short rest period, Jack went over to play the piano. "He was obviously very gifted" says Geoff, "and I later learned that he enjoyed a particular reputation for the speed of his playing. People would say to me: 'Jack could make them 'osses go faster than anybody, anywhere else'."

Another acclaimed local pianist was Charlie Williams, who accompanied the films at the **Ashbourne Empire**. Les Allen recalls that as well as tinkling the ivories for the pictures, Charlie would entertain the audience in the breaks. Les recalls that "the words to popular songs would appear on the screen, and Charlie played the tune several times until we knew them... songs which come to mind include *I'm In Love With Sheila O'Shea*, *The Whispering Pines of Nevada* and *Side By Side*."

Les also remembers that Charlie Williams' popularity was such that when he was mysteriously sacked, there was a near riot during Charlie's last performance. However, the audience's anger was eventually quelled, and his replacement Charlie Gosling turned out to be just as good. Not only that, Les believes Charlie managed to get a good job in Blackpool.

One local woman who tried her hand, albeit briefly, at silent film accompaniment was Hilda Webb (née Ratcliffe). Sometime during 1920, her mother Alice spotted an advertisement in the paper for a relief pianist at the **Derby Cosmo** on Upper Boundary Road. Although Hilda was only 14, proud Alice believed her daughter had the talent (and the sheet music) to not only give it a go, but also to make an impression. The few shillings a week pay would help, too. Although Hilda had performed publicly before, this was a fresh, unique challenge. Nervously clutching her music, she entered the 'scruffy little cinema' and passed the audition. A pianist like Hilda Ratcliffe would have been expected to deliver mood and colour to a range of pictures. However, she doesn't remember seeing a score provided with any of the films, so had to rely on her own stock music. "I never got a run-through either" says Hilda, "all I had was the titles, and a rough idea of the type of film."

As there were advertisements in between the various pictures, Hilda had time to check her list – a news reel called for drama, so Hilda would produce the appropiately-titled *Fire, Fire*; a romantic drama was usually complemented by the stock favourite *Hearts and Flowers*; for a solemn picture, Listz's *Liebestraum* matched up well; and for an action picture, Hilda launched into marching music. There was plenty of available sheet music designated as suitable for westerns and slapstick comedy, but there were occasions when the 14 year-old got well into her stride, and improvised. "I never got stuck" Hilda proclaims, "and I was quite well-received." However, in spite of an insistent mother, young Hilda Ratcliffe got fed up after a few months, and left The Cosmo, never to return. The job had become dull and routine, but Hilda recalls her brief spell with some affection.

It was obviously no more than a routine task for Billie Wood to supply the piano sounds to the silents at the **Alexandra** in Swadlincote. His memory of the time conveys not even a whiff of nostalgia, even though he performed for 11 years, playing an instrument known as a 'patent annexe', a cross between a piano and a conventional organ. Billie bluntly states: "I never liked the pictures. I liked the real things in life." So why did he do it for so long? "I just played for the money. I received £2 7s 6d a week – a fortune in those days." It was certainly a fortune compared with his 'real' job as mechanic at Netherseal Colliery, where invariably there was only sufficient work for three shifts a week, at only five shillings per shift.

Although the smaller, less endowed cinemas employed only a pianist, larger ones used either a band or an orchestra. Sometimes a 'band' would simply include a pianist augmented by a violinist or a drummer (or both). An 'orchestra' could comprise up

Riding High

'Pop' Buxton remembers a menagerie of odd live acts which entertained the Alfreton Odeon audience in between the films. One week, there appeared on stage an animal heralded as 'The Unrideable Mule', with invitations for the audience to mount the beast and stay on for at least one minute. Before you could say 'hi ho Silver', young 'Pop' Buxton was up on his feet. This 'have-a-go' enthusiasm was based on the fact that 'Pop's' father used to regularly take his son to see a friend who kept donkeys. One of them was reckoned to be unrideable, so the plucky 'Pop' used to spend hours trying to master it. He never did, but he thought he had learnt enough to take on this so-called 'Unrideable Mule'. As it transpired, this much-trumpeted animal was a soft touch compared with the donkey in the field, 'Pop' stayed on the mule for the requisite 60 seconds, and won a big prize.

to seven or eight musicians. At Derby's first purpose-built cinema, the Midland Electric, a seven-piece orchestra was led by Billy Albright, a talented violinist who wrote numerous scores himself.

In his history of Erewash Valley cinemas *The Thrill Of It All*, David Roddis salutes the Evans family of Ilkeston. John Evans, part of a family well respected in local musical circles, became involved in the Scala when it opened in 1913. But not solely as a musician: he graduated from caretaker to manager, remaining until his sudden death in 1944. Furthermore, his talented son Wilfred, a cellist, was to make his mark both in management and musical direction. He played at both the local Scala and Globe, as did his younger pianist brother Ernest. Possibly because of Wilfred's reputation, the Globe Orchestra was feted by the *Ilkeston Advertiser* even before the cinema opened, predicting that any patron would 'see good pictures to the accompaniment of refined and enervating music, the combination of which can scarcely fail to produce a highly beneficial effect upon his nature'.

Although the Globe only lasted until 1923, Wilfred and brother Ernest gave the Scala Orchestra an enviable standing. One letter from 'A Music Lover' was typical of the kind sent to the cinema, praising 'your splendid little orchestra which discoursed some delightful music during the showing of the pictures', and comparing them favourably with other orchestras he had heard in large cities across the country. 'Will you kindly tell them' he concluded, 'that as one who stands for good music without fancy stunts and blaring saxophones, I think their playing is a credit to Ilkeston'.

As David Roddis also points out, not so much a fancy stunt as a useful gimmick was brought to the **Palace Theatre**, Long Eaton (still running as The Screen Cinema): in 1922, a permanent organ was installed, Derbyshire's very first.

The **Derby Alexandra** also had a unique musical attraction, or at least it was to Ern Baxter. Sam, the concertina player, was an albino. Ern and his pals used to watch out for Sam when he came walking down to the Alex, and implore him to play, 'which he almost always willingly did, sitting on a window ledge with a bunch of fascinated kids'. That source of fascination was not so much his music as his shock of white hair and extraordinary pink eyes. One evening,

Toys

There are numerous accounts of the generous handing out of oranges and apples to young cinemagoers of the 1920s and 1930s. But some picture houses went further. As a youngster, John Hassell ensured he was a regular attender at both the Alfreton Empire and Odeon because he knew that come the end of the year, he would get better Christmas presents than he ever had at home. If you had enough stamps on your attendance card, you were guaranteed a gift. For boys like John, these included metal wind-up toy buses, bikes and other vehicles. John's one regret is that he never hung on to these toys, as he considers they would be of some value today.

Food of the Gods

H.L.Burt of Riddings savours the memory of a visit to the Somercotes Premier as a youngster in the 1930s. Even before he and his pals cast eyes on the big screen, they would delight in beholding all the goodies on display at Bates' sweet shop near the cinema. If he had as much as one and a half pence jingling in his pocket, he felt rich and excited, because entry to the pictures was only a penny, leaving a halfpenny to spend at Bates'. There was a sumptuous choice – Dolly Mixtures, Chocolate Chewing Nuts, Jap Filberts, Liquorice Torpedos, Locust Bean, Tiger Nuts and many other varieties, all in little paper-lace edged wooden boxes, and all priced at two ounces per penny. Master Burt usually settled for an ounce of Tiger Nuts, as they lasted longer than sweets, always wrapped in a hand-made cone-shaped bag. He would then take his place in the Premier queue, which would surge forward as soon as the door was opened. After presenting his penny to a 'dour-faced lady' in the pay box, he found a vacant seat on one of the long rows. As he eagerly awaited the start of the show, Master Burt would perform a short, pleasurable ritual: "my hand delved into the paper bag in my pocket, found a couple of my precious Tiger Nuts, popped them into my mouth and for a few moments I savoured their nutty, milky taste."

Monica Blood also recalls buying her sweets at the local shops before entering her local cinema. She also remembered to take the wrappers off: "the slightest rustle", says Monica, "and everyone round about would turn on me and go 'sssshhhhh!!!'."

However, there was plenty of noise at other cinemas, caused directly by food: stories are commonplace of kids dropping monkey nut shells on the floor, simply because it made a super noise when walking on them on the way out.

There was a consistently annoying noise also caused by food at the Bakewell Picture House at the turn of the 1960s. So irksome had it become that Robert Bowler's usherette mother decided to take matters into her own hand. She used to take time out to pop every crisp packet with a quick jab of a knitting needle. Fellow usherettes were forever grateful: no more would a playful youth blow up his empty crisp bag and burst it at the moment she walked by in the dark.

John Bradford attended the matinées at the Swadlincote Rink, and although he usually spent his spare penny on sweets, occasionally he had a fancy for something more savoury, so he called in at the Co-op butcher's shop and bought a penny faggot.

An unusual penny purchase at the Somercotes Premier is explained by projectionist Eddie Burnham: "We used to get orange marks on the screen at some Saturday afternoon matinées. Some kids would turn up with a penny carrot they'd bought at Connie Lucas' grocer shop. When it was Flash Gordon taking on Ming, for example, the appearance of Ming was greeted with a shower of carrot ends."

A grocery shop purchase to a similar end is recalled by Swadlincote cinema-goer Graham Nutt. For the matinées at the Empire – run by John Avery – the youngsters used to buy a pound of cherries, at which point the shop assistant used to say: "Here's another pound of cherries for John Avery's neck!"

Ice-creams were, of course, extremely popular, although Pat Swift reckons that certain cinemas used to play an underhand trick: "it was common practice" she maintains, "to turn the heating up before the interval in order to maximise ice-cream sales."

Leslie Halliwell, who wrote a nostalgic account of his cinema-going days in the book *Seats In All Parts*, dwelt somewhat critically on the quality of the ice-creams served up by the cinemas: "The tubs contained hard, dull, tasteless stuff, and the Snofrute bars, being nothing but frozen juice with bits of fruit left in, tended to melt very suddenly and run through the open-ended carton right down one's sleeve. They tasted delicious, but resulted in pools of sticky mess down the carpet."

Ern was allowed to sit next to Sam in the orchestra pit, and discovered a common difficulty for the silent film musician: the closeness of the screen. Ern was astounded to find that 'it was only by craning the neck backwards that the film could be seen'. Not surprisingly, a cricked neck was a common complaint for a picture house musician.

Gladys Parkin, the pianist at the Killamarsh Palace, had no time to complain of a stiff neck, and the cinema owners would certainly have had no cause for complaint about Gladys' commitment and conscientiousness. For 15s a week, Gladys Parkin cleaned the cinema in the morning, played piano during both afternoon matinées and evening screenings, and had no time to compose herself in front of the keyboard: she also acted as usherette, showing upwards of 300 customers to their seats. Furthermore, the cinema employed variety turns in between reel changes, so presumably Gladys played on.

Dorothy Marston, who played the piano at the Alexandra in Swadlincote, had her work cut out in another way, as her nephew Len Brown recalls. It could be said that the presence of live music was useful in a picture house for covering the sound from the operator's gallery and the chatter of the audience. But Dorothy had the opposite problem: the noise from the skaters in the adjoining hall was so overwhelming that the poor woman had a job hearing herself play. This particular headache was exacerbated when the rain pattered on the corrugated roof!

That amplified rain must have proved a useful sound effect accompaniment at times (apparently, hailstones sounded like a conflagration). Swadlincote historian Graham Nutt recalls an amusing story passed down to him by former Alexandra projectionist Jim Smith, about an actual 'effects' picture sent to the cinema. It also highlights another of the unique qualities of this woeful picture theatre. One day, a film called *The Tempest* arrived, in a package containing an electric fan. It was requested that the fan be coupled with the supply and placed at one side of the screen. Also in the delivery were some ribbons and bits of metal, all to be hung just above the screen. Obviously, the idea was that as the film was rolling, the audience would experience a tempestuous wind while sat in their seats, thereby enhancing the realism of the picture. Jim Smith duly set everything up, and once the lights were extinguished, the fan came on and did its work. The Alexandra audience had truly been struck by a tempest. However, some patrons got more than they bargained for. The temporary wind machine had not only whipped air around the ribbons, metal bits and faces of the audience, but had also fetched down the accumulations on the Alexandra roof. Here was a genuine,

early case of the 'shit hitting the fan': when the lights came up, Jim Smith noticed that years of dirt, dust and cobwebs were sitting on the faces of the first five rows. "It looked just like a miner's matinée" quipped Jim.

Sound effects were available as an adjunct to the music from a surprisingly early date, evidenced by a glance at a 1912 catalogue from the pioneering British cinema suppliers Walturdaw. This firm sold all manner of products – arc lamps, ash trays, projectors, poster frames, ticket machines and tip-up seats... even a 'Singing Bird' for picture house entrance halls. A cage with two musical birds, 'which sing the latest songs of the day' cost £10 17s 6d, with average takings for the cinemas estimated at between 15 to 25 shillings a week. Walturdaw also sold an impressive set of 'Sound Effects', comprising largely metal-based gadgets that could reproduce a wide range of noises: a glass crash (the cheapest available effect, at 2s 6d), baby cry and bird whistle (3s each), pig grunt or train whistle (3s 6d) up to the slightly more expensive hen cackle (5s), galloping horse (8s 6d) and church bell (9s). For the more affluent picture house, a rain machine could be purchased for 11s, a thunder sheet for 15s, with a cathedral chime clocking in at £4 4s, complete with light oak frame, or only £3 15s if you were content with a frame of stained walnut. Although these multifarious effects were billed as 'a revelation' by Walturdaw, they were hardly going for a song.

The **Belper Picture Palace** had a large panoply of sound effects, untypical of a small town cinema. However, expenditure on effects was never a problem: the picture house percussionist Alf Davies used to make them all himself. Alf's son Peter retains a vivid memory of the myriad objects his father fashioned and built, and which in the 1920s must have considerably enhanced the enjoyment of all the silent

Alf Davies, percussionist and supplier of sound effects at the Belper Picture Palace.

Fire Down Below

Dick Pymm, long-time projectionist at the Derby Gaumont, chortles at the memory of an incident which brought new life to the phrase the 'hot seat'. One of the many gimmicky features of the Compton organ was the illuminated seat. One evening, a flustered-looking musician suddenly packed up playing, went back down under the floor, and sent an urgent message to the management – 'My seat is on fire'. There had been an electrical fault in that area. Fortunately, no lasting damage was done to the seat of the organ or the organist, and there was a humorous, coincidental coda: immediately following the incident, the Gaumont ran a trailer for their forthcoming attraction – *Fire Down Below*.

film programmes for the audiences who gathered in the Palace on King Street.

During the day, Alf Davies was a photographer. In the evening, he would sit behind the drums just in front of the Belper Palace screen, with his fellow musicians 'Mamie' Miller on piano, and John Miller on violin. It wasn't long into Alf's residency before he brought his obvious talents as a craftsman to bear, and began turning his hand to the construction of various instruments that could reproduce the noises Alf could 'hear' on the screen but which were silent to all in the seats. It was all very well giving the audience the emotional tone of a piece of action through music, but how much better for the patrons to also experience the slams, bangs, booms, claps, clatters and crashes! This thinking resulted in Alf Davies becoming a one-man orchestra of sound effects.

Peter Davies remembers a room in the family house where his father stored his arsenal of effects: "when you walked in, it was like stepping inside the Nautilus." So what kind of hand-made equipment was in this metallic array? The simplicity of the construction often belied Alf's ingenuity. For instance, although the effect of rain came from a metal drum of dried peas, the actual number of peas was important, and the question of tempo was crucial: a slow turn gave the impression of a trickle, a fast turn was a downpour. There was also a drum with dried sand: "When my Dad got to work on that drum," says Peter, "it was as if the sea was lapping at your feet." Another basic requirement was wind, again reproduced via a drum, and the effect of two canvas belts rubbing together. Once more, speed was all important: a rapid turn, for example, could simulate a storm.

Some of Alf Davies' effects were simplicity itself: a few choice nuts and bolts tossed into a tin bucket were enough to imitate the sound of various crashes. Son Peter also remembers seeing a large tin sheet, about six foot by four foot, which hung on a carrier. A controlled vibration was sufficient to produce all the drama of thunder and lightning. Alf always had an assortment of whistles (a swanee whistle had the desired humorous effect when the Keystone Cops came a cropper), a set of door catches, creaking hinges (ideal for horror films), and a sheet of brown paper, which would sound uncannily like flames when crackled right next to the microphone.

For the sound of human contact, Alf would produce his slapboard. This consisted of two pieces of wood about two foot long, hinged at one end. Brought together at the correct speed – as long as he synchronised well with the action on screen – Alf would produce a very lifelike slap on the face. This slapboard was also utilised for fight scenes, when the fist made contact with the jaw. Should the fist make contact with the stomach, Alf would strike a hard cushion placed close to the microphone.

Peter Davies also tells of how his father experimented. After some searching and trying, he eventually found that the striking of a series of half-shafts off a car best approximated the sound of bells.

Alf Davies assembled his battery of noises completely at his own expense. His conscientiousness knew no bounds: if he was confronted with an incident in a film which required a sound effect he didn't have in his armoury, he would immediately go out and create one. When one particular feature film came to the Palace, and called for the sound of bells, Alf realised that his half-shafts of a car failed to reproduce the deep resonance he required. So, he went out and obtained a shaft off a lorry. Come the next screening, the Palace must have vibrated when Alf came to strike that shaft with all his might. But it was just the thing for *The Hunchback of Notre Dame*.

As Peter Davies confirms: "People have often remarked to me just how authentic the sounds were, and how frightened they became sometimes by the noises he could create." Take the time the Palace received *Ben Hur*: Alf had a metal megaphone,

This Week of Grace

Herbert Siddons has a fond memory of appearing on the variety bill at the Matlock Picture Palace in 1938 as a Gracie Fields impressionist. He was only 14 years old, but had impressed one of the cinema's usherettes so much that she unhesitatingly recommended him to Mr Farrell, the Picture House manager, who duly auditioned and booked him. Herbert remembers having to obtain Gracie's permission to perform his act; her agent wrote back, telling him he was permitted to do an 'impression' but not an 'impersonation'. In other words, Herbert was allowed to sing like her, but couldn't dress up. So, picture the scene: a 14-year-old lad walking on to the stage in a male evening dress suit, proceeding to emulate to perfection the chirpy comic songs of a Lancashire lass-turned-movie-star. 'Gracie' received £4 appearance money, and was very well-received. Herbert went on to play the Alfreton Odeon, and continued as an impressionist, on a semi-professional basis, impersonating other acts like Carmen Miranda, this time complete with frock (and fruit, no doubt), and Shirley Bassey. He ended his performing days in 1979. Now in his 70s, he has finally lost the power to 'Sing As We Go' like Gracie Fields – "nothing comes out, I'm afraid", says Herbert.

through which he would do a little bit of singing or crooning. Once again, using his ingenuity, Alf found that if he growled through the megaphone, he could mimic the lions as they awaited their diet of Christians. However, it wasn't just the poor Christians who suffered that week. There were so many lions growling in one screening of Ben Hur that Alf's voice was beginning to crack. Yet such was the appeal of *Ben Hur* and its realistic lions that the film was retained for a second week. Alf Davies saw the screenings through, but by the end of that fortnight, he was admitted to hospital with throat trouble. His voice had almost completely seized up.

Peter Davies recalls an even funnier story, and an even more traumatic experience for Alf than his growling excesses through the metal megaphone. For western films, Alf Davies acquired a revolver. Two, in fact; after all, gun battles could be quite severe, with shots going off in quick succession. Both guns fired out a compressed cotton wool ball, and proved very effective for dealing with any rats that strayed into the stalls. One night, waiting for his cue, Alf had one revolver pointing down, forgetting that his right foot was on the clap cymbal. The on-screen gun battle commenced, and Alf swung into quick-draw action. The next thing he remembered was a tremendous jolt in his foot, and his subsequent cry of pain. Looking down, he saw a shoe billowing blood. He had shot himself. 'The show must go on' adage must have been

agonisingly felt at this point. Alf bravely struggled through to the end of the performance before receiving treatment, and carried a scar to the day he died. It is worth reflecting on the possibility that when Alf fired the fateful shot, he delivered the first moment of sound dialogue to silent films, albeit briefly, indistinctly and painfully.

By the time proper sound dialogue came to films, musicians like Alf Davies were redundant. He graduated to his own local band, the Derwent Dance Orchestra, and his reputation grew even wider. But all of Alf's sound effects became junk and, a few years later, after using the effects in the odd pantomime, they went the way of junk. Son Peter adds a rueful coda: "All I have left are two whistles."

Some local cinemas resisted the talkies for as long as possible simply because their audience seemed perfectly content with the silents and had long enjoyed the popular tradition of a live orchestra. A 'regular patron' of the Ilkeston Scala wrote to the cinema expressing his 'regret' at the advent of the talkies: 'I would much prefer hearing that delightful combination, the Scala Orchestra... I think the majority in Ilkeston prefer the silent picture plus good music'.

Within a few years, any such feelings were forgotten. The silent cinema was to lose its appeal and power as soon as that voice uttered those now immortal words: 'You ain't heard nothing yet'.

Dreams That Money Can Buy
Tastes, talkies and the 'super cinemas'

Enter the dreamhouse, brothers and sisters, leaving
your debts asleep, your history at the door.
This is the home for heroes, and this loving
Darkness a fur you can afford.

         – from *Newsreel* (1938) by C.Day Lewis.

BY the turn of the 1920s, cinema still had its critics, some quite virulent and resentful, like the renowned stage director Gordon Craig, who in 1922 openly condemned this burgeoning entertainment:

'Smears all it touches. Enslaves the mind of the people'.

Another figure of the Arts, French satirical writer Louis Céline expressed a sharply cynical view, describing cinema as 'that little clerk of our dreams that could be hired for an hour like a whore'. Poet John Drinkwater, in marked contrast to fellow versifier C.Day Lewis, whose rhapsodic rhyme opens this chapter, stated in 1923 that the cinema 'has no existence at all as an art'. In the same year, General Booth of the Salvation Army denounced films wholesale, as 'most disgusting and absolutely unfit for public exhibition'.

Maybe General Booth and his Salvation Army colleagues had cause for slight concern when even the influential trade paper the *Bioscope* had made the claim as early as 1919 that the cinema was the Church's 'legitimate competitor in moulding the character of the nation'. Indeed, by the mid-20s, the cinema was being referred to as 'The University of the Plain Man'. At about the same time, a film executive was claiming that the cinema was the 'most potent single factor in modern life'.

Most of cinema's detractors were resigned to its potency... and popularity. Lady Fowler, who officially opened the **Spondon Sitwell** cinema in 1928, said – according to the *Derby Evening Telegraph* – that she 'did not like the idea of a cinema', regarding it as 'an evil necessity'. However, 'speaking as a magistrate', she pronounced herself pleased that 'due regard would be given to the selection of films', before having the further grace of complimenting the Sitwell proprietor Mr T.Henry on the 'thought and taste shown in the decorations'.

By the time the Spondon Sitwell was opened, it was generally accepted that both

The Sitwell Cinema at Spondon.

Site of the Sitwell cinema at Spondon. Marshall Grey.

the respectability and the social status of the cinema was at a much higher level. Even the Royals were indulging in cinema-going: it was reported that 19 members of the Royal Family had been to see *Ben Hur*. By the end of the 1920s, *The Film In National Life* reported that 'a fellow of an Oxford College no longer feels an embarrassed explanation to be necessary when he is recognised leaving a cinema'.

It is not stated, though, what kind of picture that Oxford fellow would enjoy the most. One of the many springing up from the expanding film industries of the European countries, or from Hollywood? For the mass of the British cinema public, it was decidedly the latter, another source of discontent amongst the country's guardians of ethics and taste.

If you are resentful of the Hollywood film, and of America's dominance of the film market in general, you can blame World War One. Basically, British film-making shrank drastically during the war, and the Hollywood movie industry was galvanised by its opportunity to satisfy the growing demand for film entertainment; all over Europe, too, with the welcome universality that the silent film could bring.

Although Britain eventually received America's aid in winning World War One, she had unwittingly lost the battle for the film market on its own soil. The British film industry had to virtually start from scratch and, to make matters worse, was faced with many British cinemas block-booking packages of miscellaneous American films. Yet, as Audrey Field reveals in her book *Dream Palace*: 'There were few signs, as yet, that the public minded this state of affairs, for many of them were still happy to go to the pictures to see almost anything and be gregarious and keep warm'.

There is little doubt that because both the film industry was still finding its artistic and technical feet and audiences were still enraptured by the simple spectacle of the moving image, films that were deficient or weak in terms of acting, lighting, and overall direction were being served up to a largely indiscriminating audience. But crude and unsubtle as so many films were at this time, the Hollywood film-makers at least had an eye for the constituents of mass entertainment. As Audrey Field further states, there was 'an engaging gusto about even the indifferent American product which the British could not hope to match'.

This can be verified by the nature of the numerous American-based serials (mainly of the 'near-miss' adventure type) and 'comics' (particularly of the broad slapstick type), both significantly uppermost in the memories of the many Derbyshire folk who spoke to me of their cinema-going in the 1920s. Uncomplainingly so, as I have already intimated, in marked contrast with Labour leader Ramsey MacDonald who in 1923 roundly condemned 'foreign' films (by 'foreign' he meant 'American'), stating he was 'sick and tired of seeing nothing but American places, people, manners, customs and romance'.

There is no evidence that Ramsey MacDonald did anything to improve this state of affairs as the American Dream took a hold. Indeed, by 1925, British films appearing on British screens were down to a mere five per cent. A year later, historian A.J.P.Taylor remarked that few British films were making their mark, and that the movie 'brain drain' had already begun: 'Actors,' wrote A.J.P., 'soon departed for Hollywood if they achieved any reputation'.

What's more, it had all but been forgotten that Charlie Chaplin was British: a Favourite British Film Stars poll conducted by the *Daily News* in 1924 resulted in most votes for Betty Balfour and Alma Taylor, two names that barely feature in film history books. The American stars and their films seemed to satisfy the majority of 1920s cinema-goers. The reasons are simple: Hollywood saw the cinema not as art form but purely as entertainment, and produced films that appealed to the simple, undemanding tastes of the mass populace. As a British renter advised in 1927: 'appeal to the primitive emotions rather than to the reasoning faculties'.

An article in the *Bioscope* in 1922, addressed to the British film industry, seemed to be pointing out all the elements of a typically popular picture which the country's film-makers would do well to heed if they wanted to emulate the appeal of the Americans:

'There are certain things in film entertainment that can always be relied upon to please, such as romance presented with sincerity... Baby scenes always get over... All stories must end happily. There's no need to bother about logical or artistic endings. People don't go to cinemas to study logic or art. They want to be cheered up. Therefore, see you get humour into your programme. Broad humour, not coarse or vulgar, is safest, because it appeals to the majority... And don't neglect the tragic. Folks like to know that other people get into trouble as well as themselves. Women especially love a good cry. But the end must strike a happy note.'

There was even more extreme advice provided by writer Arrar Jackson, drawing on the estimation that approximately 60 per cent of the audiences throughout most of the 1920s were women, as well as revealing an appallingly contemptible attitude to an audience he obviously looked down on: 'Even if a woman is devoid of teeth, has a carcass which rattles like a box of dominoes as she walks, and wears elastic-sided boots and red flannel, she is still enough of a woman to simper at an emotional close-up, even

Queue of strikers for a free matinée at the Ripley Hippodrome during the General Strike of 1926.

if she simpers in secret.' Whether simpering or laughing, with or without teeth, audiences of both sexes continued to pour into available cinemas. Writer P.Morton Shand, in his brilliantly incisive, analytical study *Modern Theatres And Cinemas* (subtitled *The Architecture of Pleasure*), outlined an important element in the growth of cinema's popularity. Even in the 1920s, he identified that people's demand for simple pleasures was growing more insistent as a result of the stresses and strains of the age or, as he termed it, life's 'increasing strenuousness, complexity and neurasthenia' (a general term for fatigue, anxiety and listlessness).

Because 'we no longer take our pleasures quite so seriously or decorously', Morton Shand believed the cinema industry should reflect this in its approach both to the building and to its social function. The 1920s saw a culture that wanted 'to be amused and not instructed, intrigued but not edified', and that traits like pomposity were 'a welcome Aunt Sally's coconut for us to shy at'. As a result, cinemas needed to be 'comfortable', 'sober' and 'elegant' but also 'amusing' and 'flippant', without having anything that it is 'solemn' or 'serious' about them.

Although many architects' creations didn't exactly tally with P.Morton Shand's theories, these statements and others in his book are worth quoting as they insightfully identify all the salient points about the social function of the cinema, and why it proved so attractive beyond the nature of the films themselves. For example, he pointed out a crucial difference between the cinema and a rival form of entertainment, the theatre: 'There is something formal and ceremonious about going to the theatre. It is an occasion, an event. It implies more careful attire, if not evening dress'.

Rather than an occasion, the cinema was a pastime. Also, although the theatre (and the concert hall) had an atmosphere of a 'polite social gathering', the picture-house had an image which produced a more casual attitude in people. Unlike the theatre and the concert hall, says the author, 'we are ready to drop into any old cinema on any old pretext, at any old time, and in any old clothes'.

But the cinema was even more than a place where one could informally drop in, wearing one's tat. Because it was 'primarily a sort of public lounge... a blend of an English club and a continental café; at once the most public and the most secluded of places', people could go in alone, as a twosome, with children, the whole family or a group of friends; they could smoke (apparently this wasn't permitted in other European countries), drink or eat. There were also the advantages which both the proximity of picture houses and their cheapness allowed:

'One can enjoy a little nap as easily as the luxury of a good laugh or a good cry. In wet weather it is an escape from the rain; in winter a means of keeping warm. Schoolboys, whose holidays are drawing to a close, know that prevalent epidemics can often be caught there.'

However, when it comes to the actual architecture of cinemas, P.Morton Shand devotes most praise (and photographic illustrations) in his book to examples on the continent, particularly (and surprisingly) in 'semi-bankrupt' Germany. As for Britain, a German architect remarked to Morton Shand that 'your cinemas are not entities. They do not hang together. They are patchwork affairs'. The author agrees, citing a mentality in Britain that sees 'the wrong men' being entrusted with the job of building and decorating the cinemas, 'unqualified architects' who hand over the design of their decorations to 'various firms of shop-fitters, plasterers and upholsterers'. Rather than employing professional craftsmen, architects have been 'getting a little man from round the corner to do this, that, and the other job'.

P.Morton Shand rails against 'a depressingly low level of design among British cinemas', producing 'uninspired' buildings. Part of the problem, he says, is that our theatres and music halls had rarely been built by qualified architects, and that the cinema had continued this 'bad tradition'.

In his book on the history of cinema architecture *Picture Palace*, Dennis Sharp is equally as critical of the buildings of this age, accusing architects of drawing inspiration from previous examples. 'Little wonder' he wrote in 1969, 'that many draughty, ill-ventilated and badly designed interiors have fallen into disfavour.'

Taking a general view of cinema architecture, David Atwell, author of *Cathedrals Of The Movies*, states that 'the cinema can be said, with good reason, to be the most important new building type of the 20th century. And yet for the most part cinema buildings have been reviled by architectural critics, and frequently by architects themselves'.

A prominent cinema architect J.R.Leathert referred to the 'vulgarity' of many designs, while the editor of The *Architects Journal* wrote of the 'poverty' of quality in the architecture. Worse still, he stated, there were some cinemas 'in which to witness a film is like eating out of a newspaper'.

There were exceptions, of course, particularly amongst the so-called 'super-cinemas' of the 1930s. But in Derbyshire in the 1920s, there was one cinema that would have surely have gladdened the eyes of most architectural critics. It certainly found favour with Dennis Sharp, who applauds 'a remarkably early example of conservation planning' in Chesterfield in 1923. As the new **Picture House** in Holywell Street was opposite the Parish Church with its celebrated crooked spire, it was decided that the town's new cinema should blend in with its historic surroundings. 'The result', writes Dennis Sharp, was 'a unique gabled half-timbered façade that looks as if it has wandered over the border from Cheshire or Herefordshire.' The interior, too, would have been awe-inspiring to any 1920s visitor, with its lavish,

theatrical decor, elaborately ornamented stage, and decorative dome. The auditorium also housed a large concert organ, on which a young musician called Reginald Dixon is believed to have received his first organ instruction. The Picture House also comprised a restaurant, and a ballroom which, according to Janet Parsons, had "the best floor I ever danced on".

The delights of the Picture House, which Janet experienced in the 1940s when it became the **Odeon**, would have been in stark contrast to the paucity of the experience suffered by her mother and father who did their courting in the 1920s at the **Kino** in Clay Cross, where they had to perch on cold wooden benches. Also, because this makeshift cinema had no rake, Janet tells of how her parents had to endure the annoyance of "those ladies who wore enormous hats bearing feathers, fruit and flowers and who insisted on sitting very upright on the front bench and blocking the view."

Nearby Chesterfield also boasted the **Victoria** on Knifesmithgate which, like the neighbouring Picture House, had an attractive frontage, made up in mock-Tudor. According to Brian Hornsey, author of the booklet *Ninety Years of Cinema*

Site of the Victoria Picture Palace in Chesterfield in 1996. Geoff Hood.

in Chesterfield, some people recall a Tudor influence running to the interior design, 'with wall lamps after the style of London Bridge'. It was also described as a 'huge, airy building', which is no surprise as it housed 1,500 people when re-opened in 1924.

Other cinemas that sprang up in Derbyshire in the 1920s were more modest creations that any architectural commentator would have regarded with resounding indifference. In Derby and district alone, five cinemas opened in this decade: the Derby **Cosmo** (the former Cosmopolitan Hall) in Upper Boundary Road (1923), the Alvaston **Rex** (1925) on the corner of London Road and Barnaby Street, and three other cinemas that opened in 1928 – the **Popular** on Mill Street, the Spondon **Sitwell**, on Sitwell Street, and the Allenton **Broadway**, at the corner of Stamford Street and Osmaston Road. Each of these plainly-constructed cinemas was erected to fulfil an increasing public need for film and, as the Mayor of Derby, Alderman Allen Mycroft commented when he opened the Alvaston Rex, 'the local people... would now be able to get their entertainment without having to pay tram fares to town and back'.

The Cosmo on Boundary Road, Derby. Derby Evening Telegraph.

The Derby Cosmo is now a discount warehouse. Marshall Grey.

Although the original walk to the Rex entrance was a pleasant pathway decked with laurels and rhododendrons, the 650-seater picture house was a prosaic, boxy building which gave every suggestion that a crippling window tax had ruined its intended appearance. Inside, even the screen was initially bereft of curtains.

Although the Popular had a similarly flat, rectangular frontage, it did at least look more like a picture house, although the opening advert that proclaimed 'Derby's new super cinema' was probably over-estimating both its appearance and status. The 750-seater 'Pop', the only cinema to grace the area known as Derby's West End, was publicity conscious from the outset: it

Site of the Rex Cinema at Alvaston. John Osborn.

The Rex on London Road, Alvaston. Frank Walters.

The Popular in Derby's Mill Street, pictured in 1946. This was the West End's very own cinema.

The former Derby Popular. John Osborn.

advertised a 'See yourself on the Screen' gimmick where opening night attenders were filmed, with the relishing prospect of appearing on the cinema screen a week later. One hopes that the first-night patrons who discovered the late 1920s novelty of double seats exercised chaste restraint. Not so much a novelty as an 'innovation' according to the *Derby Evening Telegraph* was a 'first-class waiting room', a useful facility if queues formed and showers occurred.

Another innovation that year was to be seen at the 670-seater Allenton Broadway: the gangway floors were illuminated, aiding the progress of the patrons to their seats. The Broadway looked more impressive and edificial a cinema than its sister building the Alvaston Rex (both

Those eager faces. Children applaud a film at the Derby Popular. Paul Southall.

Present site of the Broadway at Allenton. David Barraclough; and left: The Broadway, Allenton, pictured from Osmaston Park Road. Sam Winfield.

Out in the county, there came the Cosy – to Heanor – which offered 'buffet and billiards' in the 780-seater cinema, notable for its narrow but toweringly impressive frontage. Writing in his book *The Thrill Of It All*, David Roddis refers to the cinema's bid to

were owned by the same company), but Sam Winfield, author of *Dream Palaces of Derby* contends that 'it lacked that certain atmosphere'.

replace the cinema orchestra with a Panatrope, a system by which recorded music matched the film. It was a failure, 'and the orchestra was quickly re-

Smokescreen

J.B.Thomas recalls 'an interesting by-product of the cinema' which he and his pals used to exploit by plundering picture house rubbish bins. They would scour the refuse for small lengths of film which had been discarded by the projectionist following a splicing job. The strip of celluloid was then taken to the school playground. First of all, it was inspected by all and sundry to see if anyone could name the film. Then the real purpose of their rubbish bin raid began: 'The film was rolled up very tightly and then encased in a piece of paper, with both ends screwed up like a miniature Christmas cracker. One end was then lit. The paper eventually ignited the film which, being highly inflammable, started to burn fiercely. If you then stamped on the whole package, the flame disappeared but the combustion process still continued, creating dense clouds of white smoke. Great fun!'

engaged'. It is also recorded that for the second house patrons, the orchestra performed with greater vim, having benefited from the proximity of a pub and a generously long interval.

However, that cinema orchestra's days were numbered, along with all the other musicians who had accompanied the silents (it is estimated some 28,000 musicians were put out of work), in spite of the contention in the *Bioscope* in 1928 that 'the silent black and white film will remain the staple product of the industry while sound, colour and stereoscopy will remain items of novel appeal'. But as Al Jolson had already reminded them a year earlier, in *The Jazz Singer*: "Wait a minute. Wait a minute. You ain't heard nothin' yet!" (a little known fact is that there are only two dialogue sequences in this picture; also, this first talking feature film contained only 354 words, all unscripted too, as Warner Brothers had only intended to make a film with synchronised music and singing).

Although there had been experiments in sound taking place in Europe since the turn of the century, it was Warner Brothers who launched the talking picture using the Vitaphone sound-on-disc system (and averted encroaching bankruptcy). Thus, America tightened its grip on the picture industry, ushered in the golden age, and thrust American accents and language upon us. The whole concept of talkies was anathema to more than just the likes of Charlie Chaplin. Specifically addressing the sound of the dialogue, a Mr E.Davies, a grammar school master, asked the Association of Assistant Masters 'whether we were going to lower the standard of the English language to the American nasal twang'. If we were not, he continued, 'we must either ban talking films or have them made by people who can speak what we call the King's English'. Marie Pettipierre recalls the time her family first saw a James Cagney film: "We

couldn't understand a word he said, talking so fast in a Yankee drawl; the American accent was so new to us."

On a more general note, film historian Ernest Betts denounced the acceptance of talking pictures as 'the most spectacular act of self-destruction that has yet come out of Hollywood... the soul of the film – its

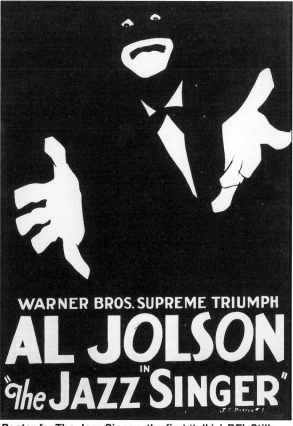

Poster for The Jazz Singer, *the first 'talkie'.* BFI Stills, Posters and Design.

"Audiences are saying it, Everywhere:—

At last, "PICTURES that TALK like LIVING PEOPLE!"

Vitaphone Talking Pictures are electrifying audiences the country over!

For *Vitaphone* brings to you the greatest of the world's great entertainers . . .

Screen stars! Stage stars! Opera stars! Famous orchestras! Master musicians!

Vitaphone recreates them *ALL* before your eyes. You see and hear them act, talk, sing and play—like human beings in the flesh!

Do not confuse *Vitaphone* with mere "sound effects."

Vitaphone is the ONE proved successful talking picture — exclusive product of Warner Bros.

Remember this — if it's not Warner Bros. *Vitaphone*, it's *NOT* the real, life-like talking picture.

Vitaphone climaxes all previous entertainment achievements. See and hear this marvel of the age — *Vitaphone*.

WARNER BROS. VITAPHONE PICTURES

If it's *Not* a WARNER PICTURE it's *Not* VITAPHONE

Talking pictures were a miracle of the 1920s. This advertises the Vitaphone sound system. **BFI Stills, Posters and Design.**

the evening of 8 June 1929, a 16-year-old called Dennis Pountain witnessed that inaugural screening of a talking picture. Young Pountain was assistant operator at the time, and had previously supplied percussion and sound effects in the cinema's musical band. He left a year later, in 1930, and ended the decade as one of the country's leading dance band vocalists, having changed his name to Denny Dennis.

Derbyshire's first talking pictures were in an all-British programme, including *Derby Day At Epsom* (apparently, the sound quality was poor, but audiences thrilled to the roar of the crowd); *Mr Smith Wakes Up*, a comedy; and *Teddy Brown and His Band* (Terry Brown was a huge man regarded as the world's biggest xylophone player – in both senses).

The Cosmo's first sound feature was *The Terror*. A *Punch* review reflected the naivety and inexperience of some of these early talking pictures: 'The only terrible thing about this talkie is its unnatural slowness... the characters speak as if they were dictating important letters'.

eloquent and vital silence – is destroyed. The film now returns to the circus whence it came, among the freaks and fat ladies'. Writer and commentator F.E.Adams proclaimed that 'talkies are merely a temporary craze, like broadcasting and greyhound racing'. Yet, by 1930, the silent film had all but disappeared, and our cinemas were being swamped by all-talking, all-singing, all-dancing Hollywood productions.

The first talkies to be shown in Derbyshire were in one of Derby's more modest picture houses, both in looks and capacity – the Cosmo. Its dull, unassuming frontage gave the impression it was a refurbished shop, although it was, in fact, a converted public hall. Its largely artless interior included seating for 650. It is more than likely that from the projection room on

No doubt because of the novelty of sound, even the credits to *The Terror* were spoken!

Actually, *The Terror* was not Derbyshire's first sound feature; that claim seems to belong to the Chesterfield Victoria, which screened *The Singing Fool* starring Al Jolson, at the cinema's Grand Re-opening on 29 July 1929. This much-talked about talkie stayed for two weeks. An unquestionably popular attraction, *The Singing Fool* became the opening talkie at several other county cinemas.

As the 1930s beckoned, cinemas across the county had been making arrangements to introduce the necessary apparatus for the talkies. The revolution was on. The Ilkeston Theatre Royal proudly advertised its first talkie *Syncopation* with the words: 'It talks, sings, dances and glitters'. However, in order to show such glittering novelties, the cost of installation wasn't cheap; the Derby White Hall, for example, spent £5,000 to put in its new projection and sound equipment (equivalent to the cost of building the Ilkeston Scala a mere 17 years earlier). Some of the early cheap 'sound-on-disc' systems (prior to 'sound-on-film') were notoriously unreliable. Len Waller remembers 'teething troubles' at the Somercotes Premier: "The synchronisation between film and disc used to be so way off at times that you had a woman on screen speaking in a man's voice! And once you got 'out of synch', it was the devil's own job to get back – much to the delight of us kids, who used to jeer with glee."

But there is little doubt that audiences greeted sound pictures with as much excitement as they had the silents. Frank Bacon reckons Heanor folk "were filled with wonder at the miracle of sound coming from the film", and he cites one instance in the early 1930s that almost replicated the experience of the audience who first gazed in disbelief at the Lumière Brothers' Paris show of 1895: watching *Hell's Angels* at the Cosy, Frank remembers one scene where the German air ace, Baron von Richtofen, flew his aeroplane towards the camera with guns blazing: "With the noise of the guns and the aeroplane engines, it was so realistic that everyone thought the plane was going to come out of the screen." Frank, and many others, dived for cover under the seats as the enemy plane 'passed over'.

Some cinemas seemed reluctant to effect the change to sound. As David Roddis discovered in his research of Erewash cinemas *The Thrill Of It All*, even as late as September 1930, the Palace, Long Eaton was advertising 'Silent Supers and No Canned Music'. It proved futile: the cinema closed, and for a time was facing conversion to a shopping arcade until it was decided the Palace should enter cinema's brave new world.

Ironically, Derbyshire's first purpose-built cinema was virtually the last to shake off the silents. Not until 1931 did the Derby Picture House (formerly the Midland Electric Theatre) make

the change. Not that the cinema appears to have suffered financially in continuing with silent pictures, as it's thought the prestigious repute of the Picture House orchestra ensured consistently good audiences.

Not only did the Picture House and other existing cinemas enter a prosperous and exciting new era, but also it was realised that now was the time for new building. For example, the new sound systems found out the inadequate acoustic properties of many cinemas; audiences were struggling to actually hear the dialogue. But as Dennis Sharp points out in *Picture Palace*, there was also a growing belief in the British cinema industry that it should 'provide the cinema-goer with greater "illusion", elegance and comfort in their buildings'. Also, audience interest was accelerating. It was time for the 'Super Cinemas'.

Whilst converting to the new sound apparatus, some Derbyshire cinemas took the opportunity of closing temporarily for refurbishment. The **Lyceum** at Whittington Moor only preserved its shell when it shut in 1932, re-opening with a completely new balcony, staircase and entrance hall (paved in marble). Coloured scenes of Venice adorned the walls and proscenium arch. Appropriately, the film choice for the Grand Re-opening was *The Big House*.

Derbyshire's first super cinema, in effect if not in truth, was a theatre that had suffered the sinking interest in live entertainment and yet at the same time had seen the potential for refloating its fortunes in talking pictures. The **Derby Hippodrome** had already been described by the *Derby Evening Telegraph* as 'the acme of comfort'. As John Taylor points out in his booklet on the Hippodrome: 'the

The Derby Hippodrome in Green Lane, pictured during its 20-year career as a cinema. It ceased to be a live theatre in 1930 until well after World War Two. **Sam Winfield Collection.**

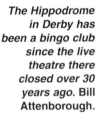

The interior of the Derby Hippodrome. Sam Winfield Collection.

The Hippodrome in Derby has been a bingo club since the live theatre there closed over 30 years ago. Bill Attenborough.

Live theatre ceased at the Hippodrome on 14 June 1930, and on 15 September, after introducing 1,000 tip up seats in the stalls, the theatre re-opened with the optimistically-titled *Sunny Side Up*, starring Janet Gaynor.

Just less than ten years later, the Hippodrome enjoyed a notable highlight, when Anna Neagle made a personal appearance at a screening of her film *Sixty Glorious Years*, in which she played Queen Victoria. Innumerable autographs were signed, before Miss Neagle retired to her Midland Hotel suite, to sleep in the same room where 89 years earlier, Queen Victoria had herself slept.

The Derby Hippodrome enjoyed 20 glorious years as a cinema, particularly for Sam Winfield, author of *Dream Palaces of Derby*, who says 'there was always a cinema atmosphere to the building, rather than that of a theatre'. John Taylor disagrees, contending that the theatre 'never really made a suitable cinema', mainly pointing to the architecture of the building, which required the free-standing screen to be steeply angled to accommodate the highly-placed projectors.

Soon after the Hippodrome's conversion to the film faith, Derbyshire was to welcome a spate of purpose-built super cinemas. This was to be an exciting era. Architecture critic P.Morton Shand, writing in the *Ideal Kinema* in 1931, encouraged cinema architects to 'imitate the United States, the home of jazz, and all big and fruity things'. Dennis Sharp, in *Picture Palace*, outlined the influence that American cinemas were to have on British cinema architects: 'Sumptuous exteriors, with interiors that included murals, original art works, chandeliers, elaborate staircases, fine draperies, silver and gold leaf, mahogany panelling, gilt and marble, deep pile rugs, luxurious lounges, comfy chairs.' In many ways, the fantasy interiors of cinemas were a reflection of many of the films being shown in them.

It is generally acknowledged that the nearest British equivalent to the American cinema moguls of the twenties was Oscar Deutsch, who created the giant Odeon circuit. By the 1930s, the name Odeon came to mean 'Oscar Deutsch Entertains Our Nation'. From six cinemas under his control in 1931 until his untimely death ten years later, Oscar Deutsch had built (at his expense) about 140 cinemas, and ran an empire of nearly 300 Odeons. One of the first cinemas Deutsch built (even before the name 'Odeon' was adopted) was the **Alfreton Royal**, which opened on 16 April 1931. The striking exterior was a one-off; later Odeon cinemas conformed to a house style, and were a lot plainer than the Royal's look suggested, with its attractive timbered mock-Tudor frontage. But Oscar Deutsch's own words (from an article in the journal *Design and Construction*) in

theatre boasted crush rooms, lounges, a Winter Garden, and a tea room'. In the auditorium itself, John points to the 'high decorative standards'; the two deep balconies with their rich baroque plasterwork, and the ornate proscenium arch would have felt palatial to any patron. Although John refers to the exterior as 'bland', the brick-built Hippodrome would still have been an imposing, eye-catching sight for anyone who walked up Green Lane. It still stands today, straddling both Green Lane and Macklin Street with an air of faded grandeur (and a noticeably unsightly Walkers Bingo sign giving off a tacky metallic silver gleam).

In February 1930, the Hippodrome's manager Ernest Vincent spelt out the dispiriting truth about the theatre's future as a live entertainment venue. Basically, it had none. There was a dire shortage of variety and music hall shows. These shows were usually booked a year in advance, but as Ernest declared, "I cannot tell you what we are showing two months ahead." And the explanation? "The talkies have scared producers." However, they hadn't scared Oswald Cray, manager at the nearby Grand: "They will never kill the theatre." The Grand is now a nightclub.

Royal Theatre, Alfreton, in the early 1930s. **T.Moss.**

Site of the Royal, Alfreton. **Geoff Hood.**

white collars were skewwhiff or not Daz-white."

Oscar Deutsch also took over the Derby White Hall, with once again his wife making her customary designs on the interior, with the cinema re-opening as the Odeon in August,

1937 are still applicable to the cinema he brought to Alfreton:

'It was always my ambition to have buildings which were individual and striking, but which were always objects of architectural beauty... we endeavour to make our buildings express the fact that they are specially erected as the homes of the latest, most progressive entertainment in the world today.'

But although – post-Alfreton Royal – Deutsch was to adopt a more formulaic vision of the Odeon exterior, it's likely that with regard to the Royal interior, his wife Lily had already begun to exert her art-deco tastes on her husband's buildings. Such was her influence that Odeon interiors were said to be 'gilded by the Lily'. As Dennis Sharp records in *Picture Palaces*, Lily Deutsch 'brought an entirely welcome atmosphere of art deco influenced taste in the selection of the colour schemes.' He also comments that 'the pastel-coloured results were always impeccably judged and chosen.' So it was with the Alfreton Royal, and as David Roddis notes, the cinema always had 'an opulent air', helped in no small measure by the highly-decorative lighting on the walls and ceiling. The cinema also had a strict air, as far as the staff were concerned. Audrey Farns-worth, who worked as an usherette, remembers the manager as "a big, bluff man who used to line us up so he could inspect us, fingernails and all. Sometimes he would belittle us in front of everyone else if our

1935. Mr Deutsch was also responsible for creating the 'Odeon Children's Circle'. Ken Taylor has fond memories of nipping on to a bus from Peartree with his younger brother Jack every Saturday morning to enjoy a children's feature film, a few cartoons and the inevitable cliffhanger serial, all for 3d. The youngsters also took part in competitions. On one notable occasion, the children were asked to draw a character from Walt Disney's Mickey Mouse films. Ken's seven-year-old brother won first prize. Ken came nowhere, but kept quiet about it, as he had in fact done young Jack's drawing for him.

Ken and Jack would also have joined in the club 'hymn':

'To the Odeon we have come,
Now we can have some fun,
We are a hundred thousand strong,
So how can we all be wrong?'

The club 'promise' was: To obey one's parents, to be kind to animals, and to make this country 'a better place to live in'. This promise was crowned by the singing of the National Anthem. Such was Oscar Deutsch's sense of patriotism that he even took the trouble of producing an official souvenir programme for Children's Circle members to commemorate the Coronation of King George VI. Ken Taylor still retains that souvenir programme, now a collector's item, and worth a good deal more than the one shilling it cost back in 1937.

The Derby Coliseum on London Road. **Sam Winfield Collection.**

Site of the Coliseum, Derby. **John Osborn.**

There was also an Odeon signature tune for the grown-ups to sing along to prior to performances, which ended with the lyrics:

'So meet me tonight,
Where your favourite
    stars shine bright,
Just round the corner
    at the Odeon'.

For all Oscar Deutsch's efforts, it was generally acknowledged that in Britain, only the interiors designed by the celebrated Theodore Komisarjevsky approached the awe-inspiring splendour and flamboyance of the US cinemas. Komisarjevsky declared that 'the picture theatre supplies folk with the flavour of romance for which they crave'; and he designed his cinema interiors accordingly, with a notable fantasy character, particularly the Brixton Astoria, which was eloquently described as 'an acre of seats in a garden of dreams' (the audience looked on both a stage and auditorium walls decorated like the exterior of a Mediterranean villa, and a ceiling of midnight blue dotted with twinkling stars, giving the feeling of sitting in the open air).

The Derby Coliseum, which opened in April 1934, could not match such extravagance. However, Sam Winfield, who had a particular affection for this building, and who had noted the fantasy character of the new picture palaces in the capital, states with undisguised relief that the Coliseum interior 'had none of the Gothic excesses' of the London cinemas. However, there was an especial Mediterranean air about the exterior of the Coliseum, which was a striking presence at the corner of London Road and Traffic Street (on its site now are the garish excesses of modern retail architecture). For an avid cinema-goer like Sam Winfield, these picture houses were 'temples'. In the case of the Coliseum, this wasn't so far from the truth. Not only did the cinema's lofty frontage of Corinthian columns give it the appearance of a Greek temple (particularly when floodlit at night), but also the original building opened in 1842 as the London Road Congregational Church.

A rascally local press created a stigma about its conversion from a place of worship to a haven of entertainment. As a youngster, Alec Turner remembers he and his brother weren't allowed to attend the Coliseum; his parents believed 'the wrath of God might cause it to collapse at any moment!' A prophecy appeared in Old Moore's Almanac that the balcony in a cinema converted from a former congregational church would fall down. Even though the opening film was *SOS Iceberg*, no calamity was to befall the Coliseum, which enjoyed a popular reputation (though perhaps not with employee Tom Spencer, who believed the projection box to be haunted).

The Foreword in the opening souvenir programme heralded the Coliseum as 'Derby's New Super Cinema', and anticipated that 'its success will provide a step to further Derby's effort in establishing itself amongst the leading cities'. The owners had certainly worked hard on several features of the cinema, proclaiming proudly that 'over 16 miles of cable and 700 electric lamps have been used', and that in the area of seating 'some scores of chairs were inspected before a final decision was arrived at and before they spelt Comfort!' It was also thought by the

The Gaumont Palace, London Road, Derby. W.W.Winter.

The former Gaumont Palace, Derby. Marshall Grey.

efforts that were being made to bring the best possible pictures to the cinema: 'A glance at our film bookings will prove that great pains have been bestowed in the selection of only good pictures.'

Furthermore, the manager believed (no doubt still in his pardonable pride), that the Coliseum was 'the last word in ultra-modern cinema theatres'. As it turned out, further words were to be spoken in the town. Indeed, the next word in ultra-modern cinema theatres shouted its arrival less than six months later, and only a few hundred yards up the road. Possibly as a riposte to the Coliseum's claim, the opening sentence in the souvenir opening programme of this rival palace proclaimed itself to be 'the very last word in modern cinema construction'.

Derby's Gaumont Palace was Derbyshire's first true purpose-built super cinema. Although the Coliseum carried all the attributes of a super cinema, both artistically and technically, it was still a converted construction, without a classic cinema appearance. But Gaumont British was a company which helped set the seal on what we would now acknowledge as an archetypal cinema of the grand, elegant style, a palace in name and nature. The Gaumont Palace took a year to construct. The souvenir programme reminded its opening day patrons that '12 months ago a number of rather dingy old buildings stood on this ground. Since then the Builders with their army of 200 men have wrought mightily and skilfully with the 500 tons of steel, the million

management 'that the cinema-going public of Derby really prefer a human orchestra to mechanical music. We think that our patrons will appreciate this venture, and your support for this policy is solicited by attendance at this cinema regularly, thus enabling this feature to be retained and enhanced.' Sadly, the orchestra (an eight-piece) lasted only a few weeks. Its acoustic instruments couldn't rise above the hubbub of a 1,250 seater audience, so the orchestra was discontinued.

The 'Resident Manager' Mr H.V.B.Goodson included his own message in the souvenir programme, humbly announcing: 'It is with pardonable pride that this new COLISEUM SUPER CINEMA is presented for your enjoyment.' He also pointed out that all cinema-goers would be made equally welcome, even if they sat in the cheap seats. He actually stated, in the polite language of the times, that 'every patron, no matter which part of the house he or she patronises, will be treated as an honourable guest'. Mr Goodwin was also out to make the Coliseum known as 'the Bright Spot', and laid no small stress on the

The auditorium of the Gaumont on London Road, from the circle. **Sam Winfield Collection.**

bricks, the 5,000 tons of concrete and the thousand and one other materials which are the bones, body and clothing of the Gaumont Palace.' Another aspect – 'by no means trifling' – was that a 'chunk of hillside' (about 8,000 cubic yards) had to be removed because Osmaston Road stood 18 feet above London Road at this spot.

According to Dennis Sharp, author of *Picture Palaces*, the buildings of British Gaumont's chief architect Mr W.E.Trent 'were all marked by a notably compact plan which in many cases overcame the problem of an awkward site. His work is among the best produced for super cinemas anywhere.' Certainly, the site of the Derby Gaumont would have been identified as 'awkward'. As the Gaumont's souvenir opening programme reveals: 'many were the difficulties which beset the architect. The peculiarities of the site had to be overcome'. In an article on the Gaumont, the periodical *Ideal Kinema And Studio* noted that 'an improved appearance has been secured in a somewhat narrow thoroughfare'. In other words, the cinema stood in a road which was not of great width; 'and a flat elevation of the large scale required by the building would have been somewhat overpowering and out of place'. So, W.E.Trent decided to recess a large middle section of the building, and set it back even more above the second floor.

Thus, for all visitors who approached the Gaumont cinema, 'a simple and dignified front is presented to

London Road'. The souvenir programme continues in its architecture-speak to affirm that 'by this arrangement of mass, a play of light and shade is introduced which immediately awakens interest and enables the proportions of the building to be appreciated'. It took no language for anyone to appreciate the magnificence of this 'mass' of attractive red brick (relieved by a little cream terra-cotta tiling), ornamental centre columns, black and white marble-stepped entrance, illuminated canopies, interchangeable neon film signs (on both sides of the entrance), topped off by sculpted panels depicting a clown, 'pantaloon', harlequin and 'columbine' (intended to represent 'the oldest known form of entertainment'), sitting either side of the imposing words GAUMONT PALACE, also lit by neon and noticeable over a wide area. A truly majestic sight.

Let us now step inside, where more wonders await... through the polished walnut and glazed doors to the so-called Entrance Vestibule, 'paved with terrazo and mosaic', and walls of 'rich Australian walnut'. One noticeable innovation was the 'Available Seat Indicator', an at-a-glance guide to the auditorium accommodation. The proprietors described this area as 'the best lit Cinema Entrance in England', with over 500 lamps 'projecting their welcome beams upon you'. Coupled with an exterior described as 'the most beautifully lit Theatre front of its size in the Kingdom', it is hardly surprising the

Margaret Lockwood receives a bouquet of flowers from a young Wendy Dudley at the Gaumont, Derby.

Gaumont boasted the title of 'Fairyland of Light'.

Some Gaumont visitors entered the foyer without a glance or a ticket: these would be people on their way to the café/restaurant, where 150 people could be seated comfortably. Here, Gaumont grandeur was reflected in an etched mirror representing the 'Dance of the Hours', and more splendid lighting – four curved panels lit by 100 lamps, and diffused window lighting courtesy of over 100 flame-coloured globes. There was also a waitress service and music, and with the café/restaurant open from 11am through till 10pm, it was proclaimed 'a pleasant rendezvous'.

The auditorium was a sight, sensation and experience that brought in cinema-goers from far and wide. It must have been a palpable thrill for first-time visitors to encounter the vast, airy, awe-inspiring magnificence of the Derby Gaumont Palace. I don't need to dwell on the minutiae of its design – just look at the photograph – and then imagine, if you can, an audience of 2,300 in such surroundings. I also need to remind you that the largest auditorium in a typical multiplex is not much more than about 350 to 400. So, multiply by five, and raise the roof, so to speak, three times. Imagine not a series of simple spotlights, but slender, chandelier-like lights, and add to your view a decorative ceiling and proscenium opening, with warm brown, tasselled screen curtains and (on the rare occasion when it was used) a fire safety curtain with a specially painted mural depicting Derby industry.

The seats were the epitome of

comfort, and the air-conditioning was state-of-the-art – the Gaumont Palace boasted of manufacturing its own climate, declaring that 'the air you breathe at the Gaumont Palace has been washed, warmed and purified'. It was calculated that about 1,000 cubic feet of air for every person was both pumped in and extracted every hour.

Not surprisingly, the projection and sound equipment was also of the utmost quality. Not for this cinema the 'tiny, ill-ventilated and dangerous boxes' which most operators had been used to. According to the Gaumont, the Operating Chamber was a 'revelation', with this roomy projection box controlling everything – picture projection, sound and lighting controls, and curtain movement. A machine called the Ross Brenograph was a feature which could be seen, in retrospect, as a way of compensating for the cinema's programme of black and white, as it flooded the screen with ever-changing colours when the opening title and credits appeared. Roy Christian remarks that as a child, he and his pals didn't welcome this effect: "If we children were forced to sit in the front rows, we used to get a bit frightened being swathed in lights."

But Roy was still excited enough by this new cinema to queue for up to an hour and a half in order to get in, remarking also that "it was the 'in' thing to be seen in the Gaumont queue." For Alec Turner, who had previously attended the 'tuppenny rush' at the Cosy down the road, the Gaumont was a revelation: "it was fantastic for those of us who had been used to hard seats and glaring lights. We sank back in the plush, gazed at crystal chandeliers overhead, and we were in heaven!"

By the time the opening day main feature *Evergreen* (starring Jessie Matthews) was rolling, patrons would also have been aware of up-to-date projection and sound. But before the films were even on screen, visitors would have been entertained by the sound of Derbyshire's first cinema organ (at least as a separate entertainment entity -the organs at the Derby White Hall and Long Eaton Palace being utilised as an accompaniment to the silent films, with also the anticipated organ installation at the Derby Coliseum being cancelled when the original building company's funds ran dry, the subsequent company deciding not to re-order the organ).

The Derby Gaumont organ was an illuminated British-made Compton, costing £10,000. For that price one got, according to the Gaumont brochure, 'a musical giant of a thousand voices, from a mere whisper to a thunderous valley of sound'. Some of those 'voices' included 'the thrilling peal of the majestic Cathedral Organ, the dazzling brilliance of the full orchestra, or the infectious lilt of a Dance

Con Docherty at the illuminated console of the Compton organ at the Gaumont Palace in 1934.

band. And all this at the lightest touch of the expert organist who controls it'.

The first expert organist was 'Con' Docherty. In fact, the brochure described him as 'a master'. Although Con Docherty played only in the first two years of the cinema's life before moving on, his name has been mentioned to me more than any other who formed a part of Derbyshire's cinema history. This is partly due to the sheer thrill and novelty of having a theatre organ in a cinema, plus the fact that it was illuminated (even the seat), and that it rose from the floor. But all that would have counted for nought had not Con Docherty been such a superb musician.

A well-known Derby keyboard musician Cyril Sprenger remembers Con with enormous affection. As a 14-year-old beginner, Cyril wrote to Mr Docherty to ask whether he could look over the newly-installed Compton, along with his school choir and music teacher. Con graciously obliged, and not only showed them the organ but also treated them to a half-hour recital. "It was a thrilling experience" says Cyril, topped off by a 'Con-trick' "When our music teacher was reluctantly persuaded to sit at the console and play a few bars for us, Con Docherty unobtrusively slipped backstage and caused the console to rise as our teacher sat playing. Was he surprised!"

The ever-approachable Con Docherty was visited by the ever-enthusiastic Cyril Sprenger at least once a fortnight. Although Cyril admits to pestering the life out of him, he remembers that "he took it all in good part, although he did once threaten that he would send my father a 'bloody big fat bill' for services rendered. But he never did."

Like Cyril Sprenger, Cornelius Docherty was a promising pianist, beginning tuition at the age of nine, and graduating to organ at the age of 16. By the time he was 18, Con was providing musical accompaniment to silent pictures at the Queen's Hall, Newcastle. Although he only played as cover for a fortnight, he was asked to stay on. Eventually, after passing an audition at Gaumont-British, Con began playing as an organ 'temp' at some of London's leading cinemas, before seeking permanent work, which came his way with the opening of the cinema in Derby. Con was a little reluctant to come: "All I knew about Derby was the horse race." But to Derby he came.

Dressed immaculately in white tie and tail suit, and demonstrating a wonderful command of the Compton, Con Docherty was an immediate hit, particularly with a young local British Celanese worker called Phyllis Hewitt. They courted briefly, and then married. Before that relationship, Con remembers an incident at the Gaumont where his popularity backfired on him. On spotting Con's distinctive figure in the Gaumont foyer, an irate-looking man made a beeline for him. Prodding him with his finger, the angry patron accused him of having an affair with his girlfriend. Con Docherty vociferously denied the charge, and eventually pacified the man, having convinced him that this relative newcomer to Derby had never heard of, let alone visited, the suburb of Spondon, where the man's girlfriend lived. What had apparently occurred was that this girl was having an affair with another man, and under considerable pressure from her boyfriend to reveal the name of the cad, bleated out the first name that came into her head. Unfortunately for Con, the girl was a Gaumont regular and, like other regulars, was very familiar with the name of the popular organist. Such was the price of fame.

So how good was Con Docherty? "As an organist he was, and still is, a very good one" says Cyril Sprenger. Cyril's father, also a good keyboard musician, always spoke highly of him. He told Cyril that Con was "a very 'clean' player, and a real musician. And believe me" says Cyril, "there is a difference between just an organist and a musician. Con was one of the best." Cyril cites his playing of

Danse Macabre as particularly brilliant, and that was in about 1992, when he was 85!

But Cyril recalls that way back in 1934, "he knew how to use the organ. Whatever he played, whether Classical or dance music, it was always beautifully executed." Cyril remembers that one piece de resistance was *Finlandia* by Sibelius. However, Con Docherty's well-loved theme tune was *We'll All Go Riding On A Rainbow*, in deference to the ever-changing spectrum of colours on the Compton organ.

Another tune Con Docherty got well-used to playing was the National Anthem. One night, however, he almost committed a faux pas. Con was in the habit of slipping out to the pub in between his turns. There was a good local close at hand, and Con had befriended a regular there, fellow-Geordie Hughie Gallacher, recently signed by Derby County. One night, while the main feature film was running, Con and Hughie were enjoying a particularly good chin-wag. "We'd had a pint or two as well" admits Con. Through a slightly bleared eye, Con looked at his watch and realised he was needed back at the cinema in order to close the show with the King's Anthem. He made it just in time to sit at the organ and press the button on the console. As if he had timed it to the second, Con and the Compton rose in view at the precise moment the slide of King George V appeared on the screen. "But then I suddenly had an aberration" says Con. As a result of his panicked rush back to the cinema and his ale-induced sense of well-being, Con Docherty suddenly launched into *Auld Lang Syne*. Luckily, he swiftly came to his senses, and using his considerable dexterity on the keyboard, Con smoothly improvised his way into the tune that everyone in the auditorium was attentively standing up to respect.

Such was the ability and finesse of this musician that Cyril Sprenger says he would have sooner listened to Con Docherty than Reginald Dixon (the famous Blackpool Tower organist was a regular Sunday guest player at the Gaumont). In 1936, Con Docherty moved to Ashton-under-Lyne, as he was in demand by the Compton company to exploit the wonders of its sensational new Melotone organ. Con was replaced by Stanley Bishop, who was himself followed by Andy Hume. Other organists made their mark, at the Derby Regal as well as Gaumont. But none left quite the same impression as Con Docherty, now a sprightly 88-year-old, living in the North-East, and still *Riding On A Rainbow* on any organ he is invited to play.

Four years on – in 1938 – the Derby Regal opened, also with a Compton organ, which similarly rose from the darkling depths. The seating capacity was impressive – 1,840 – in a plush, if plain auditorium,

The Regal in East Street, which later became the ABC. **Derby Evening Telegraph.**

The former Regal, East Street, Derby (left of picture). **John Osborn.**

and the foyer was long and luxuriant, but the Regal directors' claim that they had brought 'a luxury cinema second to none in the provinces and equalled by few in the world of entertainment' was a highly fanciful notion which lost its credibility the moment one walked round a few short corners to behold the Gaumont. Still, the Regal did provide even more palatial gleam to the picture house scene. The cinema was certainly in capable hands: the manager Harold Benzeval was a well-liked and highly respected showman who had come from the White Hall cinema with a principal aim of establishing the Regal as 'the entertainment centre of Derby and, with this end in view, he invites the co-operation of his patrons, whose criticism and suggestions will receive his personal attention'. He was true to his word. Sam Winfield tells the story in *Dream Palaces of Derby* of a regular patron writing to Mr Benzeval to point out that the sound was indistinct when sat in a certain row in the stalls. The manager asked the patron to come and see him personally, whereupon he presented the complainant with a pass covering a couple of extra performances.

Harold Benzeval remained as manager for 22 years.

The auditorium of the Regal in East Street, from the stalls in June 1938. Stewart Bale.

In stark contrast, the career of the first Regal organist was tragically brief. Wilfred Southworth was already well known to radio listeners when he came to the Regal from the Forum cinema in Birmingham, but he hardly made himself known to the Regal patrons: he died shortly after the cinema opening. One wonders what occurred during his brief spell at the Regal or whether he brought with him some deep-seated torment, because a few

The foyer of the Regal in East Street on the cinema's opening day in June 1938. Stewart Bale.

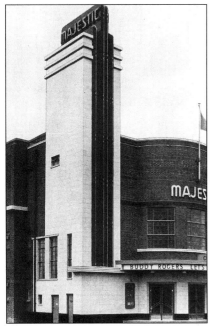

Left: The Majestic, Chaddesden, with its 70ft-tower. W.W.Winter. *Kwik Save* now occupies the site of the Majestic at Chaddesden (above). Marshall Grey.

The Gloria (above), all lit up at Chaddesden. Derby Evening Telegraph; *(left)* The former Gloria at Chaddesden. John Osborn.

weeks into his employment, young Wilfred apparently committed suicide. He wandered on to a south coast beach, undressed, left his clothes in a neat pile and walked into the sea. He was never seen again.

After the Regal, no cinema built in Derby was able to match the Gaumont in size and sophistication, although the Cavendish, which opened on Upperdale Road at the end of 1937, was an impressive effort. It had an imposingly high frontage (which more than compensated for its plainly-stated design), and a large, modern auditorium, seating 1,664 patrons who were happy to see the erection of a picture house to directly serve the suburb of Normanton.

A year later, the suburb of Chaddesden welcomed two new cinemas – the Majestic and the Gloria. On the outside, the Majestic certainly lived up to its name, as the building was distinguished by a 70 foot tower. It is said that the neon at night could be seen for miles around. The Gloria could have been designed by the same architect, as this building also had a tower, albeit ten foot shorter than the Majestic. But the Gloria went one better than the Majestic at its opening: there would have been a thrill for the first-night audience at the Majestic to hear talent show host Carroll Levis read out a congratulatory telegram from Gracie Fields (the star of their inaugural film *Looking On The Bright Side*). However, before the Gloria's opening film *I See Ice* was screened, not only was there a telegram from the film's star George Formby, but also it was read out by one of the supporting stars from the picture – Gary

Marsh – who was furthermore accompanied to the cinema's launch by another support star from the film – Polly Ward. But the Gloria's opening wasn't as smooth as hoped: the cement appeared smooth, but hadn't actually set properly, and part of the foyer was damaged. Fortunately, by then the first-night patrons were safely inside.

In the same year, when Ilkeston saw its fourth and final cinema built – the Ritz – there was an even bigger star on hand to open proceedings – Victor McLaglen – a burly star of British silent films who had already became popular in Hollywood for pictures like *Dick Turpin* and *The Last Patrol*, and was later to star in *She Wore A Yellow Ribbon* and *The Quiet Man*. Although Victor wasn't starring in the Ritz's opening night attraction, he was more than happy to be there: his nephew John was the Ritz manager.

As for the Ritz as a building, it was – according to the *Ilkeston Advertiser* – aptly termed 'Ilkeston's Luxury Cinema'. The reporter also praised the seating (for over 1,400) – 'the last word in comfort' and which also allowed 'plenty of leg room between each row'. Taking a more general and paternal view was the chairman of the Ritz directors J.L.Adams who simply described his cinema as 'a beautiful building'. As for the exterior, David Roddis is correct to note that the giant advertising tower was reminiscent of the style

The Ritz at Ilkeston in 1938.

The former Ritz cinema at Ilkeston. **Gill & Peter Dishart.**

'The interior presents a scene of exquisite beauty. One enters the roomy foyer through swinging glass doors, and immediately the footfalls are deadened by the thick rubber floor. The auditorium is lofty with ample gangways and plenty of space between the seats, which are all of the armchair pattern and luxuriously upholstered. There is an air of magnificence about the whole place, and the results which have been achieved in the space of a few months constitute a triumph – or series of triumphs – for the architect and tradesman who have carried out the work.

The scheme of decoration is blue, gold and silver, giving a delightfully soothing pastel effect.

Everything has been contrived to provide the utmost comfort, combined with utility, and the theatre will be deliciously cool in the hottest days of summer, and seductively cosy during winter's bitterest weather.'

Truly a place for all seasons. Never mind the seductive cosiness of winter, though... 'Sweet lovers love the spring' wrote Shakespeare. And the spirit of The Bard was alive in Swadlincote, as the press reporter noted that the Majestic was a red brick building which 'externally, and in general appearance, strongly resembles the Shakespearian Memorial Theatre at Stratford, on a small scale'.

Could this place be any more 'majestic'? Why, yes... the projectors offered 'the finest sight and sound reproduction it is possible to conceive'. And, just to complete the 'picture', 'The acoustics are perfect'.

In the north of the county, Buxton opened its Spa cine-

of Odeon cinemas. According to the *Ilkeston Pioneer*, the cinema's design – by Reginald W.Cooper – was 'perfect'. The newspaper also believed the Ritz would last for over a century, as the company which built the cinema – ran by Mr W.Chell – had a motto: 'Chell Built, Well Built'.

There was a similarly excitable feeling in the local press when Swadlincote saw its new Majestic unveiled in 1933. An enamoured *Burton Observer* reporter commented thus:

The Majestic at Swadlincote.

Kwik Save are also on the site of the Majestic at Swadlincote. **Geoff Hood.**

The Regal, Chesterfield, in earlier days. **Geoff Hood.**

The Chesterfield Regal building in 1996.

auditorium distinguished by apricot plush seating and exquisite decor.

As a result of his involvement in the construction of the Regal, Arthur earnt the princely entitlement of two free tickets to the opening, where he would have seen Wilfred Southworth on the rise-and-fall Compton (Wilfred, as stated earlier, was also at the console at the opening of the Derby Regal), before settling down to *Follow The Fleet* with Fred Astaire and Ginger Rogers.

Astaire and Rogers were but two stars in the Hollywood firmament bringing Derbyshire audiences flocking into its cinemas, be they new, glitzy picture palaces or old, cold, converted village halls. Everybody in the county now had a cinema of some sort nearby. More people than ever were to seek out the cinema when Britain was thrust into another World War.

ma in 1937, and Chesterfield saw the Picture House become an Odeon in 1938. Two years previously the Regal had boosted cinema capacity in the town by a further 1,900 seats, making it Chesterfield's biggest picture house. According to Arthur Savage, who helped build the Regal, the whole of Cavendish Street was demolished prior to its erection, the cinema eventually occupying three-quarters of the street's length. Arthur carries a fond memory of a palatial

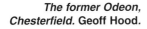

The former Odeon, Chesterfield. **Geoff Hood.**

Smilin' Through
The age of austerity and escapism

War is not only dangerous but dull and it is important to keep civilians amused as it is to keep them occupied. War work and anxiety are exhausting, and for those who have been through the last war – and hardly yet recovered from it – I think as much diversion as possible is necessary.

Letter to *The Times*, September 1939

From the moment you passed the kiosk, you were in a different world.

Brian Patton, Ripley cinema-goer

AT the turn of the century, there was not one single building in Britain specifically built for use as a cinema. At the turn of the 1940s, it was estimated there were some 5,000 cinemas nationally, with a third of them each housing over 1,000 seats.

The turn of the 1940s also brought Britain into another world war, and the already acknowledged sense of escape provided by the cinema was to intensify in the wartime atmosphere of rigour, stringency and austerity. A speech by Winston Churchill, following a visit to MGM Studios, Hollywood in 1929 can thus be seen as highly portentous:

'The motion picture is an essential part of the rapid forward march of civilisation, and as such it is standing in opposition to the brutal passions and hatred which even in our time have wrought conflict between nations'.

The so-called 'Golden Age' which had already begun in the 1930s with stars like Gable, Garbo, Cagney, Crawford, Astaire and Rogers was to shine with even more lustre in the early 1940s with the likes of Bogart, Hepburn, Hayworth, Stewart, Crosby and Hope. By 1940, annual admissions had returned to one billion a year, and by the end of World War Two, nearly three quarters of the entire populace were cinema-goers, with a third of the adult civilian population and two-thirds of schoolchildren going once a week or more often.

The Central Office of Information, which compiled these statistics in 1946, also found that 'high proportions of cinema-goers exercise very little choice or no choice as regards the films they see'. Most Derbyshire picture-goers of the 1940s confirmed this fact to me, and many cited twice-weekly visits to the cinemas as commonplace. Some went even more frequently. Beryl Carver-Smith remembers that the programme at the Chaddesden Majestic was changed three times in the week – Monday, Wednesday and Friday. "Everytime it changed, off we went." As Charles Birch of Ashbourne recalls: "If you went to both the Empire and Elite in the town, you could see four different programmes in one week, and some people DID!" Even someone going to the cinema twice a week throughout the war would have seen over 1,000 feature films, spent a total of 75 days viewing them, and another 25 days queuing.

The Richest Man in Town

Ann Hill, whose mother Vivenne Marshall was an usherette at the Alfreton Odeon, remembers hearing about the times Mr Palmer-Moore, the local squire from Alfreton Hall, used to attend the Odeon. He was either very shy, suspicious of other people, possibly contemptuous of them, or, maybe coming from a large residence, he simply liked his space. Because, every time he came to the cinema, he always took the trouble of booking two spare seats either side of him and his wife, so that nobody sat next to them.

Ripley Hippodrome and staff in the 1940s. Sam Lavington.

The cinemas weren't open at all when war was declared, on 3 September 1939, as a safety precaution. Almost as a premonition of this, cinemas in Derby town centre were plunged into darkness on the eve of the declaration: a vicious storm brought all the barrage balloons down. Katy Meakin remembers sitting in the Picture House when the incident occurred: "All the lights went out in the cinema, and we thought an air raid was on. Much excitement ensued, until we emerged from the cinema to be greeted by torrential rain. What's more, all the buses had stopped (it was past 9pm), so we had to walk home."

Ironically, the Hippodrome was screening on that very night *The Hurricane*, a re-opening attraction following the cinema's refurbishment. Arthur Blood was in the audience at the time of the blackout, and praises the swift enterprise of the manager, John Denton, who invited servicemen from the audience to take the stage and entertain the patrons. As they performed in the blackness of the auditorium, as many staff as could find torches pointed their beams on to the stage.

The Hippodrome crowd walked out into the foreboding rain to find that their cinema's blackout was to stay. *Kine Weekly* had its own say about the cinema shutdown in its 6 September issue:

'If intoxication is becoming a public scandal, if public houses have sold out of beer by 8pm, and there is nowhere else to go, then the time for re-opening the cinemas has become an urgent public necessity.'

By the middle of September, all Derbyshire cinemas had re-opened, unaffected by the ruling that those picture theatres regarded as most vulnerable to attack from the air would have to stay shut. The Derby Cavendish, however, re-opened with alternate rows cordoned off in a bid to reduce casualties in the event that a bomb might strike. This nervousness could well have been down to the cinema's proximity to soldiers' barracks, with Rolls Royce not so far away, too. Also, as at Rolls Royce, an artist (the famous Ernest Townshend?) was called in to the 'Cav' to effect suitable exterior protection: the white asbestos cinema roof was painted with camouflage

Although given the green light to re-open, cinemas were not allowed to admit unaccompanied children at any time, and closing times were earlier (the Derby Odeon compensated for this – and at the same time provided for night-shift workers – by beginning its performances at 10 o'clock in the morning). Initially, cinema admissions dropped, owing to unease with the blackout, and fear of an air raid. But as tensions eased in this 'phoney' war period, attendances returned to normal, and then went beyond the normal as civilians sought a welcome extrication from war's privations.

Naturally, the war was also to affect the cinemas themselves. Alec Turner, who was rewind boy at the Derby Gaumont in 1939, remembers spending a September week blacking out the glass entrance doors; dipping lamps in blue or amber lacquer to dim them; lowering the massive crystal chandeliers, dismantling them and placing them in storage; stripping the neon signs from the front of the building; and moth-balling the mighty organ.

Queues outside the Wirksworth Cinema during World War Two. Note the lack of advertising on the cinema front, which was a feature of the war period. Tony Holmes Collection.

Helen Mosley, who had come to work at The Kings, Ilkeston from 1938, also witnessed first-hand the wartime restrictions. For her, all the glamour of the cinema seemed to go: "All lights were extinguished, heavy curtains put on the doors in the foyer, and the ticket box was blacked out, save for a small strip of light so that money and tickets could change hands... so woe betide if you dropped your change!"

Usherettes like Helen would also have found less light power in their torches. Alec Turner remembers that once the war set in, picture houses were supplied with a battery 'de-polariser' which passed a low current through the batteries in the reverse direction, thus removing the layer of 'polarising' gas which formed round the carbon electrode each time the battery was used. However, Alec wonders why they bothered, as he remembers "it wasn't very effective."

Alec also recalls how shortages even affected the projection of films as the war dragged on. Once he graduated to the Odeon as third projectionist (one of the cinema's projectionists had been called up), he increasingly noticed that carbons for the arcs, which crucially provided the projector light beam, were not always available in the correct length and diameter: "We made do as best we could, using metal holders

('carbon savers') to burn the carbons down to the last tiny piece. This sometimes meant reducing the arc current to make the carbon last out the reel, or – catastrophe – change the carbon while the arc was still burning, which meant burnt fingers, a short screen blackout, and a rather cross manager on the house telephone!"

The shortage of a very specific, seemingly innocuous need proved a serious threat to the standard of projection at the Odeon. All projection box portholes required optically flat glass. When this became scratched beyond reasonable use, Alec Turner discovered that the cinema's supplier had no exact replacement in stock. The cinema had to make do with polished plate glass, but Alec noticed that this badly distorted the picture. He had to throw himself into a serious and strenuous search before eventually locating the particular glass required.

There was no shortage of the film cement that was constantly needed to repair torn and tattered film, which was just as well because Alec's girlfriend was pleased to discover that the amyl acetate mixture was an effective substitute for nail varnish, one of several cosmetics difficult to obtain during the war.

Rationing hit the cinema cafés. Alec Turner felt the

Laughter in the Dark

Pauline Cooper still has a laugh every time she remembers her friend Ann Rhodes, and their night out watching an Arthur Askey film at the Chesterfield Regal: "We came to a moment in the film where a chap called Alfie tripped over a mat. When he got up, his hair stuck out, and Arthur Askey said: 'you look like you've got fowl pest'. Well, my friend Ann let out this jovial laugh. However, it didn't end there. There was a small murmur of laughter from the audience, and that set Ann off again. She laughed louder, and longer. She just didn't stop, and it got to the point where the entire audience were laughing at Ann instead of watching the film. By then, you couldn't hear the film anyway. Ann finished up in a doubled up state under the seat."

A good job she didn't have any dentures in. Vivienne Marshall, an usherette at the Alfreton Odeon, remembers one lady laughing so much at a comedy that her teeth fell out, and everybody had to stay behind with their torches to hunt for them.

Cinema-goers at the Wirksworth Cinema. The photograph was supplied by Anne Butler, the smiling girl wearing spectacles to the right of the picture.

food shortages as keenly as the customers: he often used to pay for a meal which took his fancy on the menu, and invariably it was personally delivered to the projection box. However, as the war progressed, such became the paucity of choice on the menu that Alec decided to bring in his own snap.

However, Alec did benefit from the 'Butterkist' run. Although sweets and chocolate were rationed, Butterkist wasn't: "So, when the message came that the kiosk had received a supply, there was a mad dash to buy the allotted two packets per person before the supply ran out."

Missing

Graham Nutt of Swadlincote remembers an instance of cruel fun enjoyed by the regulars at the town's Majestic cinema. For a considerable time, there was a seat missing in the middle of a row (for some reason it was an inordinately long time being repaired). After a while, all the regulars got to know about this seat, and always looked forward to the time when the cinema was full. Invariably, a late-comer would appear in the dark, and if he made a beeline to this gap in the row, it was a sure sign that he was not a regular patron. Knowing full well what would happen, the other members of the audience would stand up to allow this unsuspecting soul to pass in front of them so he could make his way to the welcoming comfort of the cinema's last remaining seat (and in such a good position too, in the middle of a row!). Heads would then turn to see the victim drop down and disappear with a thump as he took his place in the non-existent seat. Exit one embarrassed patron and much chortling from the surrounding audience.

Sam Winfield recalls how food rationing affected the Coliseum café. Somewhat craftily, the manager continued to print out a full menu, ensuring that the café maintained a good rating. But when it came to actually ordering the especial delights from the surprisingly well-stocked menu, customers were disappointed to hear their requests repeatedly met with the words 'sorry, that's off'. Not that Sam minded too much: "After profound apologies were made, an extremely attractive and always bubbling blonde cook/waitress served two rounds of luscious cheese on toast, followed by jam or lemon tarts with an excellent pot of tea."

Cinema staff were called on to assist the war effort in more ways than the obvious one of providing film entertainment. In 1941, Alec Turner joined the Home Guard, often turning up for work in uniform, with respirator and rifle, ready to do an all-night stint at Platoon Headquarters. He remembers that "Sunday mornings were occupied with rifle drill, the firing range, grenade throwing etc., and then straight on to start the afternoon show at the cinema."

Alec Turner recalls that employees at the Derby Odeon took it in turns to 'fire watch'. This meant that several of them would stay overnight – about one night in ten – in the cinema building, to help deal with any fire bombs likely to drop in the vicinity. "Fortunately" says Alec, "we never had to deal with any."

Ironically, the Odeon staff were constantly exposed to a night-time hazard provided not by the enemy, but their own civil defence – smoke-screen generators, lined up along the pavement outside the cinema. "These were oil-burners" recalls Alec, "lit on moonlit nights to baffle the enemy bombers. Not only did they choke us with smoke, we also fell over them."

Alec does remember one incident which gave the town centre a fright. Having volunteered to decorate the Odeon foyer at 11 o'clock on a Saturday night, young Alec was perched at the top of a ladder, emulsioning the highest point of the main staircase wall, when a terrific bang caused his ladder to shudder violently. "A bomb! we all shouted, and off we went to investigate." It wasn't a bomb. However, it was a cinema-related incident. In the car park of the Regal, which was next to the stage end of the Odeon, stood a static water tank, holding millions of gallons of water for Fire Brigade use. It had suddenly given way, releasing the water into all the surrounding shops, and the Odeon under-stage rooms and front stalls. "It was a mess" says Alec, "but luckily the water hadn't got as far as our back-stage sound equipment and curtain controls, so we roped off the front stalls and opened as usual the next night, even though we had flood water lapping the front two rows. The show must go on!"

Sam Winfield remembers a similar problem during the war for the Chaddesden Gloria, although this cinema's flood problems were of natural origins. Because the site was poorly drained, the adjacent Chaddesden brook sometimes seeped into the stalls, affecting up to the first nine rows.

In spite of the nationwide devastation wrought by enemy bombers, relatively few cinema buildings were lost, and Derbyshire was almost completely unaffected. The only recorded damage seems to have occurred to the roof of the Riddings Regent, which was damaged by shrapnel, and to the Matlock Picture Palace booking office, which had its leaded windows completely shot out by tracer bullets as a German plane was being chased over Matlock, at one moment flying perilously close to the rooftops of Dale Road, where the cinema stood. In the wall of Farmer's shop, near to the site of the Picture Palace, you can still see

Wartime cinema-goers at the Gloria, Chaddesden. Derby Evening Telegraph.

two of the bullet holes. Although Peter Dakin regarded the Bolsover of the early 1940s as a "dark, sleepy coal-mining village", he recalls numerous enemy planes passing over. One full-house evening at his father's Carr Vale cinema, two crunching explosions shook the building. Women gasped, men stood to attention. Peter rushed to his Dad: "Did you hear that?" "You're not kidding" he replied: his father was completely covered in a layer of asbestos and arc-lamp carbon dust that had accumulated on the ceiling; it had all been fetched down in one fell swoop by the blast of two stray bombs which had landed in a nearby field.

Cinemas rarely shut down during air raids. The usual procedure was for a message to be relayed to the audience that a raid was imminent, with the offer of a refund for anyone who wished to leave. Few ever did. However, Dennis Howells remembers that his parents had made the decision that they would leave their local Scala in Ilkeston once notice of a likely raid was announced, even when a frustratingly frequent outburst of air raid alarms kept interrupting their viewing of *Mrs Miniver*. It took them four visits before they saw the film which, by a neatly ironic twist, tells of the British people's will to survive the German bombing raids!

Down the road at the Kings, usherette Helen

Mosley remembers that if a siren sounded, "a notice was projected on the screen, and the film stopped for five minutes to allow time for those patrons who wished to leave. The film was then re-started for the stalwarts who were left. There were not many at first." Gradually, however, more audience members stayed put, as they got used to the fact that most of the German bombers were bound for Coventry, Birmingham and Manchester. There was also the realisation amongst some cinema-goers that the buildings they sat in were toughly constructed. Others stayed put in a simple display of British stiff upper lip wartime spirit.

"Those of us who worked at the cinemas had to stay" adds Helen Mosley, "very often going home in the pitch-black dark while the air raid was still on. We used to put our coats over our heads in case of shrapnel. How we used to long for moonlit nights." Exactly the feeling Dorothy Bampton would have had on one particular night when, after a night's entertainment at a Derby cinema, she walked down St Peter's Street to be suddenly confronted by a large unidentified mass which she also realised was moving. Eventually, peering through the gloom with the help of a passer-by's torch, she discovered to her horror that she had only just missed being trampled by a line of elephants, performers at the nearby

Hippodrome Theatre being escorted back to their stabling somewhere in the town.

In spite of the blackout, cinema audiences swelled to an unprecedented volume. Admissions increased at a stroke when after three decades of six-day weeks, picture houses were allowed to open on a Sunday. "When Sunday cinema was first mooted, we objected bitterly" says Alec Turner. His Trades Union fought against it, but in vain. Some cinemas resisted Sunday opening: although Alfreton cinemas threw open their doors on the Sabbath, those in towns like Ripley, Heanor and Ilkeston remained shut. In the cinemas where owners bowed to audiences' wartime demands, the projectionists found their workload was more onerous than on any other day: Sunday screenings were one-offs, and usually consisted of old films. Alec Turner points out that as films came in cans and not on spools, every Sunday film had to be made up, or 'spooled', for screening, and 'plated off' for return the same day. Also, because Sunday films were invariably old copies of even older films, they needed much repair.

Some cinemas exploited Sunday opening by holding religious services immediately before the evening's screenings. Other cinemas had no screenings at all, but still opened – for concerts. The Chaddesden Gloria became a popular venue for regular Sunday variety shows, attracting some of the big names of the era – Vera Lynn, Cyril Fletcher and Sandy Powell. Many cinemas organised charity concerts on a Sunday; fundraisers for 'Wings For Victory' or 'Spitfire Week' were commonplace.

Cinemas also aided the war effort by screening training films for the Home Guard. Furthermore, John Shutte, who in post-war years became a member of the Royal Observer Corps, points out that the cinema – from the war years right through to the mid-1960s – played a big part in the passive defence of Great Britain, by opening up their doors for ROC personnel to take part in an annual test of aircraft recognition. The Corps volunteers manned observation posts all over the country, from where they were assigned to identify and monitor all aircraft movements – day and night – and report the information to regional centres. It was crucial war work, as John explains: "These centres that relied on this information were the plotting rooms seen in many wartime films, with girls pushing markers across a large map, and with overlooking officers calling up squadrons of fighter aircraft when necessary."

Early in the war years, with aircraft recognition becoming increasingly vital, an annual compulsory 'Master Test' was begun, with the Derby Gaumont providing its premises on a Sunday morning. The reason a cinema was required was because, as John explains, "the test consisted of a silent film made up of a series of short clips of aircraft in flight, followed by a few seconds of bright white screen so that examinees had enough light to enter the aircraft name on the test paper." These tests, which provided the incentive of pay awards, thus helped strengthen the standards of aircraft recognition at a critical time.

Georgina Boneham remembers seeing enemy aircraft in flight, as part of the *Gaumont British News* at the Belper Palace, as she vividly recalls the cheers every time a German plane was seen to be shot down. The newsreels came into their own during the war, and were another strong factor in the increased attendances at cinemas, gratifying the public thirst for visual information of Britain's progress in the conflict. Radio bulletins had the advantage of immediacy, and newspaper stories provided the detail, but neither could compete with a medium that provided dramatic, moving visual evidence of British troops in action (even if the words and pictures were pure propaganda).

Wyn Hope remembers that at the Langley Mill Ritz, "photos of local boys in uniform were put on the screen, giving information if they were missing in action." Wyn remembers that her husband-to-be, a Sherwood Forester, had been missing for nine months when suddenly his picture came up on the screen, giving news that he was safe and well in a German PoW camp. Also, in his book *Dream Palaces of Derby*, Sam Winfield recounts the story of a mother spotting her son in some newsreel scenes at the Derby Regal. When she told the manager Harold Benzeval, he kindly arranged for the newsreel to be shown again.

But it wasn't just our boys who were in vision: Betty Alldread had an uncle who also became a prisoner-of-war in Germany. This invariably triggered heated passions in Betty's grandma when the newsreel was shown at Crich Picture House: "If the face of Adolf Hitler ever appeared on the screen, grandma used to get really aerated, and start yelling 'shoot him, kill him, the swine!' After a while, the audience got used to this, so that every time Hitler came into vision, they'd all turn to look at her."

Although the newsreels were a vital part of a picture house programme, it was common for sister cinemas to cut costs by sharing each copy of the latest newsreel. This often produced panic in the projection box. Stories are commonplace of cinema rewind boys running, biking or bussing the vital can of film from one cinema to another (because of the still inflammable nature of celluloid, it was actually illegal for anyone to carry the cans on public transport). Sometimes the lad delegated for this duty found the timing too tight, resulting in a hastily-inserted, unprogrammed interval at the receiving cinema and an extremely out-of-breath errand boy.

However valued the newsreels became, they were regarded by some as an intrusion into the atmosphere of welcome unreality that the cinema provided. For many, that sense of escapism was satisfied not only by the fantasy nature of the films, but also through the effect of being snug, safe and shut away from the harsh world outside. There was a welcome aura of warmth, comfort, opulence and splendour that enabled people to forget the afflictions of the war, and be elevated from their dull domestic surroundings. Brian Patton, who became projectionist at the Ripley Empire in the mid-1950s, sums up the feelings shared by every local cinema-goer: "The cinema was always a cut above the place you lived in… the gold leaf glittered in the lights, the curtains were plush, the seats were comfy, and seemed to wrap around you somehow. And once the film came on, you were lost… we escaped from our harsh environment for a couple of hours."

Adrian Skollin of Heanor contends that this escapism, which can be traced back to the 1920s, was a crucial factor in the pacifying of a long-suffering nation: "Because cinema-going was essentially a working-class pursuit, and it took these people away from the hardships of life, I believe it staved off any thoughts of revolution in the country." Historian A.J.P.Taylor interestingly augments this argument in stating that 'cinema provided a substitute for real life' and 'helped people to become watchers instead of doers'.

Whatever the points for and against this debate, there is no argument that in the post-General Strike years, when there was a rapid growth in cinema building, the picture palace provided a rich respite from the ravages of poverty, unemployment, and general disillusionment with one's lot in life. In later years, the oppression of war served to enhance the need to seek sanctuary in a cinema, particularly for those of modest means. One concurring voice would be that of Jack Harding, who was brought up in Swadlincote during the 1930s and 1940s and remembers that "most Swadlincote people lived in tiny two-up, two-down cottages, in which families of ten were not uncommon, so just to have a seat of your own in a cinema was a luxury." Remarkable as it may seem, a first visit to the local cinema was for some people the first opportunity to feel a carpet underneath their feet. Dennis Sharp, author of *Picture Palaces*, believes the cinema was 'the ideal working-class entertainment, combining and offering escapism with informality, warmth, privacy in the dark and, most important, cheapness'.

Eddie Burnham raises a salient issue about the allure of a picture palace in his youth, which points up a feeling in some contrast with contemporary attitudes: "I remember seeing *Crossroads* on TV once, in the 1960s. Meg Richardson saw a group of people walk in, and then walk straight out. She turned to the manager and said: 'You know why they did that? Because this place is too grand for them'. The cinema industry never thought like that."

It is arguable that the place was less grand than those people hoped for, as sixties materialism would have produced increasing numbers of lower-middle and working class homes on a par with the attractions of the *Crossroads* motel lobby. But the grandness of a cinema in Eddie's day would far exceed cinema-goers' largely unadorned and unassuming homes. And, as Eddie suggests, the picture house designers exploited the mundane social conditions of its majority audience.

Cinema historians confirm this. In 1927, R.Sexton and B.F.Betts wrote a book about *American Theaters Today* (the kind of picture theatres that would come to influence the British architects of the super-cinemas of the 1930s), and stated that 'The masses, revelling in luxury and costly beauty, went to be thrilled by the gorgeousness of their surroundings which they could not afford in their home life'. So it would be in Derby as much as in Denver. Indeed, British cinema designer Theodore Komisarjevsky was well aware that the predominantly working-class patrons of a picture house craved a fantasy world:

'The richly decorated theatre, the comfort with which they are surrounded, the efficiency of the service, contribute to an atmosphere and a sense of well-being of which the majority have hitherto only imagined. While there, they can with reason consider themselves as good as anyone, and are able to enjoy their cigarettes or their little love affairs in comfortable seats and amidst attractive and appealing surroundings'.

Leslie Halliwell, writing in *Seats In All Parts*, argues that the cinema produced this other-worldly effect more effectively than any other available entertainment venue – the concert and music hall, theatre and palais de danse – because it was 'the most conveniently and constantly available, and it took people furthest out of themselves, into a wondrous and beautiful world which became their Shangri-La, though they never expected to find it in reality. In order to experience that world, they would willingly queue for hours; besides, it was cheaper than lighting the fire'.

He is right: film-goers were willing to queue for hours. Although audiences massed into cinemas in the 1930s, long queues were only likely to form on a Friday or Saturday night. But the growth in attendances during the war made queuing every evening an inevitable by-product of cinema-going. As Heanor cinema regular Frank Bacon observed: "You could never walk straight in at any cinema. You always had to queue." No one complained about it either. Queuing was accepted as obligatory and, during the war, became inextricably woven into the social fabric of life. It was 25 years on that I believe Pink Floyd lyricist Roger Waters distilled the essence of the habit with his line from the song *Time* from the *Dark Side Of The Moon* album:

'Hanging on in quiet desperation is the English way.'

Perhaps queuing also says something about two endemic features of our make-up, made manifest by the war: the renowned English patience, and 'resolve'. Arguably, as part of a society that was not in a hurry, and with less conflicting pressures than today, the act of standing in a queue was hardly questioned. Furthermore, the wartime attitude of 'pulling together' would have found some expression in a cinema queue. Indeed, the cinema queue evolved into a social gathering. Some people tell of wandering down to the local cinema queue in the sure knowledge that one's friend would be there to help chew over the gossip of the day, before walking off to another destination.

However, with few competing leisure pursuits that came as cheap and as convenient as the cinema, queuing for the pictures was viewed as the only option, and once got used to, it was hardly thought about. Basically, if you wanted to spend three hours in the place you loved, you soon became inured to the prospect of spending a further hour in an orderly line, even if it was in a moon-less, blacked-out, rain-sodden evening. Amelia Woodward remembers the days of the Swadlinote Rink cinema when kiddies used to queue for the matinées in the pouring rain. Her mother took pity on the line of drowned young rats and made sure she had a large towel or two on hand to rub their wet little heads as they filed into the cinema.

Occasionally a busker would come and perform for the crowd. A.E.Thompson has a memory of a couple who used to entertain the queues at the Derby Gaumont by playing tunes on a trolley-full of variously-measured wine glasses.

Roy Christian inadvertently entertained the Gaumont queue on an occasion when he was courting a new girlfriend: "A little boy suddenly came running up, grabbed me round the legs and yelled 'Daddy!' Not surprisingly, I got some rather quizzical looks from my girlfriend. I explained to her that it was a case of mistaken identity... the queue had moved a little while the boy was elsewhere, and when he came back, he went to the same place. 'Daddy' was about ten yards further up the line!"

Whether cinema-goers visited the Derby Gaumont Palace or the Crich Picture House, going to the pictures at this time not only took one's mind off the war but also provided one of the few pleasures of this rationed age, an age eloquently summed up by the wartime cinema experiences of Jose Howarth:

"From 1941 – when I was 12 – to 1945, my friends and I, who lived in Chase Road, Ambergate, used to walk up to Crich cinema and back. It took us a good half-hour, but time didn't seem to matter too much then. We weren't in so much of a hurry to get somewhere, like today. Occasionally, the cinema owner, Frank Gill, who lived in Ambergate, drove us in his car. We felt very privileged, what with cars and petrol in such short supply.

Going to the pictures was our biggest adventure. His little cinema at Crich provided such treats. The building itself was like a tiered shed; it was simple, spartan, bare, and lacking in luxury, but the films were just the same as those shown in the magnificent cinemas of Derby. The staff there were friendly, doubling up to do all the jobs, and a lovely family atmosphere prevailed. Of the films, I remember *Old Mother Riley* with Arthur Lucan and Kitty McShane, plus Laurel and Hardy, and Roy Rogers and Trigger.

After the film show, we would buy a tuppeny bag of chips from the village chip shop and walk back down through the fields back to Ambergate. If it was getting dark, we would be looking up into the skies for signs of friendly or enemy aircraft. Of course, it was the blackout, and very dark, except for the times when it was a 'bomber's moon'. We were never afraid, though, despite the lonely wooded pathway. We spent our walking time recalling the film we had just seen, an escape from our austere reality, and a learning about life which probably moulded our lives for ever."

The Pursuit Of Happiness

The glamour, the thrill... and the double seats

People saw things on the screen that they could only dream of. TV kitchen sink dramas and soaps portray a life you can see every day. But when you went to the cinema, you saw Cary Grant in a dinner-suit sipping champagne, and ordering crêpe Suzette for Ida Lupino. Half the people in Somercotes didn't have a clue what a crêpe Suzette was, never mind what it tasted like. But they all came away from the film wanting one. I know I did!

Eddie Burnham, projectionist, Somercotes Premier 1943-47

Take your girlie to the movies, if you can't make love at home.

lyrics to a popular song

FROM the turn of the 1920s, when the glitzy fantasy of Hollywood began to invade Derbyshire towns and villages like Somercotes, through to the mid-1950s when both the Somercotes cinemas – the Premier and Empire – began to founder in the face of television,

Staff and their families at the Somercotes Empire in the 1930s. **Bailey & Sons.**

the cinema exerted the most powerful influence on Derbyshire social lives. For some, cinema became not a pastime, but a passion. People didn't just go to the cinema, they lived it. Their memories testify to this...

Duncan Cross, for example, worked most of his life as a projectionist at the Ashbourne Empire, but when he was off duty, his first thought was: 'Let's go to the pictures!' What's more, if there was a good film to see that wasn't on locally, he used to cycle all the way to Derby and back – an hour each way.

From 1946, Bill Doyle, now resident in Chellaston, went to the cinema 'as regular as clockwork'. Bill grew up at a time when he could indulge his interest at countless cinemas nearby. His fond recollections depict a romantic period of cinema-going that firmly belongs to a lost age:

"I lived in Wilmot Street, and within a third of a mile, the cinemas were abundant. There was the 'Collie', as everyone called it – the Coliseum. Then there was the Gaumont, Odeon, Regal, Picture House, Hippodrome, Black Prince, and so on. I can

Site of the old Somercotes Empire. **Gill & Peter Dishart.**

The Black Prince in Colyear Street, Derby, one of Bill Doyle's regular childhood haunts. Derby Evening Telegraph.

Garland, and Mickey Rooney. I'd sometimes go and see their films many times over. Queuing for up to two hours was taken as normal to see a film. I remember queuing for three hours to see *Quo Vadis*.

In my schooldays, I attended Christ Church on Normanton Road, and left at age 11 to attend Rykneld School, at the top of Boyer Street. I mention this to illustrate the many film billboards advertising the latest attractions. There seemed to be hundreds of them, so I always dawdled on my home from school, stopping to read every board. They changed every week. They were usually on street corners, measuring roughly 3ft x 3ft, and at eye level, too. They were never vandalised, though. I would stand and stare at my heroes, reading every word on these coloured posters, taking in all the over-the-top claims such as 'NEVER BEFORE HAVE YOU EXPERIENCED SUCH HORROR' or 'THE GREATEST ADVENTURE EVER FILMED'. Many of these films never came anywhere near my expectation – but they were still great fun to read.

Every picture house had its own persona, aura and odour. At the Collie, they overdid it sometimes with a fragrant rose spray! Also, the Collie, Cosmo, Forum, Alex and Normanton came into the category of cinemas with ill-fitting carpets, rickety seats, un-cleaned lavvies and broken-down films. Whereas the Gaumont, Odeon and Regal were the better-kept, up-market cinemas.

But the Collie remained special to me. Not only was it the nearest cinema to my home, but it was also the place where I saw my first films. The Coliseum was my inauguration into the cinema, so it held a special, affectionate place in my heart."

Ann Moore reserves her affection for the Broadway, Allenton which she retrospectively admits was "a bit of a dump, and always dusty… but I didn't think so

visualise all of these picture houses vividly because if I was not at school or in bed, I was at the Pictures. Between the age of 10 and 15, I went to the cinema almost every day.

You may wonder: how could I afford my favourite pastime? Most of the money came from a morning and evening paper round. Out of my weekly wage of 7s 6d , I gave my Mum half, so I had to find other ways of feeding my addiction. I'd sell firewood: I'd nip down to the Market, and buy an orange box for a penny. There was enough wood to chop the box up into 12 bundles, which I'd sell door-to-door at tuppence a bundle. At the same time I'd ask people for lemonade bottles, as there was a penny deposit to collect. I usually took a can of Brasso with me, too, and offer to polish the brass on their doors.

To go to the cinema as often as was humanly possible, I'd usually pay the lowest admission price – 9d – and it never seemed to be any more than this for years and years. Trouble was, the cheap seats were right at the front, and I constantly suffered a wry neck and sore eyes. But it was worth it. The films I most vividly recall were those starring Roy Rogers, Gene Autry, Humphrey Bogart, James Cagney, and Johnny Weissmuller as Tarzan. Musicals were abundant, with names like Van Johnson, Dan Dailey, Judy

Site of the New Theatre, Ilkeston, now a residential home for the elderly. **Gill & Peter Dishart.**

then. I loved it, especially that one moment on a Friday night when I used to cuddle up to my Mum and think: 'another film yet, no school tomorrow, and ice-cream in the interval to come'... Sheer bliss."

Marion Toft, who also came to love it 'on Broadway', recalls how the lure of the screen brought her and her brother to misbehave and disobey their parents, and first paints a backdrop to the cinema-going hey-days she thrilled to in the post-war era:

"We went to Allenton Infants' School – that one in Lord Street that recently closed down – having barely changed since the 1940s when we were there. It cost a penny to ride in the bus from Shelton Lock. Sometimes we'd sacrifice the fare to buy a pennyworth of transfers from the newsagent on the corner. You floated them off in a saucer of water and, if you were careful, you'd get a good picture on your arm, or on to a bit of writing paper. Or you could buy a penny apple, a penny 'sucker', or a pennyworth of chewing wood. It was worth the one mile walk home for any of those treats.

It was against this backdrop of post-war austerity that we first started to visit the Broadway. Our cousin Betty lived in Allenton, that cosmopolitan centre of the universe. Betty knew everything (well, she was 12, wasn't she?), like, which queue to join for the Saturday matinée? I came to be always in that queue, in the afternoon, so that when I learnt French at Homelands a few years later, I thought one particular French word must be wrong – 'matin' could never mean 'morning'!

As we were from Shelton Lock, where our greatest entertainment was fishing for sticklebacks in the

canal, we were totally enthralled by the cinema. Betty always took us to stand in the shortest of the two queues. There were the 'nines' and the 'fives'. Most people stood in the fives. It was many times longer than our queue, and stretched round the long, blank side of the cinema building. That was where the boys jostled, shouted and fought. We suspected they used swear words, too. The manager and his son kept a close eye on them.

For an extra fourpence, you could be in the well-behaved line on the other side, barely reaching to the first shop on the main street. It was a social divide which even in those days, and at our age, we were smugly aware of.

Once, my brother and I had been naughty (some long-forgotten misdemeanour). For this, we were banned from going to the cinema that week. But that would have meant we would not find out what happened to the hero, trapped in the underground room which was gradually filling with water – the cliff-hanger from the previous week!

So, we used a knife to raid our money box and extracted some coppers. Not as much as usual, but enough to get us in. Together, we sneaked out of the

Pay kiosk at the Ritz Ilkeston in 1938. **A.Eyles.**

house. We didn't even think of the consequences of our action.

Trouble was, we had to stand in the fives! Such shame! Then, when it was our turn to pay at the box office, through force of habit we automatically started up the stairs to the balcony, the posh place where the rich ninepenny people went, our usual route. The manager made to stop us, then, recognising our innocent, eager faces, for some reason waved us upstairs. Once again, happily, we could cheer on the goodies and boo at the baddies in complete safety from the rabble down below."

But what happened to young Marion and her brother when they got home? After all, they had defied their parents. Did they get into more trouble? Did they miss the following week's Broadway entertainment with that ever-present cliffhanger serial? "Funny enough, we didn't. Our Mum and Dad were pretty angry, and we had to make up for our further misdemeanour by being extra good and doing lots of odd jobs around the house. But they still allowed us to go the Pictures. I think they realised how much it meant to us. So, cinema was a force for good in the end!"

Len Waller, who frequented the Somercotes Empire from the late 1920s onwards, was another avid cinema-goer who, like Bill Doyle, also worked to earn his way into the pictures. While some Somercotes children went round the 'posh houses' and collected empty jam jars (halfpenny for a pound jar, three farthings for a two pound jar), Len and his pal distrib-

uted handbills for the cinema. But eventually it became too much like hard work:

"You only had to get rid of a few hundred handbills on street corners in order to qualify for a complimentary ticket. Then, not only did the numbers of handbills increase, but also the Empire reduced the distributors to two people – Arthur Taylor and me. We found ourselves with thousands to give away, just for one measly ticket each. So, we began giving half-a-dozen to each passer-by. Then I discovered a hollow clothes-post, so that got rid of quite a few more. A disused boiler fireplace accounted for another pile. One day, George Nichols – the 'chucker-out' at the Empire – wouldn't let us in with our free passes. We'd obviously done our job too quickly, as he told us we had obviously not had time to hand out all the leaflets properly. We'd been rumbled."

Dennis Howells' ploy at the King's in Ilkeston was also eventually rumbled: "After purchasing your ticket, you came upon two doors into the auditorium, one on the left, the other on the right. Left was the usual entry. If, during a film's performance, you needed the toilet – which was in the foyer – you returned to the show via the right door. It wasn't long before we realised that if you went to the toilet first and entered through the right door, your ticket wasn't taken. Consequently, the same ticket got you into quite a few free shows. However, this fell through one night when the cinema got very full and found it had more tickets than seats. After that, we all turned honest."

The toilets themselves provided perfect entry into the cinema for any keen but hard-up youngsters, particularly if the public convenience was conveniently situated beyond the foyer. Stories are commonplace of the one lad in

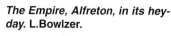

The Empire, Alfreton, in its heyday. **L. Bowlzer.**

Site of the Empire, Alfreton. **Geoff Hood.**

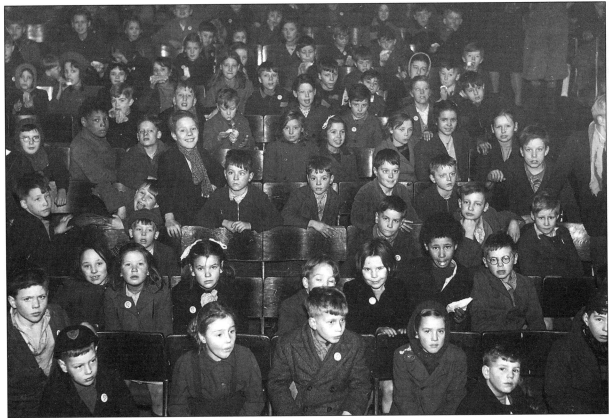

Local children settle down for the show at the Derby Popular in December 1949. Paul Southall.

the gang with the most 'bottle' innocently exchanging his hard-earned pennies for one ticket, when in point of fact those pennies were the cumulative result of a whip-round amongst his mates. Once he had entered the auditorium and taken his seat, he would simply wait for the lights to go down. Then, rising and walking as swiftly and discreetly as possible, he would slip into the Gents and unlatch the lavatory window to welcome in the fresh air, along with a snaking procession of little boys easing themselves through the opening. A quick check to see if the coast was clear – and they were in.

John Hassell admits to this misdemeanour from his days at the Alfreton Empire, which had a toilet door you could open from the inside. To make it look less suspicious, two members of John's gang would pay to get in. It was still a cheap visit all round, because as John recalls: "two of us went in, but eight came out."

Mick Peat and his pals each preferred to spend their tuppenny cinema admission at the Ripley Empire on three fags and four matches from Peggy Hayes' shop. They, too, exploited the toilet entry, except in this case, no one had to buy even one ticket to open the Gents window. All four of them slid down the coke chute, and sneaked into the cinema one at a time so

as not to arouse suspicion. Fortunately, the dark of the auditorium wouldn't have revealed their coke-dusted clothes. But these boys would eventually have to go home. Wouldn't your Mum have noticed something, Mick?... "Well, you'd just shake your coat and hope for the best."

There was never a problem at the Wirksworth Town Hall cinema, because they employed eagle-eyed Edward. As a youngster, Edward would sit innocently in the audience while his father projected the films. If the 'look-out lad' spotted any young miscreants sneaking in through the Exit doors, he would fetch his father, Edward would point them out, and Dad would throw them out.

Even those who had been honest enough to pay for their seats were prone to move about the differently-priced areas. At the Ilkeston Kings, it was realised that there was a one-row gap between the lowest-price stall seats and the dearer ones, so it was common practice to shuffle out of the cheap seats once the lights had gone down, and thus obtain a better view further back – at no extra charge, of course.

Dennis Howells noticed this ploy. He was a regular attender at the Kings, and all of the other Ilkeston

Fright

Peter Davies remembers wearing his school cap to the Belper Palace cinema even though it was at a Saturday matinée: "You see, our school caps had big peaks, so that whenever something frightening came on the screen, the peak caps came in useful to mask your eyes from the screen."

Peter had other fears, too: "If you misbehaved, the usherette's light would be upon you. The first light was a warning; the second light was followed by a crack at the back of the head."

But Peter also had to be wary of his own pals: "You had to avoid sitting directly underneath the balcony because sometimes an ice-cream carton would fall down, occasionally full of ice-cream."

However, there was a prank that would have been very frightening for any first-time visitor to the Palace matinée: "A common sight was the childrens' cinema tickets being thrown across the projector beam. It looked like a flame was coming towards you!"

cinemas. Dennis became steeped in the sensation of cinema, acquiring an extraordinarily wide knowledge of films, which eventually brought him television fame and glory as the first winner of the BBC TV *Film Buff of The Year*. I remember watching his progress in the contest, astounded by his expertise in the area of the B movie. But then he would have seen a countless number of these in his avid acquaintanceship with the pictures which began in the mid-1930s, "before the auditoriums of cinemas resembled carpet warehouses" adds Dennis with thinly-veiled contempt. His pot-pourri of memories scans an entire spectrum of the picture-going experience in the so-called 'Golden Age':

"I spent most of my misspent youth at the Pictures. Usually I went with a friend called Stan. My earliest recollection is going to the New Theatre. I can't remember the film, but I do remember the pillars in the front, and a picture which confirms this also tells me I would only have been four at the time. However, I clearly remember the choice of films my father gave me when he offered to take me into Ilkeston. At the New Theatre, Gary Cooper was starring in *The Plainsman*, supported by a black and white Popeye cartoon. The Kings had an Irving Berlin musical – *On The Avenue* – with Dick Powell, with a Walt Disney colour support called *The Old Mill*. I chose the western.

The New Theatre had a large stage and was the only cinema in town to have two staircases. I noticed that the left one was the most frequently used, probably because the other three cinemas in the town all had left-sided staircases. I fancy the ones who used the right staircase didn't come from Ilkeston.

Once at the New Theatre, I got so engrossed, I left my Cadbury's Dairy Milk on the arm of my seat. It melted into my jacket. We bought our sweets at one of the shops either side of the cinema. Confectionery takings can't have been all that good at the New Theatre because the prices in the sweet shops were cheaper than inside the cinema.

When a colour film was being shown at the New Theatre, I used to be fascinated by the coloured smoke caused by some cigarette smoker sitting under the projector's beam. I remember seeing the first Cinemascope film they showed – a western called *Rough Company* with Glenn Ford.

When The Kings installed Cinemascope they were the only ones equipped with stereophonic sound. The Kings was my favourite local. I remember my father taking me to see George Formby in *Keep Fit*. At the age of six I was going there with friends, without parental accompaniment. One of my big surprises in cinema-going occurred at a Saturday matinée. After the show, the windows were opened to let in light for the cleaners. Until then I didn't know there were any.

Eventually, I became a member of the St John's Ambulance Cadets. Each Monday and Saturday we assisted the regular ambulance man on duty at the Kings and the New Theatre. So I got a free film show twice a week. Why it was only two days a week at only two cinemas was something I never worked out.

The Ritz was advertised as 'Ilkeston's Luxury Cinema' presumably as it was the newest. Admittedly they had a large foyer upstairs, but I remember the floorboards creaking on the left-hand side of the stalls. They opened in May 1938 with *Stella Dallas* but my first experience there was when the main feature was *Dead End*, on a Monday afternoon. The irony of the title struck me when the film broke down, or it may have been the projector. After what seemed like hours of waiting, during which several

Rogue's Yarn

Roy Beech relishes the memory of what he innocently calls a 'rogue's trick' he used to pull on the Matlock Picture Palace queues. When a sizeable queue was formed, Roy would appear on the pavements, and extract a halfpenny from his pocket. This was no ordinary halfpenny: it had a hole in it, and through it was threaded a long piece of cotton. This enabled Roy to walk the length of the queue jingling the halfpenny on the footpath. The success of this prank was all owed to the fact that many people in that picture house queue had already spent money on cigarettes and sweets at the nearby shop. The sound of Roy's halfpenny on the pavement would produce an air of panic as the queuing masses spent several fruitless minutes rummaging around on the floor looking for the change that they thought had slipped from their pockets!

patrons visited the cake shop across the road and came back scoffing cream buns, we were informed by the manager R.V.McLaglen that the show could not continue. Actually, it hadn't even started, but we were given free passes for the evening performance.

It was not unusual to enter the cinema for the first house and stay till the close down. This once got me a free performance: a film broke down partway through the second house showing. It didn't bother me – I'd seen it all the way through in the afternoon, and I got a free pass for another time.

The Scala was the cinema that we all knew would close down first. We were mistaken; it's still going, the only one left in Ilkeston. It was really old-fashioned, and in the stalls directly underneath the balcony were two giant fans which in hot weather would start whirring around, killing any chance of hearing the film. Before the age of curved screens, all cinemas had flat ones, but none seemed flatter than the Scala's. If the cinema was almost full and you had to sit near the front, the film was elongated. So was your neck by the time the film was over. The Scala's standard fare seemed to be double bills of PRC and Monogram films, affectionately known in the trade as 'Poverty Row'.

There were two toilets in the Scala stalls. Through the door on the left to the Gents were a dozen or so steps leading to the contraption. One day, I was caught short during a screening. I could easily feel my way in the dark – I went to that cinema enough times, after all. But whilst stepping out boldly in the gloom, I found something was missing – the steps. They had filled them in, and I nearly broke my neck. The ladies fared no better – the one door for them led to only one cubicle. Once flushed, the sound reverberated through the cinema. Very embarrassing.

One of the Scala's attendants carried a long cane to keep unruly youngsters in check. Imagine that nowadays. Also, it was nothing to find a member of

the audience standing up, if the film was late in starting up, and addressing the projection booth with: 'You can start now, we're all in!'. This patron, along with many others, would often sing along with the adverts, like 'We eat Wheatsheaf, the best of bread' or 'The secret's in the underlift', the latter promoting the joys of a Berlei bra.

One of the joys of early cinema-going was that if you wanted to see a new release, you went to the big towns. Your local sometimes had to wait as long as three months for it to arrive there. Also, if there was nothing to suit at the local, it was only a short trip to Heanor, which had a Cosy and an Empire. Nothing doing there? Right, a quick trip down the road to the Langley Mill Picture House, advertised in the local press as 'Picture Hose (we want U in)'. Failing Langley Mill, Eastwood was a short hop, skip and jump away. Unlike today, remember, all these cinemas had a different show.

I once went to the Heanor Cosy to see *Lancer Spy*, and got in just as the main film was starting. This was at 6.20. At 7.30, the other patrons left, leaving Stan and myself waiting for the second house. Slowly, an usherette came down the aisle spraying Jeye's Fluid everywhere. Soaked, we held our ground. We were asked if we had just entered. We replied honestly. We were then informed, albeit politely, that if we wished to see the remainder of the programme, another entrance fee was required. We hurriedly left, never to darken that cinema's doorstep... well, for at least another week.

It's odd that in the days of continuous performances, you could walk in halfway through a film and when you reached that part of the film during the second showing, you would get up and leave and you would have understood the plot. Nowadays I can watch a film from the beginning and still come out confused."

Let us now consider a female perspective of this

era, with more of a romantic emphasis on the magic of the moving image, as presented to Patricia Turner of Ripley, who admits to being "awash with nostalgia" about her visits to the Ripley Hippodrome in the 1940s:

"As they changed the programme three times a week, we sometimes went three times. One bought a pink ticket (1s 3d) which rose from the slot. We then mounted the stairs, tingling with anticipation. Once settled, we began with the *Pathé News*. A resonant cock crowing was followed by a satisfyingly cultured voice, as we watched the Nazis goose-stepping, King George and Queen Elizabeth walking sadly among the debris left by German bombs in London, Princess Elizabeth driving an ambulance and Princess Margaret being led around by corgis. We then watched splendid gentlemen encased in plus-fours, hitting golf balls mightily, and Donald Campbell bouncing across lakes.

Then the lights came on and the usherettes, holding big wooden trays supported by a thick band around their necks, stood with their backs to the screen. We all scrambled down for a chocolate ice or a packet of fruity pastilles. Then the lights dimmed, and the feature film began. The huge lion of Metro Goldwyn-Mayer roared lustily, the titles flickered, and we were transported into a new world.

The Westerns… Roy Rogers stalked across the plains on Trigger, Hopalong Cassidy ambled amiably, and folksy cowboys uttered their American platitudes. The Indians – always the baddies – would ululate around their totem poles, their resplendent feathers streaming in black and white. Then, foolishly, they would set off to rid the land of the whites, galloping wildly up to a ridge where they were visible for miles. Whooping excitedly, they cascaded down and were shot by the exultant cowboys. As a gesture to the susceptible, a cowboy's daughter was often depicted sobbing over a dying chieftain's son.

Then there were the nights when we cried convulsively over Flicka the horse, hoisted in a sling and about to die – though, of course, he didn't – and Lassie, trailing across cruel terrain to end in tail-wagging triumph at the end. I always chanted 'it's only a film, not real', but still the tears poured.

There were the endless musicals, like the ones starring Sonja Henie, whose Scandinavian features beamed under blonde hair as she was drawn across artificial ice on her sleigh before reaching a frozen lake; here, she cavorted effortlessly on her skates, sometimes with a partner, other times alone. There was Esther Williams, who whatever romantic path she followed, invariably reached a pool and swam with lithesome grace, before being joined by other swimmers who invariably formed patterns on the water and pretended they were water-lilies or large circles of splashing dolphins. There were also the musicals where gentlemen always wore bow-ties and tails, and ladies shimmered down flights of steps as the orchestra hectically traced their steps. These ladies, usually clad in pink ostrich feathers, suddenly swooned into a rotating circle.

There was one woman called Kathryn Grayson whose contract stipulated she must sing an aria from an opera in every film she starred in. So, after zinging through various jazzy routines, she incongruously burst into Violetta's dying trills.

As for the straight romances, I remember a suave actor called Robert Cummings, leaning over a lady in evening dress which reached her neck at the front but left her back bare. He breathed to her: 'you have a lovely back', but I could not understand how she was so well upholstered at the front but had no bra straps. I decided it had to be a clever filming device. There was Carmine Miranda balancing a huge turban of waxed fruit on her head, her breast and lower parts encased in a glittering, tight-fitting drapery while her midriff gyrated in wild abandon. She sang such gems as:

'I know my life will begin
The very moment I'm in Argentina'
I'd swear she never left Hollywood.

Filled with these delights, we sallied forth, a huge throng descending the stairs which were overhung with a mirror in which one could eye the crowd or inspect one's face for the ravages wrought by weeping.

I cannot remember why the Empire was less frequented, though I can remember standing one Bank Holiday in hot sunlight for at least an hour to see a musical. We were happy and uncomplaining as we poured into the cinema to trample across the bare-boarded aisles into the primitive tip-up seats.

Of course, you had to go to Nottingham for the major films with the sophistication of Loretta Young, William Powell and Myrna Loy; the smouldering eyes of Merle Oberon; or the legs of Betty Grable. But Ripley offered hours of pleasure and I look back happily to a time when communal enjoyment gave an enchantment which no 'earthy, realistic' television soap could ever capture. It was the make-believe which glittered in the imagination."

The fantasy element prevalent in the pictures of the time provided a deliverance from the drabness of domesticity and an escape from the exertions of work. If you were in love with the cinema, you were in tune with another world that made you forget, if only for a few hours, the deprivations and disappointments of life, "where such things as Income tax existed." This was in stark contrast with the more modern movie world, as Eddie Burnham sees it: "The

Cold Justice

David Wigley remembers an incident concerning the Matlock Ritz where a happy coincidence saved his bacon – and his cold feet: "During the winter of 1975-76, I was a very young police constable, and my duties involved pounding the Matlock town beat night and day. One particular bitter winter's evening, when there was hardly anyone about, I decided to pop into the cinema, just to get warm. The usherette, who knew me, allowed me to stand inside the auditorium, in a little dark corner, with my radio turned right down. Of course, as soon as I was beginning to warm up, I heard a faint crackling on my radio. It was the duty inspector wanting to meet me, just for a 'routine supervisory visit'. In other words, he was checking up on me, just to make sure I was doing my job, going round checking locked doorways etc. He asked for my location, so I told him I was on foot patrol on Causeway Lane. He said: 'I'll meet you there in two minutes'.

In a panic, I dived for the nearest fire exit, which brought me out on to a side street – Steep Turnpike. The Causeway Lane entrance to the Ritz was down the road. I dashed around the corner and there, parked in front of the main cinema entrance, was the duty inspector in his patrol car, watching for me. I thought: 'I'm in trouble here'. He got out of the car, walked over, and I saluted smartly. He asked to see my pocket notebook, to make sure it was up to date with half-hourly entries. He was going to sign it to show that he had met me.

I was just waiting for this almighty rollicking when, all of a sudden, a car pulled up right behind his. Who should get out but the superintendent from divisional headquarters at Alfreton; he just happened to be passing, and spotted us. We engaged in jovial banter, and as the Super turned to go, I waited for the delayed dressing down. Let's face it, I didn't look either cold or wet. The duty inspector knew where I had been. It was at this point that the Super turned to me and said: 'PC Wigley, I've been reminded of something having stopped outside this cinema: it might be worth your while popping in there every now and again, just for ten minutes'. I looked at him, blankly. 'Sir?'

'Yes, Wigley, pop in to make sure they're complying with fire and safety regulations'. He gave a little wink, got back in his car and drove off.

The Inspector stood there, flabbergasted. There I was, expecting to be on a disciplinary charge for neglect of duty. As it turned out, the Inspector couldn't even give me a ticking off after that! So, I had a lucky escape. From there on, whenever I felt cold (and there weren't many places you could go inside in those days), I used to nip into the Ritz. And I'm sure other officers have followed suit since!"

trouble with films today is that they show too much of the worst part of life. I blame people like Sam Peckinpah and Michael Winner. Let's go back to glamour, fantasy and romance."

Wilf Holt, another ardent film-goer of the 1940s and 1950s, also laments the passing of that age: "The magic has gone." Whilst acknowledging the sophistication of today's films, Wilf wearily feels a cynicism that was blissfully absent when he stepped inside his 'fantasy castle', as he terms it. He doesn't even favour the greater realism of modern movies. Wilf and his contemporaries didn't go to the cinema for that: "We went to the pictures to live in a world where villains were punished and not paid, lovers always lived happily ever after – at least till the end of the credits.

And it was all there waiting at the bottom of our street."

In younger years, Wilf Holt and his pals could be found in that same street, playing out fantasy games based on whatever picture they'd just seen: "If we had just watched *Zorro*, we all had masks, cane swords and raincoats round our shoulders. I especially remember a film called *Man and His Mate*; it was all prehistoric monsters and people talking gibberish. We kids loved it, and afterwards, we all made axes out of roof slate and bits of privet."

Stories are commonplace of youngsters re-enacting the antics of the multifarious adventure flicks they saw. An afternoon spent watching Tom Mix or Roy Rogers would be followed by impromptu battles

Usherettes pictured outside the Cavendish cinema in Derby in 1951.

what we did there you couldn't do downstairs... we always came with an orange and three elastic bands each. Once we got upstairs, we ate the orange, got out the three elastic bands each, looped them around our fingers, strode to the balcony front, and twanged the orange peel on the unsuspecting tuppenny mob. It was especially satisfying if you hit someone you knew. The manager invariably rushed upstairs to deliver a few expletives, but we never got thrown out. There were always a few who got tossed out, but that was mainly for rampant high spirits. We never tore up seats or anything like that. Seeing the *Lone Ranger* was the highlight."

In later years, Ernest Sutton's attentions would turn away from juvenile twanging of orange peel to adolescent yearning for the fruits of passion. Put more prosaically, he'd be looking for girls to date, and the cinema became the obvious, ideal centre for any courting activities. As Roy Christian concurs: "If you asked a girl out, you would invariably court her at the cinema." As Eddie Sutton himself points out: "Although we had radio for entertainment, you had to stay indoors for that. And radio was pretty hopeless if you wanted to date a girl." Where better to take your sweetheart than to the cinema? Or where better to go to attract one? Brian Patton and his Ripley pals had a regular weekend strategy: "Four of us used to go into a local pub, have a couple of pints of mild, then go and buy some peanuts, before taking our seats in the cinema. If we saw a girl we fancied, she'd have a peanut thrown in her direction. It worked, too... that's how I met my wife. She gave me a dressing down, mind you."

David Walters didn't get anything like as much joy out of girls in Matlock. David recalls the occasion when after hankering for a date with two girls that he and a pal had taken a fancy to, they plucked up enough courage to ask them out, to the local Picture Palace. The two boys dutifully walked them from the bus stop to the cinema, and then treated them to balcony seats. As soon as they were inside, the one girl said: "we're just nipping into the toilet; we'll see you up there." David handed them their tickets, bounded upstairs, and took his seat, heady with anticipation at a grope in the dark with the girl of his dreams. David takes up the story: "Ten minutes passed, and there was no sign of our dates. By this

between Cowboys and Indians with toy pistols and bows and arrows; if it was pirate pictures like *Captain Blood* or *Sea Hawk*, then it was out with the wooden swords for swashbuckling exploits. Brian Spare remembers that at the Melbourne Empire, "any passer-by who saw the children emerging from the Saturday matinée could tell what had been on. For example, if all the children had their coats tied round their shoulders, it meant that the *Superman* serial had been shown and every boy was trying to mimic the hero."

Ever since that first children's matinée inside the Derby Mickleover Infant Schoolroom in 1900, youngsters have been a substantial, important and integral part of the cinema-going world. Hollywood saw to that. In the early 1940s – at the time of British cinema's highest admissions – 43 per cent of boys and girls were going to the pictures at least once a week. For kids like Eddie Sutton, the thrill was as much in the going as it was in the viewing, summed up by his abiding memory of a regular Saturday trip to the Swadlincote Majestic as a young lad:

"I always associate the Majestic with Brooks Buses. I lived out at Linton, and at a quarter to two, we caught the Linton bus to Swad. I had sixpence on me, a small fortune then – threepence for the cinema admission and threepence for the bus ride. But we became money-conscious. Although it was a penny halfpenny on the bus all the way to the cinema, we discovered that if you got off earlier at York Road, it was only a penny. So, we got off there, and ran the rest of the way to the cinema. Most of the time we'd arrive at the same time as the bus, even though we were panting like mad. We'd do the same coming back as well, thereby saving a whole penny for sweets.

At the Majestic itself, we could have saved that penny by going downstairs – it was only tuppence, but we always paid threepence to go upstairs. You see,

The Sandwich Man

Betty Alldread, a former usherette and cashier at the Crich picture house, remembers her brother Brian becoming agitated by a certain element in the many films they would see. At some point, a family would invariably gather round the dinner table to eat. Brian had a big appetite and would inevitably turn peckish at the sight of all this scoffing. After a while, he decided he'd had enough. So, prior to every film show, he made up a large pack of jam sandwiches. Thus, every time a meal scene appeared on screen, Brian would tuck into his own food supply. As soon as they got up from the table, he would put them away. If, later, anyone began to eat, out would come the sandwiches again!

time, the film had started, so we walked downstairs to look for them. No sign. We trudged back upstairs and watched the remainder of the first half. Come the intermission, the lights came up. That was when we saw what those girls had done. They were down in the pits, necking with two blokes. I was never very lucky with dates at the cinema."

David Walters should have taken Ernest Sutton's lead. Ernest was an early believer in female equality. If he ever courted a girl, he arranged to meet her inside the cinema, so that she always paid for her own seat. But, if truth be told, Ernest pleaded poverty: "With only half a crown to spend, a bloke couldn't afford to buy the woman a seat as well."

"When we began the 'dating game', the cinema was always the arranged meeting place" says Vera Wragg, who frequented the Matlock Picture Palace. But there was no question of paying for oneself. Not only that, but "we girls expected to be taken in to the more expensive seats on the balcony (2s 3d) or, at a pinch, the 1s 9d seats underneath the balcony." But never in the cheap 9d seats, "as it would be too embarrassing, even if the expected box of chocs was thrown in!"

One of the perks of a balcony ticket was the alluring prospect of grabbing one of the double seats. Most Derbyshire cinemas, acknowledging the picture house as a popular place for courting couples, discovered that the provision of double seats was a decided allure. Some cinemas installed several across the back row; others weren't quite so generous: "There was only one double seat at the Belper Palace" says Kathleen Wragg, "so there was always a scramble for it!"

Courting heaven was in the shape of two cinema seats moulded together like a small sofa, blissfully free of an arm rest in the middle, to ensure a clear, clinching embrace. Imagine the thrill of being thrust together in the privacy of the dark, with no parents likely to burst in at an inappropiate moment, although according to Olive Gilbert, there was, at the Chaddesden Gloria, the occasional rude interruption from an usherette 'hanging over the back, grinning'. However, most usherettes were there to keep a discreet eye on double-seaters to ensure they didn't go too far.

Some did. According to one anonymous picture-goer, double seats were 'the place where you learnt the difference between boys and girls'. One usherette, who also wishes to remain unnamed, recalls finding a pair of knickers on a double-seat once. The Matlock Picture Palace seemed to acknowledge that the double seats were not there for watching films from, because according to one regular, if you sat in them,

Slightly Scarlet

Patricia Turner recalls a red-faced night in Ripley, when her mother's friend 'let slip', so to speak: "The film show finished. We rose as was customary to the strains of *God Save the King* and then proceeded to make our way out. The friend, who was heavily pregnant, had undone her skirt during the film. As we paid our respects to his Majesty, it had slid down. It was not until she caught sight of herself in the mirror that she realised a display of pants and suspenders was hardly decorous. Squawking with embarrassment, she rushed up to retrieve the dropped skirt.

you couldn't see the screen. In *Dream Palaces of Derby*, Sam Winfield recounts an incident which caused an usherette to shriek "come out, we don't allow that sort of thing in here." What sort of thing was going on in there Sam wasn't able to ascertain, although the hasty exit of a red-faced young couple suggested it was more than an exchange of butterfly kisses. Joe Vowles recalls an embarrassing incident at the Chaddesden Gloria when the house lights came on without warning, and attention was focussed on the kerfuffle coming from the back row. Patrons gazed on an unscheduled X certificate sight as blouses and trousers were hastily re-buttoned.

However, that was in 1957. The men who courted during the war and a few years beyond have assured me in their numbers that their intentions were polite and honourable in an age when promiscuity was largely unknown as a word, let alone an act. Many contend that they merely kissed and cuddled, and uncoiled as soon as the main feature came on.

Although young Olive Harrison (now Gilbert) 'spent many a happy hour on the double seats with the latest beau' she was a little nervous about being escorted by a Petty Officer in the Navy to the double seats in the Chaddesden Gloria to then discover, to her horror, that the main feature was the raunchy 'sex western' *The Outlaw*, starring the cleavage-hugging Jane Russell (Bob Hope once described her as 'the two and only Jane Russell'). "It was embarrassing" says Olive, "but I squirmed and shut my eyes." As it turned out, the Petty Officer didn't get carried away by the eye-widening delight of the leading lady – "there was a kiss and a cuddle, but no hanky-panky" – and maybe the root of Olive's embarrassment can be deduced by her comment that Jane Russell's endowments "did make my 32b seem nothing to write home about."

Eddie Sutton recalls a time when it was 'hands off' as soon as the main feature *Fanny By Gaslight* came on – this, after all, was her choice. Up on the screen, the Swadlincote Majestic audience sat back to watch the beastly villain James Mason, a lecherous man with a twinkle in his eye, and with evident designs on the heroine. Suddenly, attention turned to the double seats at the clear sound of a slapped face. There was the culprit – Eddie – feeling not only his cheek, but also the daggered gaze of 100 accusing eyes. Here was a young man on a double seat who had just been slugged by his date. He had obviously been 'trying it on' with the girl. Eddie sank back in his seat in embarrassment, amidst the keenly disapproving audience. But young Eddie Sutton was quite innocent of any hanky panky. Not that his simple explanation would have been believed. So, if you were in the auditorium that night, it is time the truth was

known: during a quiet moment in *Fanny By Gaslight*, a bored Eddie leant across to his date to offer his opinion on the picture. Not liking what he had said, she slapped him one. Honest.

Terence Green had a similarly red-faced twin-seat moment when he took his girlfriend to the Chesterfield Victoria. He bought his girl a box of chocolates, and decided he would tease her by withdrawing the box every time she reached for a chockie. But amusement turned to anger: at the third attempt to secure a sweet, enough was enough, and Terence's girlfriend yelled at the top of her voice: "OOOH! STOP IT!." Not surprisingly, all balcony eyes turned to the couple.

All eyes would have been on Anne Eames and her partner one night at the Matlock Picture Palace when they occupied the delight of a double seat embrace and ended up, as Anne terms it, "in an undignified heap on the floor." In fact, they had hardly touched each other. The seat had collapsed. This would not have surprised Duncan Cross, the Ashbourne Elite projectionist who took on a number of odd jobs in the cinema. One very necessary task was checking the seating for security, particularly the courting seats. "They required attention almost every day" comments Duncan, adding, with metaphoric appropriateness, that the double seats seemed to particularly suffer with 'a weakness at the knees'.

Courting couples were but one element in a wide cross-section of cinema-goers, but any young man seeking a date would have been recommended to try the local picture house. A survey by the Central Office of Information in 1946 of cinema-going habits (*The Cinema And The Public*) revealed that 62 per cent of the cinema audience were aged under 40 and, in turn, 62 per cent of the audience were women. Naturally, the make-up of the female audience would have been mixed – with husband and/or children, or with male and female partners – but the social respectability of the cinema would have encouraged many single women to spend an afternoon or evening at the local picture house. There were certainly plenty of single women who frequented the two Ashbourne cinemas. As town councillor Charles 'Bertie' Birch observed: "A woman never went into a pub alone, but she was alright in a cinema."

As a 16-year-old, Jose Howarth thought nothing of frequenting the Derby Odeon on her own. Watching the screen, young Jose was having her life moulded. She freely admits to having fallen under the seductive spell of the movies: "We loved all the film stars and tried to imitate them and their catch-phrases." This imitation extended to both manners and dress. One movie star – whose name is lost in the mists of memory – encouraged Jose to wear a gardenia (albeit artificial) in her hair. But there is one star who Jose can certainly recall: "I always looked up to Greer Garson." This red-haired, Irish-born, lady-like actress won an Academy Award for *Mrs Miniver*, was nominated for a further five Oscars and, according to Leslie Halliwell, had 'gentle, aristocratic good looks'.

'If you are as pretty, clever and kind as Greer Garson, you may easily marry the son of a steel magnate, even though you are a housemaid.'

'I shall never act like Greer Garson, but I still try to laugh like she does.'

'If the Gods had been kind, yours truly would have the figure of Marie McDonald, the face of Heddy Lamarr, the voice of Katherine Grayson, the feet of Eleanor Powell, and possessed the talent of Greer Garson.'

These are quotes from *The Sociology of Film*, published in the 1940s, in which sociologist J.P.Mayer allowed the cinema-goers of the time to express their feelings about film and the way it has shaped their lives. *The Sociology of Film* – and another J.P.Mayer publication *British Cinemas And Their Audiences* – provide searching and fascinating evidence of the extraordinary, inseminating influence of Hollywood pictures, and the remarkable extent of wish-fulfilment they instilled in the minds of its watchers. Values, tastes, morals, manners, attitudes, and appearances were either noted by the film viewer or subliminally received by them. Even simple acts of politeness and kindness; the rudimentary way a leading man parted his hair or his leading lady swayed her hips; the proper way to arrange the cutlery on the table or the right way to hold a cigarette – 'When I begin to smoke, I shall do it like Katherine Hepburn in *Philadelphia Story*'; even basic, common sense advice – 'After watching *Phantom Of The Opera*, I remember keeping a safe distance away from the acid bottles in the school chemistry lab for quite a while afterwards.'

Everything up on the screen was a tip, a guide or a stimulus: 'Leslie Howard made love kindly, Clarke Gable was tough and a go-getter, Cary Grant gay but dangerous, Ronald Coleman ministerial, Errol Flynn impossibly venturesome and Bob Montgomery the ideal gentleman. I looked for all these qualities in my friends and measured them up by it.'

Film fanaticism was fuelled by the availability of movie magazines. Nellie Mellors of Belper always bought *Picturegoer* 'to read avidly about the stars, who always seemed so young to me, even though so many of them were in their thirties. There were also – pre-tabloid – gossip sheets, about stars who genuinely lived glamorous lives'.

Many tried to imitate those lives. As Hollywood took its hold on impressionable minds, Dr Doris

Odlum told the Christian Cinema Council that many girls were spending money on dressing up like film stars. There was a danger, she said, that girls brought up in drab surroundings would get it into their heads that all that mattered was glamour.

Many girls allowed the glamour queens to get to their heads, quite literally. One could quite easily walk down a busy Derby street in the 1940s and see Garbo 'bobs', 'Maria' cuts and Colbert fringes. Or a Matlock street... Vera Wragg, who lived in the town during her cinema-going days, freely admits to she and her girlfriends 'trying to emulate the stars by styling our hair in a similar fashion to theirs'. Mrs B.Hawley of Heanor says that film stars were 'a part of our lives' and that she tried to copy some of the hairstyles of Ingrid Bergman, June Allyson, Patricia Roc, Rita Hayworth, Lana Turner, Ava Gardner, Anna Neagle, Margaret Lockwood, Betty Grable... and a few more besides!

One female cinema-goer was able to direct her boyfriend in the correct art of holding and kissing after watching the way Robert Stack embraced Deanna Durbin in *Her First Love*, and to herself note the 'little tricks' such as closing the eyes when being kissed, curling her boyfriend's hair in her fingers or stroking his face, 'exactly as I've seen my screen favourites do in their love scenes'. Deanna Durbin's influence spread even further. Indeed, she won a Special Academy Award in 1938 for 'bringing to the screen the spirit and personification of youth'. One young film-goer admitted that 'if I found myself in an annoying or aggravating situation, which I previously dealt with by an outburst of temper, I found myself wondering what Deanna Durbin would do, and modified my own reactions accordingly. She had far more influence on me than any amount of lectures from parents would have had'.

Indeed, many of J.P.Mayer's subjects tell of the attributes of etiquette and behaviour one would expect them to have picked up from parents but that they actually acquired from their movie-watching, be it touching one's hat when meeting someone, becoming better-mannered at the dinner table, or cleaning one's teeth every morning. Dialogue exchange in films taught one girl to 'speak so as each word I say can be understood without someone having to say to me "pardon".' Another girl claimed that owing to exposure to films 'my vocabulary has increased and I can hold my own in conversation' (one filmgoer, though, acquiring new words for her vocabulary, remembers that her parents were quite shocked when she first used the word 'scram' in front of them).

Some films and film stars went beyond mere advice in the social niceties, and altered film-goers' whole

There was plenty of choice for cinema-goers in the Derby area during World War Two as this page from the Derby Evening Telegraph *of 28 October 1944 shows.*

behavioural systems. One woman says that if she had not seen Anne Sheridan's films like *Navy Blues*, *Juke Girl*, *Wings For The Eagle* and *The Man who Came To Dinner*, "I would probably have made a mess of things by being shy and uncertain." Another woman had her life changed by viewing Jennifer Jones in *The Song of Bernadette*: "I made a resolution to love all that was beautiful and clean in mind."

More material inspiration was provided by a look inside film characters' homes. One woman, obviously anxious to improve her marriage, gazed yearnfully at the latest in modern appliances and thought: 'How pleasing for a husband to come home from work to a neat and pretty wife, owing to many labour-saving devices, than to a wife who is tired and looks it, too.'

But housewives didn't need to merely dream. The movie world may have felt unreal and unreachable, but there was much that they could do, by just acting on the fillip a film provided: 'Recently when the whole world looked dark and after a particularly trying week of hard work, I dropped into a local cinema to see *Cover Girl*. I felt amazingly refreshed, tackled the necessary household duties and then – I made over one of my very old dresses (inspired by a dress worn by the star), arranged my hair a la Hayworth, and faced the world with new pep! And thanked my lucky stars I was living in this film-made generation'.

Men were affected, too: 'Perhaps the greatest influence on my own fashion is the way Gary Cooper or Brian Donlevy brushes his hair'. One boy was not only encouraged by the Pictures to put grease in his hair, but also to keep his clothes clean and to always strip to the waist when he washed. B.Ellis tells a touching tale of how he was rescued from derision by his Western hero:

"William Farnum saved my bacon. At a very tender age, I had been detailed to attend a family wedding, as one of two page boys. This meant wearing white blouse, short velvet trousers, white socks and new black shoes – that sort of attire. Afterwards, those velvet trousers had to be worn out. How could I appear in them in front of my pals? About the same time, I saw that in one William Farnum Western, the great man was wearing corduroys. That was good enough for me. So, in boy-ish gun play, I announced that I was William Farnum. My short velvet trousers – the next best thing to corduroys – were accepted."

Frank Bacon noticed in Heanor that when gangster movies were in vogue, so were the local lads, strutting about town sporting trilby hats and long white raincoats and yelling 'come and get me, copper!' to the neighbourhood bobby. Belper picture-goer Charles Mather discovered that girls were so impressed with Fred Astaire that "lads used to save up their money and buy a full-length Melton overcoat with a white silk scarf."

Although Charles believes his generation got 'a false impression of America being the land of milk and honey', he appreciated the way cinema 'provided a break from the poverty, frustration and humdrum of life'. One of J.P.Mayer's subjects echoed many cinema-goers' feelings when he declared that films 'made me want to be a somebody, not just a someone in the daily pattern of life'. Eddie Burnham not only acknowledged that fact, but took inspiration from it: "People who lived a drab life wanted to go somewhere that was a little up-market. And they got that not just from walking in the cinema, but watching the stars. My favourite was Cary Grant; he wore a dinner suit when he went out. When I was a kid, I said: "I'm going to be like him – I'm going to wear a dinner suit and go out to posh places." And I did, eventually. I aimed high.'

Others gazed on high, and idolised. One of J.P.Mayer's case studies admitted to a Ginger Rogers fixation that was all-pervasive: 'I dreamed of her at night, thought of her all day, filled my scrapbooks with hundreds of photographs of her, hummed her songs, fluffed my hair out in daring imitation, locked myself into my bedroom and *was* Ginger Rogers.'

Many women became infatuated by male stars. One girl was so besotted with Bing Crosby, she thought of him 'constantly… I wonder what he is doing at different times during the day. When I see Bing on the screen my heart thumps'. But there were the inevitable disappointments and let-downs: 'For a whole year I thought, talked and dreamed films and Errol Flynn became my screen idol. His good looks, handsome physique and, most of all, his moustache all helped to make me feel as if I was in love. However, when the war broke out, I found that my idol had feet of clay and would not join the army. Thus ended my infatuation and I have never liked the man since.'

There was certainly a downside to cinema-going: despair at the unattainable fame, wealth and glamour portrayed on the screen, with the concomitant dissatisfaction with one's lot in life; or simple disappointment with the way on-screen life failed to transfer to reality. One woman had a disillusioning experience early in life that echoes the yearning of Mia Farrow's deprived film fan character in Woody Allen's *Purple Rose Of Cairo*:

"I am still teased about an incident that happened one Saturday afternoon. I wanted to go to the cinema very early and said that I couldn't stop to have lunch as I would be late. My grandmother was rather bewildered as it was about 12 noon and the cinema didn't open until 1pm I was asked why I couldn't wait. I very solemnly replied that I wanted to see Jean Harlow going into the cinema."

Even if the film stars weren't residing in the neighbourhood, they could still encroach on the minds of young girls, leaving them thoroughly unhappy: 'Many were the nights I cried myself to sleep because John Howard, Preston Foster or Robert Taylor were so far away'. Other girls experienced discontent in relationships with the opposite sex: 'After seeing the polished lover on the screen, it is rather disillusioning to be kissed by a clumsy, inexperienced boy'. Another girl was quick to discover that her male idols 'were so much more gentlemanly and dashing than the callow youths I knew'. It affected one woman so much that she found herself drifting 'from one mundane friendship to another – always dull and prosaic. I have finished some really very pleasant friendships because of this intangible longing for something different: something based, I suppose, on my very early idea of love. Perhaps one day the right boy will scatter this fruitless idealism, imprinted so strongly by the films. I hope so'.

The many films that filled viewers with thoughts of perfection led to disapproval with more than one's

immediate partner. One cinema-goer declared that films 'have taught me to look down on my neighbours; I think them ugly, fat and ignorant'.

In terms of environment, many inhabitants of places like Alfreton, Heanor, Ilkeston Ripley and Swadlincote would have emerged from their picture houses and immediately felt the yawning gulf between the exhilarating skyscraper cities depicted on screen and the comparatively drab, languid skylines of their own towns. But there would be many cinema-goers who would have enjoyed the heady glamour of the silver screen world but cleared their head as soon as they walked out of the foyer, not only to accept the reality of their lives but also to greet it: 'If I gaze enraptured at the gilt palaces of the movie queens, my envy is merely momentary. To me, it seems an unreal world and I do not yearn for a closer inspection. I rarely regret the return to earth. There is too much beauty around me – the countryside, the garden, music at the turn of the knob.'

Other film-goers were not fooled by the appearances of the stars.

One woman was well aware that, in

most cases, the pure, perfect look of the movie queens was a combination of make-up and 'powerful floodlighting', so that if 'we were to use make-up to such an extent as the movie stars do, we would look ridiculous freaks'.

If you put your head in the clouds while in the local dream palace but kept your feet firmly on the ground once you emerged into the cold, hard light outside, then movie-going in the golden age could be a pleasure and a thrill without leaving one hankering for the unfeasible, unreachable heights. But below the perfect summit there were still attainable ledges. You aimed for what you could realistically obtain from the pictures. Leslie Halliwell, writing in *Seats In All Parts*, tells how he gained both welcome advice, a little bit of learning and that little bit of sparkle to his life, and all without taking it all too seriously:

'Real life was fascinating, but untidy and sometimes sad; the kind of life shown on the silver screen had dramatic progression, and its loose ends of plot were always tied up (well, nearly always). It was highly moral, and it taught me such things as how to behave at table, how to speak to a lady, and what was involved in various kinds of adult activity. For instance, to be a reporter you had to wear your hat in the house, and know more about crime detection than the police. It gave me an idea of what happened in history, admittedly a hazy one since Disraeli and Voltaire and Richelieu and Rothschild all seemed to look like George Arliss. It gave me a taste for the rhythms of popular music and the styles of American wisecracking. It introduced me to hundreds of people who were handsomer or wittier or more clearly defined than anybody of my real-life acquaintance. It gave me things to dream about'.

The above-mentioned morality of movies was an important, all-consuming factor from the mid-1920s through to virtually the early 1950s. As late as 1953, the censors refused a release to Otto Preminger's *The Moon Is Blue* because the script contained words like 'virgin', 'seduction' and even – horror-upon-disgust – 'mistress'. Even before the notorious Hays Code of 1930, there were certain guidelines to follow, as shown by the guidance given by Herman Mankiewicz to fellow writer and Hollywood arrival Ben Hecht in 1927: 'In a movie... the hero, as well as the heroine, has to be a virgin. The villain can lay anyone he wants, have as much fun as he wants, cheating and stealing, getting rich and whipping the servants. But you have to shoot him in the end.'

It was thus perfectly acceptable for the Swadlincote Majestic Programme of 1933 to attract cinema-goers to its support picture *Come On Tarzan* (the actual name of Ken Maynard's 'human' horse) with the words: 'See Ken Maynard's famous horse trample on

the villain!' Herman Mankiewicz's words of advice also mirror the incongruousness of the Motion Picture Code that was introduced three years later, and although it had little effect at first, it was exerted with rigorous gusto from 1934. Basically, it was a morality code, administering rigid restrictions on any films that dared to deal with issues of sex, crime and religion.

The most ridiculous aspect of Hays' thinking extended to depictions of bedroom scenes. Double beds were outlawed on screen, and even if bedrooms were shown, the men and women who moved within them had to be married. Even then, the husband was not allowed to sit on his wife's bed unless he had both feet on the floor. And if the couple kissed, there was an eight-second limit; and only one kissing position was allowed: both lovers had to be standing. Even married couples also had to abide by this ruling, and they could only kiss each other goodnight if they performed this innocuous ritual outside the bedroom.

One can chortle at the absurdities of Hays' strict conditions, which produced a rash of exasperated film-makers, but the audiences who flocked to see the Hollywood fare that was permitted by the Code didn't feel there was anything amiss. Cinema-goers lapped up the simple, sentimental, wholesome decency of it all, and generally admired the ethical messages. A case study in J.P.Mayer's *Sociology Of Film* reflected the consensus of opinion:

'Film taught me all the things I should like to associate with life: crime does not pay; the wrong-doer getting his just desserts; kindness pays; love-thy-neighbour; plumping for the "small man"; making the best of life; "true" love wins in marriage; the mild and honest man triumphing over the immoral, unscrupulous man; all the ideals worthy of life.'

Those words help to explain why so many who were exposed to this kind of film fare rail against contemporary pictures. Although many ex-cinema-goers who have contributed to this book have made sweeping and damning generalisations about the make-up of modern movies, their contempt and discontent stem from a long, adoring association with a dream factory.

The last word here belongs to Eddie Burnham, who as the Swadlincote Premier projectionist from 1943, helped deliver that dream:

"When you took a girl to the Pictures, you were close to your girl; you could sit and hold her hand, and you could both drift off into another world. When Cary Grant was on, you were Cary Grant. When Dorothy Lamour came on, she was Dorothy Lamour. That was the secret of cinema-going, and I wish it would come back. If it did, I'd start going back to the cinema."

The Smallest Show On Earth

The not-so-super cinemas... the village halls, flea pits, bug hutches and small-town wonders

The Crich cinema was very basic, I remember. The manager was Harry Major, a blunt down-to-earth Yorkshireman who looked like Wallace Beary. One night, the projectionist didn't turn up. Harry decided that sooner than give the audience its money back, he'd put on the show, with my younger brother Brian, who was an apprentice. I was reminded of that night when I eventually got to see The Smallest Show On Earth, *where Peter Sellers plays a hapless projectionist in a run-down picture house. Well, everything went wrong. Basically, Harry didn't know how to project. He put the reels on upside down. One reel went backwards. The end reel went on in the middle. By then, the audience was restless, banging on the floor, shouting: 'We want pictures!'. My brother vividly remembers Harry peering through the projection room peephole and saying: 'We've lost 'em lad... they're going'. So, in the end, the audience did get its money back.*

Betty Alldread, usherette at Crich Picture House

WHEN word got round that there was this new-fangled entertainment called cinema, everyone wanted it, and some wanted to be in on it. So, the picture house came to both big city and small town... and even the village. As early as 1919, the magazine of the National Federation of Women's Institutes – *Home and Country* – printed an article entitled 'The Cinema In The Village', in which a 'great Statesman, well known in connection with Agriculture' is quoted as saying: 'We shall never get the people back to the land or, having got them, keep them there, unless we have a Cinema in every village.'

The WI reporter Mary Horne quaintly referred to cinemas as the up-to-date equivalent of circuses, and declared that it would be an ideal world whereby rural inhabitants only had to walk a couple of miles to 'share in the pleasure of seeing the latest thing in the "Topical News", the recent air race, the most popular boxing rivals, the wonders of the latest invention, the marvels of nature, life in other countries remote from their own, and the most thrilling of drama and mirth-evoking comedy'.

Women's Institute readers were told that building a cinema in one's local village would not be a waste of money. 'Far from it. From the nation's point of view, is it not better to spend something on retaining healthy fathers of families on the land, rather than let them wander off, with heavy hearts, but with stead-fast determination, to people other lands?' Quite.

For Mary, the expense of a cinema would be justified if it merely diverted a man's spending from the public house. In fact, although Mary's WI connections, rural existence, and stilted prose suggest she was a sheltered, conservative thinker of the time, she had the foresight as early as 1919 to recognise not only the potential influence of cinema on lives, but also the little-realised realities of a future life where working hours would shorten, and leisure hours lengthen. This state of affairs, warned Mary, 'will only tend to greater discontent, unless provision is made for mental stimulus'. Country folk, she contended, would not be content to commune with Nature. To prevent a narrow outlook 'as regards the doings of men', the cinema had an 'indisputable' claim to enter village life.

Mary also made this potentially big step seem surmountable, pointing out that guidance on equipment and installation could be sought through the Cinema Re-Creative Circle, whose aims were the 'uniting in a definite and concerted effort, on practical lines, all clergy, teachers and social welfare workers, in order to harness the unbounded force of the Cinema in the interest of right thinking and noble living'. Furthermore, where there was electric light

A scene from **The Smallest Show On Earth,** *starring* **Bill Travers and Virginia McKenna, who take over a run-down cinema and set about making it popular.** BFI Stills, Posters and Design.

available, Mary quoted an outlay of only £30 for 'machine and necessary accessories', with a small portable machine suitable for a room accommodating 500 people having been specially manufactured for the Re-Creative Circle. The same Circle was also on hand to offer advice on operation, programming and film hire.

Where could one show films, though? Why, the 'Parish Room' of course, suggested Mary, and even if there wasn't a suitable fire-proof projection room, a collapsible and portable one could be obtained for £18. More ambitious parish councils might want to erect a new purpose-built hall, but Mary – ever-sensitive to the preservation of rural landmarks – warned that the village green – 'sacred to quoits, geese and infant cricketers' must not be profaned by any sort of hut. In fact, Mary's suggestion of an alternative site was made to seem almost idyllic: 'If it is a little way "down the lane" all the better. Why deprive the young people of the pleasures of seeing each other a bit of the way? If, by moonlight, all the more romantic; if by bulls-eye lantern, all the more amusing. Some homes may be two or more miles from the Cinema but what matter when people are young?'

Mary Horne's article could conceivably have galvanised three Youlgreave villagers. A first attempt at cinema in the Peak District village was made by the Toft family in the early 1920s, according to Youlgreave resident James Fryer who learnt from his late parents that the three Toft brothers Eli, Vernon and Sidney 'were very enterprising in anything mechanical'. Sidney also had a flair for anything electrical. So, invigorated by the burgeoning interest

in cinema, they swung into action. Although mains electricity didn't come to Youlgreave until the end of the decade, there was a supply available from the nearby village Co-op. As James Fryer recounts: "The progressive Co-op management had installed a diesel generating plant with storage batteries to light their five-storey shop and warehouse, along with some private houses... and the village hall. A suitable 110 volt DC supply was therefore available for the projector light." Setting up a temporary box at the rear of the village hall, in which they installed a hand-cranked projector, the Toft brothers put on a show. It wasn't a presentation on a par with the picture house in town, as these films were genuinely silent: no pianist could be found to accompany the action on screen. Not that it would have overly concerned an audience viewing motion pictures for the first time. They would probably have also exercised a deal of tolerance towards the numerous breakdowns, which were usually signalled by an announcement to the audience that 'Sid has gone up to the workshop for some tools'.

However, Sid and his brothers eventually moved on to other enterprises as two men from Chesterfield took over and appointed William Rose as 'caretaker' and 'secretary', which probably meant he was also commissionaire, cashier, usher, rewind boy and sweet salesman. A new projector was installed when mains electricity arrived, and William's wife Margery was known to play a bit, so she got the pianist's job.

The Youlgreave villagers might have spent some time communing with nature, but communal thoughts were increasingly directed towards the action inside the village hall. Fired by the enthusiasm for film shows, a new projection room was built over a fresh entrance and pay-box. Sound projectors were introduced, and a record player linked to the amplified sound system. Who needed Bakewell Picture House or the Matlock Cinema House? The cinema was a profit-going concern, too. James Fryer's cash book records show that the cinema made a whopping great ten shillings in May 1927, and even reached the giddy heights of four pounds in September of that year.

James recalls that when George Ollerenshaw took over as projectionist, 'a rather professional show was produced', on both Mondays and Tuesdays, with a change of film for Thursday and two houses on a Saturday. It was a complete presentation, too, with one or two 'shorts', a Gaumont British newsreel, and then a feature film.

When George Ollerenshaw was directed to work in Chesterfield at the outbreak of World War Two, his assistant Kenneth Moseley took over, and James Fryer came in as assistant. James recalls that black-out arrangements were distinctly makeshift, with thick army blankets forming a light trap at the cinema's entrance door. What James also remembers is that the inadequate working conditions in a village hall were compensated by its homely advantages, namely a large, refreshing jug of tea, brewed on the premises by Margery Rose, always brought to two grateful operators almost stifling under the dry heat produced in the limited space by the arc lights. "We also got several rounds of toast" adds James, "but by the time they got to us, they were always cold."

Margaret Folley remembers that, eventually, "proper padded cinema seats were fixed at the back, but they had to leave a space in the hall for other functions." This meant that when it opened as a cinema, they filled the space with foldaway chairs. The hall seated about 300. "I always remember it packed" Margaret recalls, "even with a poor film, it was three-quarters full."

The wooden chairs were 6d, the partly padded ones were 9d, while an extravagant outlay of 1s 6d brought one the luxury of a plush tip-up seat. Once the audience was in place, Ken and James would give caretaker William the nod and he would plunge the hall in darkness – 'no dimmers in those days' – and the show would begin.

William Rose would sit silently at the front of the stage chuffing his pipe. Although a well-known and likeable man, all the children feared him – 'one look from Bill would bring silence'. The cinema itself went silent soon after the TV aerials began to interrupt the village skyline but, even here, in a small, secluded patch of pastoralism, Hollywood came knocking and was welcomed in. The seats could have been comfier, though.

In spite of Youlgreave's early start, the county's first village cinema was established even before Derby saw its first purpose-built picture house. Peter Dakin recounts how his grandfather John, who lived in Chesterfield, built houses in Carr Vale, near Bolsover, and not only decided to build a 'show place' in the village, but also moved there with his family of ten to run the show. He placed an advertisement in the local paper on 10 April 1909, announcing 'Animated Pictures and Refined Entertainment' at the Central Hall. As John Dakin had 'purpose-built' the place, he could have laid claim to erecting Derbyshire's first proper picture house, but stage shows were to dominate in early years before the emphasis was switched to moving pictures. It was a true family affair: John Dakin appointed his son as manager and projectionist, and his daughter played the piano.

Tragically, only 18 months after his enterprise had begun, John Dakin was a broken man. Just before the Christmas of 1910, following a children's talent competition, a group of children who had attended the show were struck by a train as they walked over an unmanned railway crossing. Two were killed: a little girl, and her brother... who had won the contest. As Peter Dakin recalls: "Grandad immediately closed the hall, and it was said he never got over this incident."

But the 450-seater cinema re-opened, and thrived, particularly during World War Two. Greer Garson in *Mrs Miniver* played to a packed house and had a noticeable effect. "After that" says Peter, "the place was full to capacity", even though a proportion of their regular patrons had to walk several miles to get there. They put up with a lot: power cuts were plenty, occasionally effecting an hour-long wait, and sometimes when the power was there, the film wasn't: panic stations regularly ensued when the late picture failed to materialise, prompting a taxi-dash to Chesterfield and back. But such was the loyal, family-based dedication to the Central Hall that Peter saw youngsters grow into courting couples, and their children appear at the kiddies' matinées. The cinema even installed Cinemascope. But as Peter concludes: "TV eventually came along, and you know the rest... I remember a local wireless shop owner commenting to my Dad: 'I'm not touching television – it'll never take off'." Carr Vale Central Hall has now been pulled down, an empty site, awaiting sale.

Not far from Carr Vale, some three miles to the south-east of Chesterfield, is the village of Grassmoor, which also supported a cinema – the Palace, a singularly inappropriate name in the eyes of relief projectionist Roy Beech, who at one time went to prepare the films for showing: "It was like a Nissen hut. It was largely colliers who used to frequent the place. I never liked going there, because I spent a large part of the morning repairing the broken seats."

For David Harrison, a regular attender in his adolescence, it was 'a dark, formidable place, commonly called "The Bug Hutch", and run by a draconian couple, Fred Dickens and his wife.' Fred's demeanour seemed to be summed up by the metal plate he kept on the wall stating that anyone caught swearing was liable to a fine of £5, pretty uncharitable for any youngster who kept the cinema afloat with regular ninepenny visits. Although David doesn't remember the manager ever imposing this weighty fine (in spite of the obscenities that greeted the regular breakdowns) Fred Dickens still fell well short of the usually benevolent image of the cinema manager: "He was a miserable old sod" recalls David, "coming amidst us at all times flashing a large torch, turning the beam on anyone who, in his eyes, had committed a misdemeanour, and threatening always to throw us out."

David recalls that he and his mates were simply high-spirited, but there was a prank they used to pull: "On a signal, we all used to beat the red plush seats causing large clouds of dust to rise, much to the annoyance and wrath of Fred."

What could possibly sound worse than a 'bug hutch'? Why, a 'blood tub', of course. Minnie Gilmour remembers that this name was given to the Langley Mill Picture House, which opened around 1916. The epithet suggests that rather than attracting various insectivorous intrusions, here was a cinema that drew in vicious fighting men. In point of fact, it was nowhere as thrilling as that: as David Roddis observes, the Picture House had been built on the site of the local abattoir. As a cinema, it was, by all accounts, a quite ordinary place. It is now a showroom for windows.

Langley Mill's other known cinema – the Picture Palace – must be one of the few in the country to have earnt a mention in a book penned by a celebrated English novelist – D.H.Lawrence. As David Roddis points out in his book *The Thrill Of It All*, the Eastwood novelist began writing *The Lost Girl* in 1912, the same year the Langley Mill Picture Palace was built and opened. Interestingly, there are also lines in the novel which may reflect Lawrence's own lack of enthusiasm towards the cinema per se, referring to the cinematograph as being 'but one item in the programme, amidst the more thrilling incidents... of conjurers, popular songs, five-minute farces, performing birds, and comics', with the further reference to 'the dithering eye-ache of a film'.

In the story, the daughter of a draper finds work as a pianist in a wooden building her father had bought, referred to as a cinema and variety theatre in 'Lumley', described as 'one of those depressed, negative spots on the face of the earth which have no pull at all', as well as 'a damn, god-forsaken hell of a hole'. In reality, the Langley Mill Picture Palace was also owned by a draper (from Eastwood, too) and. furthermore, was an edifice described as 'a bundle of old wood'. Not surprisingly, the building burnt down. David Roddis believes its fate might have owed something to the crude heating provided by its stoves, on which patrons used to roast chestnuts.

No chestnuts were roasted on the radiators which provided the heating for the Sitwell cinema in the village of Spondon, but they still had a specific use at one time in the early 1940s. Although there was nothing crude about this village cinema – as Molly Rainbow remembers, "it was reputed to have one of the best sound systems of any cinema in the Derby area" – there was a certain inelegance in the way usherette Mrs Perkins would keep order during the youngsters' Saturday matinées, when the film stopped and Mr Bell the projectionist was struggling to put the next reel on. To quell the uproar, as Molly recalls, "this dear lady would rush up and down the cinema, clutching a wooden coathanger, with which she would rattle the old radiators along the walls" (appropriate, then, that uppermost in Molly's memories of the matinée films is a weekly serial entitled *The Clutching Hand*). However, adds Molly, "in spite of Mrs Perkins' rough words, we all thought the world of her, and she was just as fond of us."

An extraordinary number of cinemas thrived in villages in the north of the county, and most were not only well-patronised, but also well-loved, even if they had only basic decor, unreliable projection and bum-numbing seats. Kay Wragg has fond recollections of the Castleton village hall cinema, previously a Wesleyan chapel, even though she had to spend her early years sitting on wooden chairs at the front, waiting to graduate to the chapel seats at the rear which were commandeered by the courting couples. The power lines which supplied electricity to the hall were susceptible to storms and, along with the occasional Act of God, the show was frequently halted through the action of the projectionist, when a newsreel appeared in the middle of the main feature. Kay also remembers that the people who ran the Castleton cinema gave shows at other times of the week in both Bradwell and Hathersage.

Eyam also had a temporary site for pictures – at the Mechanics Institute. Pat Robinson used to pay ninepence to sit on a wooden form. "If you were wealthy and paid an extra shilling, you could sit in the red plush chairs at the back, but wherever you sat in the place, it was always cold." Pat also has a memory of a mother who, along with her young family, never missed a picture; "and yet next morning she would be begging for a loaf and jam at the grocers."

Rose Page recalls the time when Lana Turner worked in the kiosk at the Staveley Regal: "Well, she was called Lana Turner by my Mum, as she was a pretty blonde who wore brightly-coloured lipstick." Actually, there could well have been a film star who hailed from Staveley during the silent era – a photograph of a G.W.Blythe, 'Gold Medalist and Miner Hero' and star of a film called *The Toilers*, hung for many years in the Staveley Empire foyer after its screening in 1915.

Eckington was another village in the north of the county to have two cinemas – the Picture House and Electra. Swadlincote also housed two picture houses. The Premier was regarded as the smarter, more up-market cinema; the Empire was less decorous and more down-market. "We felt posh at the Premier" says one-time projectionist Eddie Burnham. "The

Empire, on the other hand, was a bug hut. We also had a balcony, which the Empire didn't have, along with well-lit corridors with posters of forthcoming attractions and scenes from films. We had proper decor, too – a nice, wide foyer, with a rubberised floor." However, that foyer floor – with its large black and white patterning – had its downside, which Eddie felt every single morning: "Yes, I always remember those patterns because I was terrified of the cleaners, and when I arrived after they'd spent the early morning scrubbing, I always used to take great pains to only walk on the black bits."

Fortunately for the cleaners, when the local miners came en masse to the Premier, it was prior to their shift rather than directly after. The Premier, like many other picture houses in proximity to a pit, catered for the colliery workers. Len Waller remembers the incongruous feeling sometimes generated by one of these 'Miners' Matinees': "Imagine leaving the cinema after a Busby Berkeley spectacular, climbing into gritty pit clothes and going down the mine. I remember thinking: 'one moment it was *Gold Diggers of Broadway*; the next it was *Coal Diggers of Somercotes*'."

Like both the Premier and Empire in Somercotes, many other Derbyshire village cinemas, even in the more remote areas of the county – particularly in the north – enjoyed popular support from residents. They also, again like Somercotes with its Empire and Premier, sported the kind of grandiose titles more suited to neon-clad city cinemas, like the Empress at Chapel-en-le-Frith, the Savoy at Tibshelf, the Regal at Langwith, the Picturedrome at Hadfield, the Palace cinemas at Clowne, Creswell and Killamarsh, and the Empire cinemas at both Glossop and Shirebrook. There was also the Oxford cinema in New Whittington, the Dronfield Electra, Pilsley Ritz, and Tideswell Picture House.

Ken Kind of Pilsley has a memory of his aunt calling on his mum and saying: 'Shall we have a bob's worth of dark, Edna?' It was the signal for a visit to

EMPIRE, STAVELEY
MONDAY, February 1st, 1915.

G. W. BLYTHE,
GOLD MEDALLIST AND MINER HERO,
In Novel Scene, "THE TOILERS."

A film star of the silent era from Staveley? This advertisement was for a production at the Empire during World War One.

the village Ritz. As a visitor to the Pilsley cinema himself, Ken recalls the sight of the projectionist-cum-attendant Jack Hayward, who must have been frightening to some of the smaller children. Jack, known as 'Vondo' (for reasons Ken never knew) had only one tooth, a fearsome fang-like protrusion in his lower jaw. He also had only one arm, which required him to hold the strip of admission tickets in his mouth and rip them off with his one hand. Ken recalls a cheeky lad called Joey Walker who was often heard to say: 'Gnaw us a ninepenny off, Vondo', to which he would receive the threat of a boot up his rear. "Vondo was also the local bookie on the side" Ken recalls, "making him the only one-armed, one-toothed, bookmaking projectionist I've ever heard of." Are you sure, Ken?

In spite of the taunts he received, Vondo usually got the last word in. A favourite trick of his was to move amongst the audience near the end of the show and shout: 'Anybody for the ten past nine bus to Clay Cross?... Yes?... Well, you're too late – it's just gone.'

It would be no surprise to find Clay Cross residents bussing it to Pilsley for the Pictures: Clay Cross had two cinemas of no fond repute. Even though the YMCA Hall was converted around 1950, it didn't last long, closing down about eight years later. By all accounts, it would not have been missed. "It was a Mickey Mouse operation" remembers Michael Wood. "The projection room was made out of fireboard with thick blankets to dull the sound." The hall was unwelcoming and rather run-down, with staffing provision similarly basic: even though Michael was only of school age, he sometimes had to run the cinema on his own. "Many times I used to go straight from school, open up the cinema, put a record on, take the money and then start the show. Come the interval, I'd put another record on, and get out the ice-cream tray." Michael ran the cinema virtually throughout the winter months because the manager Pat Cooney lived out at Parsons Cross on the north side of

Sheffield, and very often couldn't make it because of the weather.

Pat Cooney eventually went on to acquire the Pilsley Ritz. He also took over the Riddings Regent, another cinema which few remember with any great affection. John Scott confirms its reputation as the local 'bug hut', particularly when it had gone to seed during his spell as assistant projectionist in the mid-50s. "It was very rough inside, we never got any repairs done, and the curtains were operated by two house bricks on a rope. Also, the films we got nobody else wanted, and they were so old, they always used to break down." John also recalls that very few Riddings folk ventured out to the Regent in the winter: "It was so cold, people used to sit on the radiators rather than the seats." No wonder that Regent usherette Cynthia Leek has an abiding memory of an old lady who used to come with a hot water bottle under one arm. And if the films were awful or there was a breakdown, out came the item she brought under the other arm – her knitting. It would have been interesting to see the results she would have produced in the dark of the Regent.

The Melbourne Empire – 'an old warehouse' tucked away behind Quick Close – also isn't remembered with any pride by the locals. "The velvet drapes probably looked nice when they first went up" says John Moore, "but I don't think they were ever taken down to be washed. Yet Mrs Hunt, who ran the cinema, used to turn up in a Jaguar, wearing a fur coat. The other two cinemas she ran were flea pits as well, I'm told." However, the Melbourne Empire contained much greater horrors than the odd flea. Brian Spare remembers the time the silence of a dramatic moment in a picture was broken by a lady screaming and jumping on her seat. Was she anticipating a scary scene? No, she had already had one, and it was much more frightening than anything the Melbourne Empire would have ever flung on the screen: a large rat had run across her feet. John Moore also remembers the odd rat scuttling across the balcony.

As John further recalls: "it smelt like a place that had been closed down a long time." Ironic, then, that one of the jobs handed to Bet Greatbatch was to sniff anyone who came in to ensure they were not bringing in fries purchased at the chippie next door for fear they would 'stink the place out'. Brian Spare does recall one feature that made the Melbourne Empire unique. However, it was not a feature any other cinema would have wished for – the room was bent in the middle. As a result, Brian thinks a photograph of the place would be interesting to see. It appears no one bothered to take one.

Crich Picture House was no architectural wonder, either. Also, the acoustics left a lot to be desired: if the rain should beat down with sufficient force on the corrugated iron roof, ears would be straining to hear the dialogue. The soundtrack would be even more indistinct if those ears were covered up, which was often the case in the cold winter months. As former usherette Betty Alldread remembers: "The limited heating, coming from the radiators at the side, didn't seem to reach the centre of the cinema, even when they were on full pelt. People sat there with their overcoats, caps and scarves on, and collars up, forever mumbling: 'it's bloody cold, youth'."

But still they came to the 500-seater cinema. Betty remembers that many villagers came so regularly that they eventually laid claim to certain seats, "and there was a big sulk on if someone else sat in them. If they didn't move, we'd hear cries of 'if I can't have my favourite seat, I'm not coming here anymore'. They'd go and sit somewhere else, and as soon as the person in 'their' seat got up to either fetch an ice-cream or go to the outside toilet, they would slip into the seat. The funny thing was, there was never much objection to this."

Crich Picture House was well patronised not only by the villagers, but also residents of Fritchley, Whatstandwell and even Holloway. Mrs K.Dore stayed with her grandparents at Holloway during World War Two, and even walked the long distance to the cinema, preferring to spend her bus fare on sweets. "Nowadays, having driven from Crich to Holloway, I marvel at not only how far it is, but also how dark and lonely it must have been for me. But I suppose we hadn't been taught to be afraid, so we weren't."

Following the war, a possibly unique feature for a village cinema was created at Crich Picture House: a room adjacent to the pay-kiosk was converted into a café, serving afternoon teas and light grills and snacks. This temporary extravagance would have been in marked contrast to villages like Brailsford and Kirk Ireton: they didn't even have a cinema. But from 1948, they got a film show once a week, thanks to the Elite Mobile Cinema, run by Geoffrey Dearle and his wife Norah.

Looking for a change from his market gardening occupation, Geoffrey decided to indulge his life-long interest in films (he was given a 35mm toy projector at the age of ten) having espied an opening in the cinema business. He had become aware of several villages deprived of film entertainment. In fact, he was living in one – Barrow-on-Trent – where he discovered that the villagers' opportunities for visiting neighbouring town and village cinemas were frustrated further by an inadequate bus service. Although Barrow was but six miles south of Derby, few residents sought out the town's picture houses.

Geoffrey had heard of mobile cinemas (during the 1940s there were estimated to be around 70 of them operating at any one time) so he invested in a 16mm 'Debrie' sound projector and a stand with built-in 78 rpm record player (for interval music), a portable screen and two large speakers, along with the requisite accessories like film carrying cases and lengths of electric cable. All fitted snugly into his 10 hp Hillman saloon. But Geoffrey was all packed-up with nowhere to go. So, after an encouraging inaugural show in Barrow Social club room, he went canvassing nearby village halls. Before long, he had added Turnditch to his rota, followed by Hulland Ward, Kirk Ireton, and Brailsford. When Hanbury in Staffordshire joined the list, the Dearle's travelling cinema was a six-day-a-week operation, with a day off on Sunday.

Outlay consisted of the hiring of rooms (between 15s and £1 rent per hall per evening) and films. Geoffrey always booked a programme of films for the week, costing out at between £15 and £20, rising to £25 if the feature film was in colour. But the expenditure did not stop there: "Overheads were considerable" Geoffrey recalls, "with publicity, petrol and maintenance costs. There was also a large amount of daytime work connected with the shows. Each day, we usually ran the films through at home to check for breaks and other faults. What's more, because we only had one projector, the various reels for the show had to be made up on to one large reel; the feature film was between five and seven reels alone. And then we had to split the show up into its separate reels when we returned it to the film company. We had to advertise the shows, too. We had many of our posters printed by a local firm but occasionally I would hand paint them. These then had to be taken out and displayed in the vicinity of the villages."

The trusty Hillman usually wheeled into the awaiting village an hour before the start to allow for setting up, but as venues like Turnditch Women's Institute weren't designed to the same specifications as the nearby Ashbourne Elite, the travelling Elite soon realised they were required to arrive a lot earlier in the summer months in order to black out the windows. Fortunately, there was plenty of blackout materials left over from the war years. Norah would also need time to set out the table from which she sold ice cream and sweets during the interval. Admission was 1s 3d, with children half price (Geoffrey and Norah also used to provide private shows for childrens' parties).

The Dearles soon learnt of another timing essential. Although the various villagers became avid film-goers as a result of the Elite Mobile, Geoffrey always had to start his shows no earlier than 7.30pm. Woe betide if they began half an hour earlier: the rural inhabitants would only just have finished their daily fix of *The Archers*, which was considered compulsory listening in the rural regions at the turn of the 1950s, and always finished at 7.00pm. But the latest gossips and gripes in the Bull at Ambridge were soon forgotten when the villagers walked down to the hall, wrapped themselves in blackout material darkness, and wept as Trevor Howard and Celia Johnson realised their's could only be a *Brief Encounter*. Other memorable and popular favourites which come to Geoffrey Dearle's mind include *Love Story* with Margaret Lockwood and Stewart Granger, *Genevieve* with Kenneth More and Kay Kendall, and *Goodbye Mr Chips* with Robert Donat. Any films starring George Formby drew a large crowd, and if there was a Will Hay comedy, the vicar of Turnditch was always in the audience.

A local vicar was always in attendance at one village show brought by Maurice Woodcock and Glynn Williams, whose mobile cinema operated at the same time as the Dearle's. However, this member of the clergy was there to check over the moral content of the pictures. As Maurice recalls: "he instructed us to bring nothing but 'U' certificate films, but even when we did, he still sat through to inspect them!" However, at no time did the vicar raise any objection, suggesting that he might have wanted an excuse to be seen idling his time down at the village hall picture show.

Maurice and Glynn operated from Staffordshire, but served a few Derbyshire border villages like Etwall and Hartshorne. Like Geoffrey and Norah, they weren't in it for the money. Maurice himself was already working as a projectionist, and threw all his spare time into the mobile shows: "As a lover of the pictures, I simply got pleasure out of seeing people enjoy films." Also, the people he served weren't simply those who had difficulty in getting transport into town: "We found that there were many villagers, particularly farmers, who worked late and didn't have time to go into town. But with us, all they had to do was cycle down the road to the village hall." There was another decidedly rural element to these film shows, as Maurice remembers: "If the villagers had no money, they would hand us a carrier bag of beetroot, cabbage or other produce. I never got a chicken, though!"

The other rural element that the mobile cinemas confronted was the weather. Geoffrey and Norah Dearle's little Hillman spent many a winter gamely battling through ice, snow, and fog, but it only let down the villagers once – at Kirk Ireton (but at least they had the Barley Mow pub to drown their sorrows).

The mobile cinema comes to Etwall. **Sam Winfield Collection.**

One mist-laden Turnditch eve, Geoffrey and Norah made it to the Women's Institute, but the pea souper outside had thickened considerably. Packing up their gear and gazing nervously out at the forbidding fog, a concerned voice from the audience warned them not to venture home on such a night, and invited them to stay overnight. The lady happened to be the companion of Lady Inglefield who lived in some stately elegance over at a large house called Flower Lilies. This kindly soul rang through to the house to obtain Lady Inglefield's permission, which was duly granted, and Geoffrey and Norah retired to the kind of palatial splendour they had probably only visited on their mobile cinema screen.

As this was the winter of 1953, the Dearles might well have noticed a television set sitting in the corner of one of Lady Inglefield's rooms. TV had begun to appear in country sitting rooms across the county and, within a few short years, the village hall curtains closed on all mobile cinemas. For Geoffrey, it was the end of the rural road at the turn of 1956. But this selfless, caring spirit, venturing out to the villages to

produce the magic of cinema from the back of a Hillman saloon won't have been forgotten.

Bill Kitchener is probably still remembered in Poolsbrook, a small mining village in the Staveley area. Rose Page tells of how her father brought untold pleasure to young villagers with his mobile show, albeit on a smaller scale to Geoffrey and Maurice's operations. In fact, Bill simply took his projector and screen down the road to Poolsbrook school or church hall to screen pictures mainly for the local children. From just after the war right through to the late 1950s, Bill's film show was the only entertainment to be had in the village. It was a sparse, unsophisticated set-up: 16mm silent films were projected on to a screen stood on a chair, bench or whatever was available. Entrance charge was only a penny or tuppence, and if any children couldn't even afford that, Bill hired them to come and set the chairs out and tidy up afterwards. Entry was thus earned. Costs were duly covered, and if there was any money left after the hire, postage and package of films, Bill Kitchener would then take the children out of Poolsbrook to a Forest football match or a town panto. Bill Kitchener, a true local hero.

John Avery is not so much a local hero as a local celebrity, in the South Derbyshire town of Swadlincote. After only a short apprenticeship in the cinema business, John swiftly rose in the ranks to manager of both Swadlincote picture houses – the Majestic and Empire – before gradually realising a long-cherished dream. From 1974 to 1992, John Avery was manager of the London Palladium.

As a wartime rewind boy at the local Ritz, John could not have imagined for one moment that instead of merely gazing on Hollywood screen stars like Bing Crosby, Bob Hope, Frank Sinatra, Yul Bryner, Dorothy Lamour and Jane Russell, he would actually be enjoying their flesh and blood company. From a very early age, John Avery got used to company: his family ran a busy pub in 'Swad' – The Bear, on West Street, next door to Lushes Fish and Chip shop, which was, in turn, next to the Empire Cinema. John's immersion in the public house experience was to shape his career: "I got used to the idea of serving the public. I always wanted to be of good service to people."

John's public service aspiration began modestly. His early encounter with the cinema world was not entirely inspirational. The Swadlincote Rink was 'a tin shed showing films that were scratched to hell, and to add to the general fustiness were children who smelt of orange peel'. But his head had been turned, more by the thrill of the sheer business of entertainment than by any starry-eyed notions of getting into the movies. The Burton Ritz offered him his first opportunity in 1941, when he was barely 14. John was engaged on the thankless and unfulfilling task of film reel rewinding. "My father was not pleased. He wanted me to have a 'good' job, a straightforward one. I don't think he ever forgave me until I got to the Palladium." Any thoughts of high employment would have felt a distant dream the day young John felt the wrath of the chief projectionist: "I dropped some film cement on the projection room table, and sealed together an inch of film." That thick strip of cemented celluloid was from a film called *Thunder Rock*, but the irony of the title was lost on his superior. The chief projectionist would never bring himself to forgive his apprentice, and John Avery to this day will never bring himself to repeat his language.

John can barely bring himself to remember his three years as a 'Bevan Boy', which took him out of the cinema and down into the pit at Gresley: "I wasn't very good at it, and I don't think I ate for a week. I was pretty hopeless. They quickly put me on top, and I became an electric welder."

On the day John Avery was demobbed, he took over as assistant manager at the Majestic, Swadlincote. "Within six weeks I was the manager. I was the youngest cinema licence holder in the country... in fact, you couldn't hold a licence under 21." John was 21. He had big ideas – for publicity, in particular. Barry Woodward remembers that prior to the screening of the film *Hasty Heart*, a large heart made up of flowers was placed in the centre of the stage, around which the curtains were festooned. A typical promotional stunt was the hiring of a float in the local carnival on the theme of *The Blue Lamp*, a forerunner of *Dixon Of Dock Green*. It won a prize, too. A prize for sheer corn was called for when a film screening was introduced with the startling sight of a large live donkey shuffling on to the stage, closely followed by a man carrying a dustpan and brush. The ideal prelude to the film *Great Expectations*. "Very corny, I know" admits John, "but the audience loved it."

The audience also knew that the Swadlincote cinema was too small for the large ambitions of John Avery. When he made his name at the London Palladium, Swad resident Graham Nutt says he got "a retrospective sense of a man who was 'on his way'." At the point of his achievement, Graham began to remember the little 'touches' John had introduced – not just the publicity flourishes but also the ever-present fresh flowers in the foyer, and the scrupulously smart turn-out of the staff, John in particular. "I always wore a dinner jacket" says John. He was adamant about this nicety: "It made a difference. There was a need for a manager to be

dressed as a manager, for someone to identify with and refer to." Bill Jones still retains the memory of John Avery's first night as the manager of the Swadlincote Empire (while still running the Majestic): "There he was in the foyer in full evening regalia, shaking hands with clients and enquiring of their thoughts on the film and the facilities of the cinema." For John, it was all part of the service: "It might be considered tacky today, but in those days the cinema was a place that provided a night out and a sense of occasion." John Avery dressed accordingly.

John Avery also acted accordingly with the times. Shortly after the turn of the 1950s, there was a need to counter the onset of TV. John also felt frustrated with the endless film screenings: "I couldn't run a cinema in the same humdrum style as everyone else, so I introduced cine-variety." Talent shows were staged – and some were filmed to encourage competitors back to see themselves on screen. John booked in acts like Max Bygraves, Sam Costa and Joseph Locke: "He always insisted on being paid in pound notes before he went on" says John, with usherette Noreen Maskery also recalling the Irish tenor's predilection for the falling down water, which usually ran to two bottles of scotch... again, before he went on. (A similar memory is reserved by John Wrigley for the visit of TV personality Gilbert Harding who 'over a long weekend ate not a morsel, but survived on whisky'.) Taking advantage of its large stage area, the Majestic even staged a circus show, which required a wall to be knocked in before the lion cage could be brought on: "The lion was docile, actually, but the chimps were vicious little sods" John recalls. He also introduced an annual pantomime; for the first time in its history, the Majestic took £1,000 in a week.

John Avery had his share of hiccups: "I remember someone dying in the queue" (he never forgot or forgave the local newspaper headline – 'He Never Saw Roy Rogers'). He also grew concerned about the fact that in later years, the Majestic had begun to fall apart; for example, "the gangways were ordinary flagstones and had begun to lose their level and become noisy." But those odd moments aside, John retains a warm glow of nostalgia for his Swadlincote days, when he regularly packed both picture houses, the Majestic in particular. John even flouted the regulations to ensure that as many people as possible came through the doors: "I always packed the standing room in. We sat people on the steps in the circle, and because there was always a continuous programme, we fed them in as seats became empty... nothing can beat the atmosphere of a packed cinema, with one thousand people laughing or crying together." John experienced the sensation of success in Swad. But he also felt another entertainment world was beckoning him. The variety acts he had introduced filled him with a new fervour, and in 1956 he decided to move on, taking over the Doncaster Theatre, before eventually moving to managership of the most famous, prestigious variety theatre in the West End, and the world.

What of other small town cinema managers? Most worked diligently in the background, making their mark in a quiet but effective way. One such character was Jack Plumb, who began his cinema career as early as nine years old, selling programmes and chocolates at the Heanor Empire. In a short time, he had graduated to 'spot-light boy', projectionist's assistant and chief projectionist, and had worked at all three Heanor cinemas – the Cosy, Empire and Buxton's Picture Palace – before eventually taking over as manager at the Cosy in 1938, remaining there until its closure in 1961, and then seeing out his final working years as manager of the town Empire. He retired in 1968, having spent 55 years in the business. Jack Plumb was not only the epitome of efficiency, but also the soul of benevolence. Throughout most of his career, Jack and his Cosy staff collected countless thousands of pounds for charitable concerns locally.

Steeped in technical expertise, Jack Plumb also made himself available to illuminate the annual Christmas tree in Heanor Market Place. Bernard Goodwin, who became the last manager of the Empire, recalls the time when Jack Plumb's knowledge of lighting effects and his keenness for publicity were effectively combined at the time the Cosy received *The Dambusters*. However, the publicity stunt went way off beam, literally, not that it was Jack's fault; Bernard accepts full responsibility. Jack set up a home-made spotlight, and asked Bernard to sit atop the Cosy cinema roof and look after it. Bernard was awake to the idea. But not for long: as night set in, he fell asleep, and the spotlight trajectory shifted. A rash of complaints was heard from numerous motorists being blinded by the light at traffic signals next to a tavern in the adjacent town of Eastwood. The spotlight stunt might actually have been interpreted as publicity for the pub: the beam of light was falling on The Sun Inn.

Most cinema managers are remembered with affection. Not all accounts are complimentary, though. For instance, the only recorded memory of the original owner of the first Bakewell picture house suggests he ran his makeshift cinema on a shoestring, and was forced into roguish action as a result. Mr Devine's cinema – described in the *Bakewell and District Historical Journal* as a 'tin-roofed shed near the station' – was gas lit, and reports say that when Mr Devine got hard up, he ran a length of rubber tubing to the lamp standard near the station yard to get a free supply – 'until he got caught'.

Actually, it was thought that cinema proprietors could earn a tidy living from running a small town picture house or, in some cases, several of them. Nellie Mellors reckons that the owners of the Belper Palace, Will and Alice Morton, were well-off: "They must have done alright, because they owned a racehorse." Their supposed wealth might well have led to their apparent distance from the Palace patrons. As both cinema regulars Kath Williamson and Barbara Goldstraw recall: "The Mortons were very reserved and hoity-toity. For them it was just a job; they never mixed with the patrons." Nellie Mellors remembers two "very strait-laced people – you got into trouble if you didn't stand in line when you queued." However, Nellie does have the smiling recollection of Alice Morton's earrings, which were extremely dangly. Every time she handed out change, her ear jewellery rhythmically moved backwards and forwards.

Marie Pettipierre recalls that her grandfather John Burton was employed by Will and Alice at the Palace. Although Marie's recollections of the time are hazy, it is conceivable that the Mortons, who were friends of the Burtons, performed a kindness on her grandfather. John Burton was a well-known draper in Belper who lost both his shop and home in a disastrous fire. Shortly after, he was taken on at the cinema, and assigned various duties, including that of bill poster. However, the Mortons didn't provide a bicycle for John to carry out his task. He had to walk everywhere with his posters and paste. It would have been weary work having to wield a weighty bucket, although the early autumn trek to Ambergate was alleviated by a spot of blackberrying in the village wood.

In later years, John Burton's daughter also became a friend of the Mortons, and because she used to go every night to feed the Palace cat, her own daughter Marie became a frequent visitor to the cinema, which she describes in glowing words: "It was a very beautiful cinema, more like a theatre than a cinema, as it had a lovely balcony sweeping all the way around, and deep red curtains decorated with gold." The theatre feel was enhanced by its large stage, which was trod occasionally by variety acts, and even circus performers.

However, as the years wore on, the Palace sadly went to seed, and even became referred to as a 'dingy flea pit', in some contrast to the Ritz at the top of King Street. Peter Davies remembers that when the tiles fell off the Palace frontage, they stayed off, even though they revealed a deeply unattractive dark cement. Christine Walker recalls that the Palace also became known as a cinema that attracted 'a hooligan element in large proportions, with the usherettes constantly shining their torches at people who spent most of the time scrambling under the seats'. Also, sitting in the side rows was, according to Christine 'a nightmare'. Because the seats were in a state of metal fatigue, the interlocking arrangement of the tiers meant that when someone pressed back on a loose seat, the entire row leaned over.

"If you wanted to watch a film in peace and quiet" says Christine, "then the Ritz was the place, as everyone there was better behaved." The Belper Ritz, originally the Town Hall and Law Courts, was eventually converted into a fully-fledged cinema and claimed not only better comfort and sound quality than the Palace, but also better films. Peter Davies believes that the Ritz was the first cinema in the country to use back projection. Young Peter was enraptured in a particular way by his early visits: "I remember the curtains continually changed colour, which so impressed me that I went home to try and build a model cinema, using coloured bulbs to reproduce the effect I'd seen at the Ritz."

Whatever the comparative qualities of the two cinemas, both were well patronised. Because they were only 300 yards apart and on the same side of the street, it was a common sight for the ends of the cinemas' respective queues to amusingly, sometimes confusingly, merge. Both the popularity and the proximity of the Ritz and Palace were noticed by the local bus company. Kathleen Wragg recalls a bus affectionately known as 'Shottle Emma', "a rickety old bus that used to go from Belper to Hazelwood (taking in Shottle, hence its name). It always used to be there to pick up the two cinema audiences. It never ran to a timetable!" In other words, the bus emerged at the top of King Street, waited for the Ritz patrons

to come out of the last screening, then drove down the hill to the Palace, where the passengers sometimes had to wait several minutes before the Palace patrons came out.

Further up the A6, Matlock Bath housed a cinema at the Grand Pavilion, which ran cine-variety from 1910 to the end of the 1930s. Apparently, at some point, a film about Henry VIII was specially shown at the cinema, as it was shot in Matlock Bath and used local people as extras. In Matlock itself, there were two main cinemas, the Palace and the Cinema House (later the Ritz) or, as they were commonly referred to, the 'Old Picture House' and the 'New Picture House' respectively. Although the 'old' cinema – the Palace on Dale Road – became known as the flea pit or, more poetically, the 'Laugh and Scratch', it sounded a good deal more salubrious when it opened in 1913. Indeed, the *High Peak News* described the Matlock Picture Palace as 'handsome' and 'appropriately named, for its fittings and appointments are as luxurious and up-to-date as any to be found in the country'. However, this does read suspiciously like a phrase provided for the newspaper in the form of the proprietor's publicity notes; unless, of course, the *High Peak News* reporter was an acknowledged expert on cinema buildings nationwide. In later years, cinema-goers like David Walters came to regard the place as 'dingy and claustrophobic, though it was never dirty'. Well, he never picked up a flea.

The Cinema House on Causeway Lane would have seemed a grand place when it opened at the end of 1922, particularly with its much-vaunted 'first class orchestra' and adjoining 'Café and Lounge', with 'Excellent Food and Service'. Also, with its 22-feet deep stage and five dressing rooms, it was a highly accommodating venue for variety acts. Architec-

The Ritz on Causeway Lane, Matlock. It was opened as the Cinema House in 1922. Terry Hawksworth.

The former Ritz at Belper. It was originally the Town Hall and Law Court. Terry Hawksworth.

turally, it was an interesting building (some might say 'odd'), and an unorthodox design for a small town cinema: a brick-built edifice that, for the most part, resembled a well-to-do family house but where the builder had both spare bricks and a brainstorm, and proceeded to tack on a castle tower. It still stands today, sadly crying for a facelifting scrub with industrial soap. Many new passers-by might be surprised to know a cinema lurks inside, not only from its untypical exterior, but also for the fact that a small town continues to support a cinema. In spite of its occasional closures over recent years, the Ritz is still running.

Dinah Gregory was a regular visitor to both Matlock cinemas, but occasionally she and her parents ventured further afield (and maybe 'afield' is an apposite word for the memory that follows): "When my Mum and Dad were feeling really adventurous, we would take a bus to the Wirksworth Cinema. This was not what I considered to be a good decision. The place was small and seemed to smell of agriculture. Also we always seemed to bring livestock home with us – a flea."

Small and smelly? Maybe rural market towns like Wirksworth carried unavoidable farm odours which could have reached extra-sensitive noses, but although the Wirksworth Cinema fell short of the capacity of both Matlock cinemas, it could hardly be considered small. In fact there was seating for nearly 500. Wirksworth Cinema was built in 1936 by Billy Alton on the site of an old Victorian house, whose

stone was used in the construction of the building's rear. At the front, the cinema looked a neat, appealing place, with its glass doors leading to a fully-carpeted foyer and auditorium. Billy also included a dance hall, café (the Cavendish) with seating for 120, plus a greengrocer's and a sweet shop, run by Billy's wife, who also used to make her own ice-cream for the cinema. This was yet another small-town cinema that was popularly patronised, continuing in business until 1967, even with competition from the cinema that operated in the Town Hall.

Take the A5035 from Wirksworth and you will eventually enter the 'Gateway of the Peak' – Ashbourne, a charming and handsome town which housed two popular cinemas, the Empire and Elite. However, a closer look at its history reveals a sad story of a respected, hard-working picture house proprietor who left the town a hurt and penniless man, and the equally respected female proprietor whose action led to his ruin.

Edgar Stebbings was a Manchester theatre entrepreneur who moved into Ashbourne in 1912 to flex his showbusiness skills in the new cinema medium. He opened the town's first cinema, the Empire, along with his young wife, Florence, a showgirl who had caught Edgar's eye at one of the theatres under his wing. Rumours suggest Florence married Edgar for his money. What is more substantiated is that a stage career denied her proper schooling, leaving her with literacy problems. Some speak of a complete inability to either read or write.

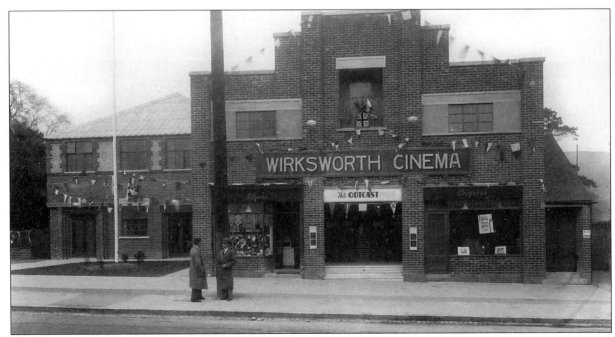

The Wirksworth Cinema in the early 1950s. W.W.Winter.

**Site of the Empire at Ashbourne.
Bob Pickering.**

These problems were to increase when Edgar Stebbings died a few short years after the Empire's opening. There was no question of Florence Stebbings trying to run the business herself, so she advertised a senior position.

One of the applicants was Frank Bromwich, a young, go-ahead man fuelled with showbusiness ambition. Mrs Stebbings was duly impressed. Because of her attendant problems, she employed Frank to run the administrative side of the Empire, booking the films and keeping the paperwork in order. According to Frank Bromwich's daughter, Marigold, her father's influence, diligence and devotion have largely gone uncredited. For instance, when the old post office and a couple of adjacent shops were put up for sale in the town's Market Place, it was Frank Bromwich who advised Mrs Stebbings to acquire the property and open a second cinema in Ashbourne. Marigold asserts that her father became 'the brains behind both businesses'. His talent extended to designing the future Elite; his application extended to overseeing the construction, including notably the wiring, a subject in which he hadn't previously been well-versed, until he assiduously immersed himself in text books on the subject.

Frank Bromwich was also known to operate the projection equipment – sometimes attending to three shows a day – and look after publicity, both designing posters and handbills, and distributing them throughout the area. There is no question that Frank was a tireless servant to the cinema. According to long-time Ashbourne projectionist Duncan Cross, Mrs Stebbings treated him like a servant; "but then she treated everybody like a servant."

Florence Stebbings made an indelible impression on both her staff and customers. Although petite, plump and frizzy-haired, cinema regular Cynthia Shemilt also remembers her as a striking, fashionable, scrupulously-dressed lady, dripping in jewellery. According to another regular Beatrice Jones, she looked as much a film star as anyone on the Empire screen. Duncan Cross recalls her "magnetic personality, which demanded attention." She also

demanded 'the utmost loyalty from her staff', and strict working practices were laid down. Duncan remembers undergoing a stiff job interview and, only a few weeks into the job, being startled by Mrs Stebbing's knowledge of his incipient relationship with a cinema usherette. She proceeded to tell Duncan, in no uncertain terms, that if their friendship was made evident in the cinema, they would both be dismissed. Duncan wasn't even allowed to walk the girl home. Mrs Stebbings laid down another curious condition: while on cinema premises, no one was allowed to whistle. She was also a stickler for cleanliness, and according to Duncan, "expected even the projection rooms to be as spick and span as everywhere else."

Considering her fastidious and keen eye, it was a wonder Ellis Watson got away with his lapse of duty as cashier. His girlfriend (and future wife) Evelyn occasionally came and sat in the box office with him and, if a few of his pals turned up, he would nip off to the Station Hotel opposite for a pint, leaving Evelyn to sell the tickets. This would doubtless have enraged his employer, but it never troubled his girlfriend. Indeed, Evelyn looked forward to her unofficial cashier duties as soon as she discovered that a penny coin covered a hole that had been drilled into the wood panelling at the back. Thus, when tickets weren't required, Evelyn peeped through the 'penny hole' and enjoyed a free film show.

Evelyn also recalls the Saturday matinées when mothers would come into town and deposit their offspring at the Empire while they went shopping. "There were some rowdy afternoons, and occasionally a fight." But not when Mrs Stebbings was

around. Her mere presence struck fear and quiet in the Ashbourne youngsters. However, Florence Stebbings was no harridan. Many town cinema-goers remember her generosity towards the children, in particular. Easter Saturday matinées

Frank Bromwich, a tireless servant to the cinema in Ashbourne, pictured in later years.

The former Picture Palace, South Normanton. **Geoff Hood.**

were marked by a mass hand-out of real eggs, courtesy of her own poultry run. Christmas matinées were free (at both her Uttoxeter cinemas as well as Ashbourne), with each child receiving a free apple and orange.

Mrs Stebbings extended her generosity of spirit to the staff, too. All usherettes were provided with not only uniforms, but also stockings and shoes. Duncan Cross remembers one incidence of her beneficence: "My 'second' at the Queen's (Uttoxeter), Tom Foster, and myself decided, 'off our own bat', that the ladies and gents' toilets needed a coat of paint. So, finding some paint, we did the job. We said nothing about this, treating it as part of our duties. However, Mrs Bayes the manageress found out and told Mrs Stebbings. When we went to collect our wages from the Elite, Mrs Stebbings had instructed Mrs Bayes to pay us an extra week's wages – something we never expected."

Her working relationship with Frank Bromwich was nothing less than harmonious. She came to rely on him implicitly. His role as factotum was extended to chauffeuring his employer everywhere, mainly between Ashbourne and Uttoxeter. They even came to share a love of antiques, and were often known to drive off to auctions in the area. Frank also helped Mrs Stebbings with her various domestic duties. By the time this was happening, he was constantly close at hand, having moved into her large household.

But this convenient, cordial arrangement did not

last. Two events were to plunge a respectable and respectful friendship into acrimony and disarray. Only recently did it come to light, through Frank Bromwich's daughter Marigold Heath writing to the local *News Telegraph*, having decided 'it is time Ashbourne realised the truth'. Mrs Stebbings was revealed to be, in Marigold's words, 'a woman who had lied and cheated her way in her business'. In the letter, she stated that: 'Unknown to my father, Mrs Stebbings was defrauding the renters (the companies who rented out the films). The Inland Revenue and the renters caught up with her, and she was out immediately. If it had not been for her age, she would have been imprisoned for fraud'.

Duncan Cross, who enjoyed a long, close association with Frank Bromwich, is adamant that "he would not have knowingly been involved in any dishonest operation", even though he did most of her clerical work. The likely source of Mrs Stebbings' fraud was the cash box. Duncan Cross says that as a frequent cashier at the cinemas, it would have been easy for her to indulge in the known practice of selling tickets twice; in other words, tearing a ticket in half in the cash box, handing the first half to the customer, and selling the other half to the next customer. Duncan believes such fraud would have been 'utterly foolish and very dangerous'. But just the kind of practice that would have alerted both the renters and the Inland Revenue, who would assign officers to make unscheduled calls on the cinemas.

Whatever the background details of her fraud, she had been found out and could not continue in the business. Mrs Stebbings offered both the Ashbourne cinemas to Frank Bromwich, who was unaware at the time of any malpractice. Had he known, he would certainly not have accepted a verbal agreement on the take-over. "Nothing was in writing" says his daughter; "he trusted her." Frank Bromwich had sensed none of her deceit. Nor her darkness...

"There was a dark side to Mrs Stebbings" says Duncan Cross, "a jealousy of her 'ownership' of her employees." One can also, perhaps, point to Congreve's famous phrase 'Hell hath no fury like a woman scorned'. Frank Bromwich incited her fury by getting married. It was not thought that Florence Stebbings' close relationship with her live-in tenant ever engendered any thoughts of matrimony, but it was clear she was torn by the break-up of a cosy, expedient arrangement. She could no longer possess him so strongly. He was to pay for it, literally, in later years.

"With no written agreement, the needle was in", says Arthur Knight, another Ashbourne cinema projectionist; "she kept wanting more than was originally stated. It was pure spite on her part." The verbal arrangement between Frank Bromwich and Florence Stebbings was based on a future paid settlement; once he had raised the necessary amount of money, she would pass complete ownership on to him. Although the Empire was to founder, and eventually to close, the Elite had long taken over as the town's main cinema. Frank threw his efforts into improving the Elite, at considerable expense. According to Marigold Heath, Mrs Stebbings – free of any written contract – had raised the agreement price several times over the years. Never recognised as a particularly good businessman, Frank Bromwich appeared to make no attempts at converting his long-standing verbal agreement – 'he was too kind-hearted for his own good', according to Duncan Cross. When Mrs Stebbings eventually demanded a final payment, Frank was floundering. He hadn't the money to pay her off and secure his long-held dream of ownership.

It would appear that Mrs Stebbings' resentment had rankled over the years, and that she was determined to ensure that Frank Bromwich would never take ownership of the cinema. This was indicated as much to Duncan Cross when, around 1960, he received a letter from Mrs Stebbings, "ordering me to see her with a view to me taking over the Elite from Mr Bromwich. This astounded me; she would never have put up with someone trying to do that to her. My reply was to flatly refuse to even consider such a proposal, pointing out her own views on loyalty. I had enjoyed a good relationship with Mr Bromwich. I couldn't betray him."

Duncan now wonders whether he should have told Frank Bromwich about the letter, because two years later, Mrs Stebbings sold out, over Mr Bromwich's head, to a local businessman, Jack Bagnall. He, in turn, struck a rental agreement with Frank Bromwich, allowing him to keep the business; Duncan took Frank aside and advised him to ensure he was never late with the rent.

There could have been more than a hint of coincidence to the timing of the take-over. It hit Frank Bromwich at a singularly difficult period: he had just invested in new seating at the Elite. He soon got in to arrears. "It was not long" says Duncan, "before Bagnall had the bailiffs in, and evicted Mr Bromwich – and the rest of us. Even though Frank had the money there for his rent arrears, Bagnall refused to accept it. And that was that."

Frank Bromwich's daughter Marigold is still bitter about the ignoble ending of her father's cinema career, a result of being "used and duped by a conniving woman." Duncan Cross feels "it was a shabby way to end a man's dreams and to bring to nothing the work he had done for the cinemas in Ashbourne." He remembers Frank suffering from ill-health in his closing years at the Elite, "in no small part due to the additional pressures put on him." One of those pressures came about when certain factions in the town ostracised him. When he decided to accept the Roman Catholic faith, he left the local freemasons' institute, of which he had been a prominent member, along with the Rotarians' group. His daughter remembers that "so-called 'friends' walked the other side of the street to avoid speaking with him." Duncan Cross is quick to point out that it was not the ordinary cinema patrons who shunned him, but "certain business people – many of whom had enjoyed years of free entertainment at the cinema, often twice a week, something they were quick to forget in his hour of need."

For Duncan, Frank Bromwich remains in his memory as "a man who had spent the bulk of his life giving his all to the success of cinema in Ashbourne." Marigold never forgets the time of the fire in the Elite engine room in 1956 when her father worked throughout the weekend to ensure the show could go ahead on the Monday. Along with his dedication to work was his devotion to charity: Frank raised considerable money for the war effort, putting on free shows for the forces based in the area during the war, as well as the children of the nearby St Monica's Home.

It is little wonder that Frank Bromwich's daughter feels resentful, and one is left in no doubt as to where the blame lies for her father's downfall: "Due to a grasping, evil old woman, he lost all he had ever worked for, including his home. He left Ashbourne a penniless bankrupt with nowhere to go." Frank eventually retired to Torquay, where he died in 1983, aged 88.

The behind-the-screen saga of Mr Bromwich and Mrs Stebbings ought not to obscure the fact that in-front-of-screen, the Ashbourne Elite and Empire enjoyed many busy, fun-filled and exhilarating years. Duncan Cross recalls the days when townsfolk came to the cinema twice a week, even if there was a six-day run which meant they saw the same programme twice. Queues were commonplace, especially for musicals, with *Gone With The Wind* packing audiences in not only when it first came to the town, but every two years thereafter when it returned.

To commemorate the man who helped bring so many cherished memories of cinema-going in Ashbourne, Marigold Heath erected a photograph and a plaque in honour of her father, Frank Bromwich, within the Elite cinema building. The rueful coda to this story, however, is that the Elite is no longer a cinema. Indeed, from the early 1950s, long years of decline were to decimate Derbyshire's picture house map. The Golden Age had gone. The dream was over.

Don't Panic Chaps!

Tales from the projection room

I always used to boast that Gary Cooper and I were in the same business – he makes films, I show 'em.

Eddie Burnham, Somercotes Premier projectionist 1943-47

MY close encounters with the Derbyshire people who kept the cinemas going have revealed them to be ordinary, decent, hard-working and personable public servants. They include all strata of personnel – managers, usherettes, commissionaires, cashiers – and projectionists? Well, they uphold all the aforementioned qualities. But they remain a breed apart. It is no coincidence that in the course of my appeals for local cinema memories, I have interviewed more projectionists than any other members of picture house staff. I soon realised why these chaps came to pour their words into my microphone: basically, they loved what they did. Most worked with a fervent dedication to duty, and remain fiercely proud of it; sometimes to the point of self-importance. Worse still, their egos will remain undeflated by the knowledge that they have a chapter all to themselves! But they deserve it: they have many stories to tell.

Projectionists were not made. They were born with a mixture of two essential elements coursing through their veins. First, a natural inclination towards matters mechanical. Projectionists have sat and showered me with technical data about the workings of the machinery as if it were as easy to assimilate as ABC. With this technical aptitude, they could have turned into industrial engineering operatives or textile machinists. However, this leads us to the second element, a fascination with cinema. Show me a projectionist who didn't love the Pictures, and I will show you someone to whom a cinema manager will have said: 'Let me show you the door'.

Granted, some projectionists will have grown to love the cinema. Duncan Cross might not have been so enamoured of film when he was first taken to the cinema aged seven, but he became the sort of fan who boasts of seeing *Top Hat* 42 times, when he was sat not in the box as an operator, but as an ordinary cinema-goer in the auditorium. Master Duncan's first experiences of the Pictures would have given away a tell-tale sign of a typical born projectionist: When I

was seven, my aunt used to take me. I remember I was always more fascinated by the flickering light that came from the back of the hall than the image on the screen. I also remember my aunt giving me a few digs in the ribs – she had very sharp elbows, too; she thought I should have been watching what was going on in front of the me. As I got older, I grew more determined to get behind there and find out what it was all about."

As a youngster, David Walters found out what it was all about when he was shown inside the projection box at the Matlock Palace. He romantically recalls it being like a horror film set: "I was shown the old carbon arc projectors, and was amazed at the mercury rectifier – a great big glass bowl with mercury, which somehow converted A/C to D/C to give you an arc. What I remember most was seeing the electricity dancing about on the top of this bowl, like something from a *Frankenstein* movie." Colin Clarke also excitingly recalls this memorable sight: "The dancing mercury would crackle and cast a vivid blue luminescence like that of a violent electrical storm."

Kenneth Roy Taylor also remembers the stark, sensational sight of the carbon arcs that crucially provided the projector light beam (nowadays quartz lamps are used). Kenneth's father, Thomas Henry Taylor, worked for 50 years as a projectionist at the Swadlincote Rink, Empire and Majestic, and was well known for his tireless devotion and splendid waxed moustache. Thomas eventually allowed his schoolboy son to enter the operating box, but he would have been sure to alert him to the dangers that lurked within, like gazing at the projector light with its quarter of a million candle power, potentially damaging to the naked eye. This light was created by the carbons, long, innocuous-looking rods, oddly pointing at different angles, as young Kenneth discovered: "You had to wind knobs to move the carbons right up to each other, so they almost touched. Together, these carbons made the same

Deep Waters

Bernard Goodwin recalls a very efficient cashier at the Heanor Empire, although she was prone to getting her words mixed up in the style beloved of Hylda Baker, leading to much unintended amusement. For instance, instead of 'corrugated iron', she'd say 'congregated iron', or 'evacuated milk' instead of 'evaporated milk'. One particularly embarrassing slip occurred in front of one of the cinema's more well-to-do patrons, who asked Bernard to tell him more about a forthcoming film called *The Deep*. At this, the ever-talkative cashier jumped in, saying: "Oh, I don't like those kind of films. Can you imagine how horrible it must be all those hundreds of feet down in the dark water to then have an octopus shoot out and wrap its testicles round you?"

bright, bluish spark that you see on a welder's torch. You had to put fresh carbons in virtually every hour. You opened the lamp housing, taking care to remove the carbons with pliers. The walls of the projector room were green with the sulphur from the carbons. On top of the projectors there was a duct to take the fumes away, but my Dad still developed a bad chest."

Colin Clarke remembers that hazard: "When the wind blew from a certain direction, the fumes wafted straight back into the arc and filled the room. Other than the door – which we would hastily wedge open – there was no ventilation. The chief and I both enjoyed a cigarette, but vowed to give up after inhaling carbon fumes."

Colin also recalls their exposure to a hazard that has only recently come to light: "Fitted to the rear of each projector were small, brass Pyrene fire extinguishers. They eventually became used in cars, until someone pointed out their lethal potency. Nowadays, Pyrene or 'Thawpit' as we called it, is banned. Unaware of the danger, we used liberal amounts of Thawpit for everything from cleaning the projectors to scraping gungy chewing gum from carpets. Many was the time, in the confined, unventilated space of the projection box, our senses would be numbed. We'd be as high as kites. Now we know why."

Colin Clarke, like most projectionists, would have begun as a rewind boy. Most cinemas came to employ boys for this easy, albeit repetitive job, although the monotony would have been tempered by the youngster's knowledge that this was invariably the first rung on the ladder leading up to chief projectionist. Before the days of automated 'cake-stand' projection systems, two projectors were used, with a feature length film running to several reels. They required close, regular attention. So, while the operator looked after the running of the machines, ensuring in particular that the film ran continuously, his young assistant would be rewinding the reels.

As well as rewinding, young Kenneth Roy Taylor would also help his father with repair of the films. In these early, developmental years of projection machinery, there was little time to rest, or relax one's guard while inflammable 35mm film – also lacking the toughness of today's celluloid, and weakened further by use – was hurtling its constant and demanding way through the gates, pulleys and cogs of a tetchy, slave-driven metal workhorse. Equipment and film stock, like the cinema itself, were still in its infancy. And equipment and film stock did not often meet eye to eye. Indeed, the first three decades of film projection are replete with stories of breaks in the show leading to blanks on the screen. Occasionally, there would be a fire risk. As Colin Clarke recounts: "When a break did occur and we weren't quick enough to shut off the arc, a pinpoint hotspot appeared on the screen, spreading rapidly as film frazzled in the gate. Many was the time I got burnt fingers preventing the flame from reaching the spool."

A blank screen would usually signal a split sprocket hole. As Kenneth Roy Taylor remembers, his father had to stop the projector, and take the film off: "We then had to take it into the rewinding room, cut the offending frame with a razor blade, clean the ends of the broken film, scrape the emulsion off, overlap it and glue it together again, with acetate – a quick-drying cement – being careful not to get the acetate on your fingers, as it was poisonous. He then put the film back into the projector and re-threaded it back into the projector gate and the take-up spool." To pacify the audience, Thomas stuck a record on the gramophone. It is doubtful if the music was heard beyond the opening seconds. A simple repair took five minutes, by which time the screen had registered a considerable orange peel and apple core count. If the job took ten minutes, the baying mob had probably turned into a lynch mob. As children could end up reading this, it is best not to speculate on what was said or done if Thomas and his son had the occasional tricky film fix which took a full 15 minutes.

Through it all, though, Thomas was a highly respected and diligent worker, devoting a 50-year career to film projection. Son Kenneth recalls that many a time, his dad would work till midnight and close everything down. Occasionally, the staff were long gone, but a few members of the audience were not. Many a time he would switch off the lights, walk through the auditorium, and stumble upon the odd slumbering youngster, who would usually take fright at being awoken by a hand in the dark. Who needed Bela Lugosi when they had Thomas Henry Taylor?

Thomas would also have witnessed a regularly frightening incident, caused by his roguish assistant Jim Smith. When they got a sizeable crowd in at the Rink, the patrons would be forced to stand at the back, unsuspectingly blocking the projector hole. In a move timed to perfection, Jim would suddenly slide open the projection hole shutter and, at the same time, yell at the top of his voice: "move to one side please, the show's about to start!" As Jim would relishingly recall: "they'd all jump out of their skins. And they never stood there again."

There was also a father/son team at the Derby Picture House (later the Ritz). In the early to mid-1950s, Brian Wilson used to assist his father Harold, the last chief projectionist at the cinema. Rewinding was the most obvious of the onerous tasks to pass on to the lad, but Brian didn't mind: he lived for Sunday mornings: "Occasionally he would ask me to go to the railway station and fetch the films when they came up from London on the overnight Saturday train." Where could possibly be the thrill in that? Well, if you lived through the early 1950s, ask yourself this: how many times did you get to ride in a taxi? "Not many people had cars then" recalls Brian, "so to travel in a taxi was a luxury."

In the earlier days of the Derby Picture House, Ron Wyke – as a 14-year-old in 1935 – used to change reels in the projection room. But he also acted as ticket collector, usher, car park attendant, food delivery boy for the cinema café, and chief stoker of the foyer fireplace. His official title was 'Page Boy'. "A 'Jack Of All Trades' would have been a better title" reckons Ron, who stayed less than two years at the cinema and drifted into the greater security of Rolls-Royce. Ron seems rueful about the years he missed: "The 20 months I spent at the Picture House have given me more memories than all my 48 years of Rolls-Royce."

Roy Bull was a year younger than Ron when he came to assist at the Spondon Sitwell. The projectionist taught him everything. A good job he did, too, because as Roy recalls: " 'Mr B' liked a drink on a Saturday, and by the time the second house was

in, he was incapable of anything." So, 13-year-old Roy ran the show. That wasn't the end of his duties, though – Mr 'Blind Drunk' had to be helped from the projection box down the vertical ladder. Roy himself was intoxicated, with wealth: "I worked six nights and a Saturday matinée, and I was paid seven shillings. I was the richest kid in school."

George Gray was only 14 when, in 1942, he became trainee projectionist at the Derby Hippodrome. It is clear the cinema should have operated a height check for all potential operators: "I was very small for my age" says George, "so I had to stand on an orange box to be able to see through the little square window." George never made the grade. It was probably just as well: he would have fallen short anyway, quite literally – the Hippodrome's massive Kalee projectors were housed in the 'Gods', and raked so steeply that the top spool box was seven feet from the floor. Film projection was a tall order, and fortunately 'long-standing' operator Tom Taylor was a suitable Harlem Globetrotting height.

Even if young George Gray was taller, he had an experience that probably told him he wasn't somehow cut out for this lark. It involved the simple transport of six big reels of film from the Derby Hippodrome to her sister cinema, the Odeon. This was a short walk from the store room on Green Lane to St Peter's Street. One day, as George gingerly emerged from the store room with six stacked reels, a slight wobble caused the top two to drop down to the ground. Off they rolled down the road. One ended up at the side of the church at the corner of St Peter's Churchyard. Fortunately, that canister had stayed shut. But George was not so lucky with the other one. Not only had the film begun a descent down Green Lane, but it had also opened at the point of impact with the pavement. Like a scene from a Mack Sennett silent, George went chasing the reel as it swiftly unravelled itself down the Green Lane incline. The frantic pursuer eventually caught up with the can, and gathered up the yards of celluloid, returning to the store room to rewind the issued film before anyone saw it. Crisis over. Which words might have spilled from young George Gray's mouth at the start of this mishap? 'Blood and Sand'? They would have been fitting – that was the title of the film.

Unlike George, young Alec Turner did make the grade, graduating to chief projectionist at the Hippodrome. Imagine a cinema-crazed 14-year-old who found that his first job – at a furniture factory – offered scarce time and scant money for picture-going. Worse still, he found himself out of work (through shortage of orders), with no job in sight. After four weeks on the dole, a desperate Alec made his plea at the Employment Bureau: "Haven't you got

Blood of a Poet

John Hyde of Chellaston (whose ode to Derby's disappeared cinemas appears elsewhere in this book) remembers a memorable evening at the Gaumont Cinema in 1970 when he went to see *Bonnie and Clyde*: "I went straight from work on this particular Friday evening and had had nothing to eat – a factor which may partly explain what consequently happened. Towards the end of the film, there is an horrific shoot-out and, although a blood donor for many years, I cannot stand the sight of blood (not in copious amounts, anyway). I studiously avoid such TV programmes as *Your Life In Their Hands*. As the volley of shots rang out, spraying the car containing the two criminals, I suddenly realised that I must have fainted momentarily. Never having fainted before, I did not really understand what had happened. I knew I had to get away from the horrors being depicted on screen and went, somewhat dazedly, towards the Gents which were at the bottom of a fairly long flight of stairs. I remember walking towards the urinals... the next thing I knew was a voice saying: 'are you all right, mate?' I looked down and saw spots of blood dripping on to the tiled floor, soon realising it was MY blood (as Woody Allen was later to say in the film *Bananas* when he realises he has been wounded and gazes down on the blood he has leaked: 'hang on a minute – shouldn't that be on the inside?'). The man belonging to that voice escorted me to the office of the manageress. She telephoned the DRI which is, of course, only a few hundred yards away, along London Road. The ambulance arrived shortly after and I was admitted to hospital. It would appear that, as I fainted for the second time, I fell backwards on to an old-fashioned, cast-iron radiator; something sharp caught me just above the right ear and, as I slid down, caused a crescent-shaped wound up into the scalp. When the nurse finally got round to me, it took something like 23 stitches to suture the cut. I was X-rayed and told I must stay in overnight. I was woken at regular intervals throughout the night to ensure I was still 'compos mentis'. Whilst lying on the trolley earlier that evening, I made up a limerick (I write poetry as a hobby). Each time I was awoken, I recited the limerick, proving that my memory was okay. It amused the nurse no end. Now, after 25 years or more, I still remember it:

> There was a young fellow named Hyde
>
> Who went to see 'Bonnie and Clyde'
>
> He went to the loo
>
> And when he came to
>
> "My God! I have fainted", he cried.

All the above is perfectly true, and I still have the scar to prove it. Recently I made my 73rd donation of blood – but I still can't watch operations on TV."

anything?" The official didn't think so: "Rewind boy at the Gaumont – you won't want that."

Eddie Burnham yearned for a cinema job, and thanks to the war and a word of recommendation from his cousin Ernie who vacated the trainee post at the Somercotes Premier, Eddie was taken on as rewind boy while still at school. He revelled in his status: "I used to like standing on the cinema steps and preening myself like the cinema manager. All my school mates would turn up, say 'hello, Eddie', and tell their girlfriends how well they knew me, as if I was someone really important." He did become

important, rising to chief projectionist at 16, "which was actually against the law" admits Eddie, "but there was a war on."

The war also gave women the opportunity to gain entry to this previously preserved male domain. The Swadlincote Majestic projectionist Walter Smith taught his own wife how to operate the box, and she happily projected pictures throughout the war. Alec Turner remembers the Derby Odeon recruiting an evacuee from Hastings, Dawn Grant. The only problem Dawn encountered as a woman was not operating the box, but getting into it. It wasn't the steepness of the ladder leading to it, either, or the fact that her climb might have revealed more than a slip and suspender. But it was still a source of embarrassment: entry to the projection booth was via a door near the Circle entrance, marked 'Gents'. Alec remembers the confused reaction from onlookers as an obvious female figure strode 'manfully' through the door. Alec was too polite to ask Dawn about the reaction she got from the gents the other side of the door.

Having gone through another door, Dawn would also have to negotiate a steep flight of concrete stairs. But there was an even worse prospect to face once inside the projection room. A door led outside to some small flat roofs, with nothing to prevent anyone falling off the edge, and it was a walk someone had to make several times a day: a small cubicle on the roof housed the turntable which provided incidental music between films. As Alec Turner recalls: "Come hail, rain or snow, someone had to go out there to set the records when needed."

Pity also the poor rewind boy at the Ashbourne Empire. Because of fire and safety regulations, there was not enough room in the projection box to permit a rewinder on the bench. There was also no room for it anywhere next door. So, the rewind room was situated below, which meant the projectionist's assistant had to trudge up and down a steep staircase at least six times an hour throughout the evening's programme.

John Moore reckons the Melbourne Empire must have broken all fire and safety regulations by providing only a vertical ladder up the back of the cinema to the projection box. "The projectionist had to clamber up there, put a rope down, come down again, fasten the reels of film to the rope, and haul them up."

Also, as the projectionist's box was only a matter of inches above a balcony back seat, John recalls how it was a common occurrence for someone either to put their hand up to blot the picture out or, if they had a more artistic upbringing, to give an impromptu performance of shadow puppets, so that the occasional giant duck would appear to join in the action on screen.

John Scott recalls a similarly ill-situated projection box when he worked as an assistant at the Riddings Regent. Basically, it was stuck outside. "If a fire had broken out, and the door was blocked, we'd have had to climb over a railing on the balcony and go down a steel ladder. But the ladder didn't go all the way – there was a six foot drop down to the floor." Luckily there was never a fire.

Even in the best cinemas, some projection boxes were inconveniently placed. Michael Wood spent a

disillusioning six months as a projectionist at the Chesterfield Odeon: "The projection room was underneath the balcony, which meant there were no windows. Sometimes I was in there from nine o'clock in the morning till half past ten at night."

Even with access to daylight and no vertical ladder to climb, projectionists were still cooped up in difficult and onerous conditions. John Taylor recalls that his father Tom, chief projectionist at the Derby Hippodrome in the 1930s, occupied a room where 'two big projectors each consumed the energy of ten electric fires, which together with the other electrical equipment, the 150 amp arc lights of the projectors, the heat from the auditorium, and the radiant heat from the sun (the projection room was right on top of the theatre) must have been exhausting for the

Derby's Cinemas – A Bygone Age

by JOHN HYDE

The old Odeon, transformed to a BHS,
The Black Prince is Duckworth Square, no less!
(Which formerly bore the Empire name
Before 'Widescreen' and 'Cinemascope' came).
While the Picture House in Babington Lane
Was a supermarket, Wilko's and 'suites' again.
The Regal's façade can still be seen,
An ABC cinema with superb screen,
With just bingo and dance, the Gaumont's intact
Which, once, Derby's avid film fans packed.
Allenton's Broadway is a food store now
And the Hippodrome, yet more bingo – wow!
The Coliseum has become a pub
Serving not good films but beer and grub.
Stylish Cavendish, another supermarket site
Where queues stretched well into the night.
The Popular closed its doors at last,
The march of 'Progress' moved too fast,
Sitwell, Forum, Cosmo as well
Were there for their regular clientele.
Gloria, Majestic, with names so proud
For years served Chaddesden's movie crowd.
A far cry, too, from Alvaston's Rex
Is the modern, hi-tech multiplex,
Derby's picture palace, once all the rage
 Have long faded into that golden age.

operators'. Tom would also have had to absorb the heat and perspiration of up to four other work colleagues.

Then there were the oppressive pressures. In this stifling atmosphere, responsibility for the required precision of projector and carbon arc changes, and sound and vision synchronisation must have weighed heavily on any projectionist, knowing the wrath of a packed auditorium would seep into the box should any mishap occur. John Taylor recalls the diary his father filled in the time when, as a 20-year-old, he took over from the chief projectionist, who was on holiday. "The only entry in his diary one day were the stark words: 'Lost the changeover.' These were the only words he could enter. It must have been devastating for the poor lad, with 1,500 or so patrons booing and jeering his efforts to sort the problem out."

Tom Taylor would have counted his blessings had he seen the operation at the Wirksworth Town Hall, only a few years before he joined the Hippodrome. Edward Saint recalls how his father Arthur looked after the running of the town hall cinema shows: "He operated a hand-powered projector housed in a metal box which had to be assembled before the show and then dismantled afterwards. The projection light was supplied by limelight using town gas and oxygen. As

the lime – which was in the shape of a cotton bobbin – burnt away, it was turned on a spindle to a fresh spot. As the machine was hand-powered, you can imagine what happened as the operator got tired; the picture would be in slow motion, until a change of hands restored it to normal speed." As each reel came to an end, a caption appeared on the screen: 'End of Part One. Part Two Will Follow Immediately'. The word 'immediately' was maybe a touch optimistic, because with only one projector, the operator had to remove the reel from the machine and, as Edward recalls: "he struggled to fit a new reel in what was now a very hot machine."

This operation is in marked contrast to the 'super-cinema' operation that accompanied the coming of sound. In terms of projection facilities, the author of the Derby Gaumont Souvenir Opening programme in 1934 commented that 'no part of a Cinematograph Theatre has been improved more in recent years.' The writer even gave the projection box a fanciful name that no self-respecting projectionist would dare embrace – 'Operating Chamber'. It was described as a 'bright and perfectly ventilated room' and a 'revelation' compared with the 'tiny ill-ventilated and dangerous boxes in which operators worked in the early days.'

The Sweet Smell of Success

Recollections of a cinema occasionally usher in the memory of a certain smell or aura to the place. Two picture houses in the same street could have a different odour to them. Bill Doyle, a frequenter of many Derby cinemas, says: "A walk into one of the less fancy Derby cinemas would bring a musty, dry sensation to the nose, whereas in the grander palaces, you smelt something cleaner and sharper." For Len Waller, a walk into the Somercotes Empire produced "an exciting smell of dust, plush, old carpet and stale scent; it was unique."

Patrons who wandered into the Derby Picture House on Babington Lane would pick up the delightful aroma of tea and toasted tea-cakes drifting down from the cafe balcony, but once inside the auditorium, the air would be sweeter (and, maybe for some, sicklier). As Mrs E. Mellors remembers: "During the intervals, one of the usherettes would come up the aisles with a gorgeous perfumed spray, and I have wondered since if it was a forerunner of today's air fresheners. I can still smell it." Mr A.E.Thompson has a similar memory of the spray cans coming out at the Saturday matinées in the Allenton Broadway: "We kids used to get squirted all over with the stuff We couldn't understand why at the time, though I suppose the combined pong of so many children must have been a bit overwhelming."

It appears, though, that the cinema sprays were usually employed to ward off fleas and flies. When Pauline Cooper asked what the Derby Empire commissionaire was spraying in the air, he replied: "Bug Pink." Adds Pauline: "It was a substance called Flit, containing an ingredient called DDT and it was dispensed from a drum-shaped container with a pump-action handle. Mind you, the Empire was still referred to as a flea pit."

The Young Ones

My cinema addiction, which my Uncle Derek created when I was only four, was re-fed and finally confirmed a few years later when I moved up to the East Midlands. At the age of 11, I became an ABC Minor, largely thanks to Lorraine Atkin. Puberty is a mysterious condition: one morning I turned up at school and decided I fancied Lorraine. Michael Horsborough had a similar spasm of adolescence and professed a yearning for Lorraine's best friend, Marion Bell. Michael was my best friend, so that made life perfect. We then knew we had to contrive a way of making our new-found affection felt. That same day I remember being in the blissfully happy position of standing behind Lorraine in the dinner queue, so I kissed her hair. Don't ask me why; it was a totally stupid and embarrassing thing to do, but, as I say, puberty is a mysterious condition. However, it was then I had one of those thrilling revelations about the opposite sex. "She smells gorgeous", I thought. Years later, John Gordon Sinclair repeated that line in *Gregory's Girl* after falling for Dee Hepburn; I always think of Lorraine when I watch that film (you see, there's a movie for every moment). Having performed this daring deed, I was, oddly, too much of a coward to ask her out, so Michael Horsborough did that bit, but he needed to ask Marion Bell out anyway, so didn't feel bad about it. I can't remember who suggested going to the ABC Minors, but as I turned out to be a film writer, we'll say it was me.

Saturday morning couldn't come quickly enough. My first recollection would be of the massive queue. The look of some of the kids in that queue either then turned me into a snob or confirmed the fact that I already was one, because after spending the first few visits in the stalls, we decided to spend the extra pennies on a balcony ticket. I distinctly remember coining the phrase: "sixpence downstairs if you were poor, ninepence upstairs if you were rich." Frankly, some of the kids in the sixpenny seats looked, well, a bit rough. They didn't actually frighten me, but the female attendants specially drafted in to curb their rowdyism certainly did. These women who patrolled the aisles were harridans. All of them wore tight hair curlers and flowery aprons, and each of them was a fearsome, evil variation on Andy Capp's missus. I can't help wondering if they also wielded rolling pins, but it would have completed the image if they had. As it was, these appalling women with death-ray glares and vicious intent never seemed to venture upstairs (simply because they were better behaved in the balcony, I suppose) so we soon moved in with the nice ninepenny crowd.

Although I can remember a stacked confectionery tray, my recollection of its entire contents are overwhelmed by the single memory of the tuppenny Everlasting Strip, a long, thin, gooey stick of succulent toffee. It took ages to eat, and even longer if we first staged a little contest between us, namely 'who could stretch their Everlasting Strip further'?

Before the film programme got under way, we had a few turns. It always seemed to be the same lad who would get up on stage and mime to a pop song. He had a guitar, and a spotlight, on him, and I was dead jealous; I was a nobody in the ninepennies and he was somebody on stage, earning wild applause for doing very little other than move around a bit and open his mouth. I don't think he knew the words to half the songs either. I vowed to go down there one day and strut my stuff, but I always chickened out.

There was one more entertainment before the film show commenced: the ritual singing of the ABC Minors song. I have lost the tune somewhere in a deep recess of the brain, although I remember it had the old-fashioned flavour of the Ovaltinies song. However, I need little help forming the words, as most of them are etched on my soul in neon colour, with a bouncing ball underneath the lines:

'We are the boys and girls well known as
Minors of the ABC!
And every Saturday we line up
To see the films we like and SHOUT with glee.
We like to laugh, and have a sing-song
Such a happy crowd are we-ee
We're all pals together
We're minors of the ABC!

That last line was always a noisy one. We then settled down for the show, which always began with a cartoon (Bugs Bunny, Tom and Jerry *et al*) or a Laurel and Hardy and ended with a feature film, invariably a Children's Film Foundation effort. All I can recall of the main feature was the odd Famous Five adventure (or a similar kind of picture where a group of spunky kids would play at detectives and end up nabbing a villain), and westerns. Really, not a lot was different from the silent matinées of the 1920s, with a vociferous audience cheering on the good guys and booing madly at the bad. I remember one dreary western which brought the manager out on to the stage. Basically, there was no one decent to cheer or boo in this picture. It was boring as hell, and so we kids had looked for other things to do. Even as posh kids in the balcony were throwing ice cream cartons around. So the manager stopped the film, and told us we'd all go home early unless we calmed down. The prospect of losing Lorraine's company earlier than usual was too dreadful to contemplate, so it certainly shut me up. We dutifully saw out the world's worst western.

We shared something else with those 1920s matinée kids: a serial. It was the Adam West/Burt Ward *Batman and Robin* serials that made the most indelible impression. I cringe when I watch them now, and recall ludicrous scenes where the Bat-phone would ring at the desk of the Gotham City Commissioner, leading to the blindingly obvious statement: 'that's probably Batman'; the endless fights where nobody died in spite of the violence of the exchanges, all of them accompanied by a bubble containing the word Biff! Bang! or Wallop!; or the time when the jobsworths of Gotham City Hall bowed their heads as our two heroes entered the building, as if they were Gods. But, then, they were! And yet look at the way they treated us. We were constantly thrown into mad anxiety with the cliffhanger finale when Batman or Robin – or, in an appalling week, both – were facing certain, painful death. So you just had to come back the following Saturday. Even when Lorraine Atkin became weary of ABC Minors and threatened to go off and do something else on a Saturday morning (like go and play with Ian Donnelly), I couldn't be anywhere else but the ABC. I would never have laid it on the line by saying directly to Lorraine: 'sorry, but Batman's in a mess, and I've got to find out how he gets out of this' (for a mature 11-year-old with a date, that kind of comment wasn't on), so I must have pretended to go off Lorraine to give me the excuse of a regular fix with the caped crusader and his awful predicament. To be honest, the outcome was usually a let-down, of the 'one-leap-and-he-was-free' variety, but through it all I contracted the cinema bug and have never forgotten Batman for that.

It has been three decades since those Saturday serials. That has made me think: we grown-ups who were weaned on cinema in those simple, unsophisticated times probably possess a wider-eyed sense of wonder about a feature film like *Batman Forever* than most 1990s youngsters. After all, we have witnessed over a long period of years the astonishing growth in movie technology. A kid who has been brought up with computer games will take more for granted than the likes of me, who used to think the glow of the Bat-phone was pretty neat.

Those Saturday mornings at the ABC Minors seem like a lifetime away rather than a generation gaps worth. I have no souvenirs to remind me of those days. No luminous ABC badge. No wrapping from an everlasting Strip. Not even a piece of Lorraine Atkin's hair. Lorraine was great to be with. I felt ten feet tall going into the pictures with a girl who liked being with me. Alright, I didn't pay for her to go in, but I'm sure she appreciated me. By the way, our three hours together in the dark were not a signal for a snog-fest. There were no double seats, we were only 11 and still a bit shy and innocent and, of course, there were films to watch.

After less than two, all-too-short years, I went off to one grammar school, and she to another. What say we give this parting more of a romantic, cinematic flavour? We said goodbye on that tarmac. I was cool about it, and she got on that plane. "Here's looking at you, kid." We never saw each other again. Well, we did actually: she became friends with my big sister. Lorraine Atkin now lives in another part of the country. I bet she still smells gorgeous.

not avert that sudden blank screen experience. Matlock Ritz projectionist David Walters remembers a screening of *The Virgin and The Gypsy* where halfway, the film broke. "Suddenly there was nothing on the screen. So I closed the curtains and brought the house lights up. By this time, the manager had come flying in with 'what the devil is going on?' I told him what had happened, and he said 'you don't close the curtains and put the house lights on, under any circumstances. You repair the damn thing as fast as you can, and continue with the film.' After about two minutes, I got the film going. The next day, I saw a colleague at work who had been to see the film that previous evening. 'Did you enjoy it?' I asked him. 'Yes, it was brilliant. Only one thing, though: I got up to get an ice-cream, and by the time I'd got back, I'd missed five minutes of the second half. That was the shortest intermission I've ever known in my life."

David also has recollections of films arriving in the wrong cans: "You could have a cowboy picture suddenly turn into a love story." A later Matlock Ritz projectionist, Robert Bowler, has a memorable experience of a cowboy picture he projected perfectly – right until the nerve-wracking, knuckle-chewing climax, when the film broke. It was a screening of *The Good, The Bad and The Ugly*: "We got to the last thirty seconds, where Eli Wallach is left dangling. It's an unbearably tense moment, where you're wondering what Clint Eastwood is going to do next. Just prior to that point, I'd finished wiping the machine down, and put the cloth in my back pocket. Suddenly I heard this grating noise, and smelt burning. The cloth had gone in the motor, and the film had stopped. I had to rip the film off and start the machine again. It took three or four minutes to warm up again, during which time 40 or 50 people were screaming and yelling at my door."

But even the most sophisticated facility could not account for human intervention. For example, a film poorly maintained at one cinema could spell disaster for the next cinema. As a young apprentice at the Matlock Palace, Michael Oxley reveals how careful one had to be with the film reels: "As a wind-on boy, I had to spool the film by hand on to an empty reel and run my fingers along the edges, to check for splits in the celluloid. If there was a piece sticking up, I had to stop the film, cut out the offending frame, and rejoin the film. Any 'lift' in the reel used to cause the film to break while being projected, and suddenly you'd have 60 yards of film round your feet in no time. Also, the film used to break quite often, mainly because it was old and because other cinemas hadn't spliced it properly."

David Walters, who worked at the other Matlock cinema – the Ritz – remembers being left in charge for the first time. He was only 17 at the time: "The first night went smoothly. On the second night, I had the trauma of the film breaking. I panicked, daring not to stop the reel until it ran out. In the end, I was literally knee-deep in 20 minutes of film."

To avoid drowning in celluloid, projectionists had to be patient, scrupulous – and sacrificial. Eddie Burnham remembers entering the Somercotes Premier at 9am to receive a copy of *A Place Of One's Own* starring Margaret Lockwood. By 4pm, he had skipped lunch and worked through his afternoon off, trying to put the film together as a result of broken sprocket-holes and badly-made joints. Eddie was only too aware that if such imperfections ran through the projector, they would catch in the gate and rip. "The last thing any projectionist wanted was a sudden blank screen, with an audience booing and demanding their money back."

Sometimes, even the most fastidious checks could

Is it the curse of the cowboy film? The John Wayne western *Hondo* figures in a story passed on by Jean Tighe about her husband Arthur when he was assistant manager of the Regal Cinema in the early 1950s. *Hondo* had drawn a packed audience. The first reel went on, the crowd hushed, and there was Wayne, tall in the saddle. However, back in the booth, the projectionist had made a horrifying discovery. The last reel of the film was missing. The projectionist alerted Arthur, who pondered the options. He may well have thought about the progress

Splash!

Derek and Jennifer Lovatt witnessed an amusing coincidence while attending the Swadlincote Empire in the mid-1960s. The 'B' film on the programme portrayed the comic antics of a sea lion who in one scene was frolicking in a fountain, with much splashing around and spillage of water. However, as the film moved on to a totally different scene, Derek and Jennifer – sat in the balcony – couldn't understand why the sound of splashing water could still be heard. Had the synchronisation faltered, causing the soundtrack to slip behind the action on screen? No – the couple then noticed that in the row just in front of them, water was splashing for real. Was this a crude, experimental example of what Aldous Huxley predicted for the cinemas of the future in *Brave New World* – 'The Feelies', where audiences would feel the same sensations as depicted on screen? No – quite simply, the roof was leaking; the torrential rainstorm outside had found a way inside. The balcony audience burst into laughter, causing much confusion in the stalls as the 'B' film about the sea lion wasn't THAT funny. There was further hilarity when the manager emerged with an enamel bucket to catch the drips. Derek and Jennifer noticed a certain nonchalance on the face of the manager as he coolly walked over to the balcony fountain, giving the distinct impression that it wasn't the first time this bucket had seen action in the Empire balcony.

of the very story up there on the screen: it was to build to an Apache uprising. Arthur might then have reached the conclusion that if the screening was to be abandoned, the film's events could be repeated in the cinema. There was nothing else for it. He didn't want to lose his scalp. The Regal had to find a spare copy of that reel. It seemed an unlikely prospect; if another cinema had *Hondo*, it would surely be showing the darned thing at the same time as them. Still, some frantic 'phone calls were made. Eventually, it was discovered that a Nottingham cinema had the film and – God bless them! – it had arrived for a screening the following day. Arthur Tighe sprang into action. A taxi was summoned. Off he went, into the sunset. He came back, in true movie fashion, in the nick of time. Arthur Tighe rode into town with ten minutes to spare. The projectionist laced up the missing reel, and the audience cheered John Wayne to the end. But he wasn't the only hero in the cinema that night.

The audience were not so lucky one night at the Somercotes Empire. If you were in the Thursday night audience the year the Empire screened *So Long Lettie*, here comes the explanation for your ruined evening. Len Waller remembers how his disgruntled pal Arthur plotted the perfect revenge on the chief projectionist who, following a row, told him never to darken his box again. Len was witness to Arthur's devilish prank: "He waited until a Wednesday performance. After it was over, we left the cinema, and waited a while before returning up the side alley. Arthur knew that the new reels of film would be stacked in the foyer, ready for the Thursday

changeover. He got in through a side door, and went straight up to a pile of six film cans. After studying the labels carefully, he slipped something under his jacket, and we were out. Come Thursday night, the film *So Long Lettie* was being screened. The projectionist wasn't so happy when he opened the film can containing the final reel. Nobody saw the end of that film."

Michael Wood, who projected pictures at various Derbyshire cinemas – from the Chesterfield Odeon to the Pilsley Ritz – also used to cut film out, but in a much more subtle way. And, it was an admirable example of a projectionist who really looked after his audience – or at least those who had buses to catch: "Sometimes you had to be conscious of when the last bus was due, so once I became familiar with a film, I used to wind a few of the film reels on, and also make an early changeover on the reel that was running, cutting out a couple of minutes each time, hoping the audience wouldn't notice. So, if you started half an hour late, you could still finish at the same time!"

James Fryer and Kenneth Moseley sometimes shortened the film shows they put on at the Youlgreave Village Hall cinema, but their motives were less honourable, a little selfish and entirely forgivable to any flesh and blood male who reads this explanation from James: "Ken and I were teenagers so we had an interest in the opposite sex. If certain girls were sitting in the back row of the seats, we would drop notes through the viewing windows, asking them to meet us after the show. If the reply was positive, we would cut the sixth or seventh reel out of

The Dead Don't Die

The first feature-length film I saw at the cinema – in 1961 – carries one notably nostalgic memory, even though the picture itself *The Singer Not The Song* starring Dirk Bogarde and John Mills, proved a dull, dour experience for a six-year-old.

I particularly remember the sight of both priest and bandit biting the dust at the film's climax – a startling experience for the sensitivities of a young viewer who had only previously attended children's Saturday matinées, where death was unheard of.

This was also noted by my seven-year-old sister Lynette. As we were ushered out of the cinema, she contemplated the long queue eagerly awaiting the next screening and, turning to my mum, asked: "what are they doing?"

"Going in to see the film, of course" was the plain reply, leaving Lynette to point to the poster and splutter the immortal words: "But why? Those people are dead." I still retain the vivid image of flush-faced parent hurrying us away from the daggered looks and a potential lynching at the hands of a rioting mob.

the programme. This gave us an extra ten minutes with the girls before they had to be home. Parents were very strict in those days; fortunately, the girl who became my regular date could run like a stag."

Michael Oxley had girls on his mind both in and out of the projection box at the Matlock Ritz. It didn't take Michael long to discover the real purpose of the Ritz balcony: in the warm evening weather, it was ideal for sitting and watching girls go by, while the projector whirred inside. To avoid any mishaps, the projector was fitted with a useful warning 'ting', just within earshot of the young talent-spotter out on the balcony.

Sometimes, what was on the reels kept Michael firmly in the box, eyes trained through the viewer towards the screen. He still remembers the thrill of receiving a Bridget Bardot or Gina Lollobrigida picture, because as a projectionist, he was able to retain a little piece of them before they went away: "We had a viewer that you ran the film through, frame by frame, so if you got one of these films, I used to cut out a favourite frame and keep it." He wasn't the only one, either. This practice occurred at several cinemas, which meant that when the audience came to the juicy bits in the film, their viewing would be upset by numerous jumps in the reel. As Michael

Orders Are Orders

While working at the Derby Odeon Pennine in the 1970s, Carl Chesworth was asked to go to the Council House to collect the Odeon's Cinematograph Licence. It contained some rather draconian conditions. Athough the licensed operating hours from Monday to Saturday imposed no harsh restraints, the Sunday hours – 2.30pm. to 9.30pm – were rather restrictive. For example, when the Odeon received the 192-minute epic *Dr Zhivago*, they realised they could only screen it once on a Sunday, as the length of the complete programme exceeded three and a half hours. That wasn't the only frustration: "It also meant we couldn't put any music on until 2.30, so our customers had to walk in to silence." Worse still, there was the prospect of silence at the end of the evening: "If we had a film timed to finish at the designated time and, for some reason, we experienced a delay, we were supposed to switch off the sound at 9.30. Mercifully, this never occurred."

What did occur, though, complied with the Licence's stipulation concerning Good Friday screenings. A cinema could only open on Good Friday if a clergyman was present to give a short service to the audience before the final programme. So, the Odeon duly booked a local vicar, who came along and delivered a short address to the cinema congregation.

further recalls: "I remember a scene in Bardot's *Yield To The Night*, where she first appeared naked, albeit only from the back. By the time we got the film, there wasn't much left of that scene!"

Most projectionists remember scenes from a film rather than the complete entity. Any trainee projectionist who believed he had got a ticket to endless free film shows was soon alerted to the reality. If anything, because of interruptions, pressing maintenance tasks and the flurry of concentrated work required before, during and after reel changeovers, there would be continual frustration at snatching a view of only certain sequences of a film over the period of its run. Only by the last reel of the final night's screening might the projectionist have come to piece together a film's jigsaw of scenes. If he was lucky. Furthermore, the constant whirr of the machines, the hum of the arc lamps, the stifling heat of the booth, the restricted and largely inadequate view through the glass, and the need to stand or perch on a tall, hard stool were hardly prerequisites for a cosy night out at the pictures. Although, as Eddie Burnham says, a projectionist became very knowledgeable about films – "you show me any film still between 1935 and 1955, and I could tell you the film" – he would never have viewed that film with quite the same pleasure as the folk in front of him, sunk back in the plush.

Projectionists would sympathise with my position as a film reviewer. I am constantly countering the claim that I lead both a lucky and cushy life sitting and viewing new films for free. Aside from the fact that I have to go away and write about them, I have to endure the fear, frustration and tedium of countless sub-standard pictures. For every memorable movie, there are about three I would not entertain thoughts of seeing as a normal cinema-goer. It would be worse for the projectionists. I only see an unfavourable film through once. Imagine, then, the plight of Michael Oxley, who found Laurence Olivier's *Richard III* one long, yawn-inducing bore on a first run-through. However, as the Shakespearian play was a set text, Michael found himself earmarked for extra daytime screenings for schools. He put that show on 32 times. How he must have begged for Bardot that week, as he sat idling his time in the box.

But a projectionist wasn't shut away all day. As fellow Matlock Ritz projectionist David Walters contends: "the projection staff used to run the cinema." Granted, it was a necessity during David's time because "the manager spent most of the time cavorting with an usherette", but it was not unusual for a manager who was otherwise busy – on official duties, that is – to leave the projectionist in charge.

Also, as Eddie Burnham maintains, "the projection-ist had to be a Jack-of-All-Trades." Colin Clarke reckons the booth operator was also "carpenter, electrician, engineer, chief stoker and general dogsbody." The projectionist was invariably exploited when various repairs were needed – screwing seats back into the floor, changing light bulbs – or servicing 'The Beast' – the diesel engine that drove the generator, a task that befell Colin Clarke every three months: "It lay on a concrete bed 12 foot by eight foot. The fly-wheel (an eight-foot diameter, two-ton chunk of cast bronze) was sunk into a deep recess in the floor. I often envisaged it flying off and demolishing half the cinema. To absorb spilt diesel, a litter of sawdust covered the red painted floor. Hand cranking it was a problem. The locking notch on the shaft was worn, causing the handle to slip off under pressure. More often than not, I landed face down in my best clothes in oily sawdust. After eventually breathing life into 'The Beast', Colin also had to contend with the monster in the cellar – the central heating boiler: "It really was a monstrous affair, covered in a three-inch layer of asbestos. If the coke supply arrived before we did, the delivery boys would fill the stairwell with two tons of the stuff. So, when I arrived, I would have to clamber over the coke and shovel it into a bunker the other side of the cellar. The boiler could eat a hundredweight of coke and still beg for more. At Christmas we used to roast chestnuts on it. Sometimes I had to beat a hasty retreat when down-draughts filled the cellar with choking sulphur fumes. But when we got good houses and poor ice-cream sales, my orders were to 'keep stoking'."

A projectionist was a scientist as well as a stoker, if Eddie Burnham is to be believed. "You even had to be skilled in the physics of trajectory" says Eddie. "One woman came in early one morning, looking rather flustered. She'd come to the cinema the previous evening, and to attract her friend's attention four rows in front, she had dipped into her handbag, rolled a piece of paper up into a ball, and threw it at her. What she didn't realise until she got home was that the piece of paper she'd extracted from the dark of her bag in the low light of the cinema was a five pound note – that was nearly five weeks wages for me. Luckily, by working out where the paper ball would have landed after hitting her friend's head, I mulled around amidst the piles of paper, and found it."

Eddie 'Jack-of-All-Trades' Burnham also remembers the time a new screen was required for the Somercotes Premier, having turned a mucky shade of nicotine brown owing to the free-smoking patrons. However, owing to the war, a replacement screen couldn't be found. So, it was out with the Walpurmer white emulsion. Another odd job done.

The Key

Although the Derby Superama – later the Odeon Pennine – was regarded as the most modern, state-of-the-art operation, this did not extend to the labels on the film transit boxes bound for the Odeon. Carl Chesworth, projectionist at the Pennine, recalls an amusing and astonishing telephone conversation he had with an employee at the cinema's Film Despatch department.

"I hate making up the labels to your cinema" said the gruff worker to Carl.

"Why on earth do you say that?" asked Carl.

"Well, just look at your address – Odeon Pennine Cinema, Colyear Street, Derby." Carl was mystified. "What's wrong with our address?"

"Too many Es."

"I beg your pardon?"

"You've got too many Es in your damned address."

What is this man saying? thought Carl, "E is the most common letter in the English language. What can he be complaining about?"

"Let me explain" said the film despatcher: "The E on my typewriter doesn't work. It types a blank. So every time I type up your address, I have to fill in by hand eight bloody letter Es."

Bernard Goodwin remembers a job that turned out odd in the other sense. Perturbed by the fact that the neighbouring Empire cinema had Cinemascope and the Cosy didn't, the manager Jack Plumb decided swift action was called for, so he hauled in his assistant Bernard on a Saturday morning: "We had to fix some cinema screen material on to the existing screen. To keep it there, we used a material similar to masking tape. We put it on the joint, silver-painted it, along with the rest of the screen, and it looked pretty good." The Heanor Cosy now had Cinemascope. Well, sort of. But it was extremely short-lived: "Halfway through *The Dambusters* that night, the chief operator thought there was a hair in the projector gate. In fact, it was the masking tape peeling off from the top of the screen. Slowly, it peeled off more and more until it was about three-quarters of the way down, and there it stayed for the rest of the night."

Projectionist's pride would have been hurt that night. For any conscientious operator, presentation was everything. So was cleanliness. Michael Wood remembers arriving in the morning and "cleaning everything" in his projection box. "It was immaculately kept – you could eat your dinner off the floor." But this was more than a matter of punctiliousness: "You were getting Grade 1 film and you couldn't afford to have foreign particles around scratching the film."

The most dedicated projectionists worked at all hours. But was it dedication, or maybe something else? "All projectionists must have been a little mad" reckons Duncan Cross. "I know I must have been. It wasn't a particularly social job. In fact, it was anti-social. And what other group of people would have shut themselves away in often small, cramped rooms with all that hot equipment, looking out on another world through a port hole?"

But it was bringing people another world that provided part of the satisfaction for projectionists like Duncan: "In the cinema business were the film-makers, actors, cameramen, cinema builders, the manager, usherettes and so on – the projectionist was the last vital link in the whole process, a link made up of thousands of skills which came in reels of film. From that projection room, you could transport people all over the world, on dry land, in and under the sea, and up in the air. You could make them laugh and cry; you could frighten them, and thrill them. You took them out of their existence."

This romanticised view of what might be seen as a rudimentary duty is shared by many projectionists who operated in the heyday of cinema. And for Brian Dawes, who was chief projectionist at the Belper Picture Palace in the 1950s, there was a difference in the presentation then: "Today's cinemas have dull lighting, a simple screen, with no curtains and no atmosphere. In my day, there was a sense of showmanship involved in putting on a film." That same sense would have tingled in Duncan Cross' veins because for Duncan, working in a cinema got under his skin, and affected everything he did: "There were times when you had to be at the cinema, giving all your waking hours to the job. It had to come before anything else. My wife seldom got a night out, and it raised a few arguments sometimes. But it was all tied in with that old adage 'the show must go on.' Even when I wasn't projecting films, I was going to see them, at other cinemas! One of the highlights of a projectionist's life was visiting another cinema and going to see somebody else's projection room. It was also an education to go and watch someone else's show; you could sometimes spot things that you yourself were getting wrong."

Eddie Burnham did the same thing: "If I went to the pictures myself, at a rival cinema, and, say a bit of blue appeared in the corner, I'd whisper smugly to my mate, 'he's got his carbons at the wrong distance'." Back at his own cinema, there was always, for Eddie, a "satisfaction in doing the job well, like having a spot-on changeover from one projector to another." And if Duncan Cross was satisfied with the evening's presentation, he would give his projectors a little pat before switching them off for the night. "They were more than just machines" says Duncan, "they were beautiful pieces of machinery that took on the personality of something alive. They were my friends."

One projectionist who himself became a friend to many people in Amber Valley was Harold Brown, who was known affectionately as 'The Lantern Man'. Beginning his career as a rewind boy at the Riddings Regent, Harold worked 61 years, accumulated a wealth of film knowledge – "he was always called on to settle an argument" says Bernard Goodwin, his last manager – and acquired a reputation for working with any kind of projection equipment, borne out by his constant relief work and his spells as operator at the Alfreton Odeon, Ripley Empire, Somercotes Premier and Heanor Empire. His warm personality endeared him to the locals – he could never walk down the street without being stopped by a passer-by once recognised – and his charity work was renowned, to the extent that in his last years, he was given an Esther Rantzen *Hearts of Gold* award for his services to disabled people.

Harold Brown, like Duncan Cross, Eddie Burnham and others were prepared to receive only adequate pay for a job that also cost them their social lives, because they knew they would, for the most part, receive a special kind of remuneration from their audience. As Eddie recalls: "You had the pleasure of seeing happy faces coming out of the cinema." This was the reward that drove Duncan Cross on: "Often, when we had a good night with a sizeable audience, I used to give a hop, skip and jump on the way home."

But before everyone went home, there was the customary playing of the National Anthem. For any projectionist imbued with that sense of pride in his presentation, this was the final part of his presentation, and everyone was expected to honour it, even the young rascals of Somercotes. Len Waller was one of those rascals: "Before they played the National Anthem, there was a stampede to get to the doors. We just didn't want to stand still! However, the projectionist soon got wise to this, and he used to whip that National Anthem on sharpish as soon as the main feature film displayed those words 'The End'."

Decline And Fall
Competition, catastrophes and closures

Cinema took people out of their homes... TV reversed this process and took them back again, usually into homes which by then were a good deal pleasanter to live in.
Ernest Betts, from *The Film Business*

I had stars in my eyes... visions of the old-style cinemas with organs and art deco styling. What I didn't see, until later, was an ordinary small town cinema that could never return to those days.
Sam Lavington, manager of Ripley Hippodrome (1983-91)

BY the turn of the 1950s, most of the Derbyshire population had a cinema nearby, continuous performances obviated the formalities of booking, and admission costs were extremely modest. Whatever one's age, sex or socio-economic status, the cinema was cheap, convenient and accessible. Leonard England, director of 'Mass Observation', an organisation which investigated life, habit and opinion in Britain, published a document in 1949 entitled *What The Cinema Means To The British Public*, which stated that the cinema-going habit in post-war Britain had become so widespread that: 'It is in danger of being accepted as institutional, and beyond the scope of query or study.' It was also noted that:

'Virtually within the lifetime of the pioneers of the kinematograph, the cinema has become such an influence that 17 out of every 20 people in Britain now admit that they go to the pictures, occasionally at least.'

This was a remarkable statistic compared with other social habits. There were more cinema-goers than smokers or drinkers, they outnumbered both pub and theatre-goers, less than half their numbers went to church, and nearly as many read a morning newspaper. Also, a survey of provincial newspapers revealed that the second most popular element for readers were the announcements about local films, one person in five giving this as their main reason for buying the paper at all. Leonard England was thus observing a hugely popular leisure pursuit, but one that was hiding its startling popularity, and receiving less recognition than it merited:

'A book that sells a quarter of a million copies is front page news for days, but a good many films are

seen by this number of people in one cinema alone during its West End showing in London, and later it may be shown in a maximum of a further 2,000 cinemas as well.'

Leonard England's article also quoted a 'recent' survey which showed that one person in every six in Great Britain said that picture-going was his or her favourite occupation. This was borne out, the report noted, by the many ways the populace spent money on films – beyond the mere purchase of cinema tickets. At the end of the 1940s, there were 27 journals devoted to films aimed at the general public, with many more catering for the more specialised film viewer. Of the weekly mass market magazines, the most popular were bought by 400,000, and read by twice or three times as many more people. Even a 7s 6d book of the film *Hamlet*, which in cinema terms was a limited success, sold 40,000 copies. It was also revealed that the zither music soundtrack to *The Third Man* had sold 300,000 copies before the film had ended its countrywide release, that the largest free-gift scheme organised by a British advertiser since the war was centred on a booklet which revealed the horoscopes of the film stars, 'while the makers of a famous beverage feel safe in using a film star in their advertisements without even giving his name'.

What Leonard England also discovered was how widely the cinema-going habit had spread. Namely, that those people who lived in country districts and in towns with a population of under 4,000, went to the cinema 'only slightly less often' than those in the bigger towns. Considering, he noted, that town dwellers had sometimes three cinemas 'within

When cinema still brought great events to people. Queues form at the Spondon Sitwell for the film of Queen Elizabeth II's Coronation. **Sam Winfield Collection.**

walking distance' (certainly true in Derby, Chesterfield and Ilkeston), while those in rural districts had considerable transport difficulties, this was a 'remarkable' statistic.

What would have been just as remarkable at the time was the notion that cinema attendances would decline within the next two decades as dramatically as they rose in the first two decades of cinema's life. The 1946 of 1,635 million admissions dropped to 1,182 millions by 1955, and by 1965 the figure had shrunk to 327 million. In terms of weekly attendance, the falling off of patronage seems all the more severe: 31 million patrons a week at the end of the war had been reduced to only 6 million.

Numerous cinemas, too, were closed and converted to other uses, mainly bingo. Many cinemas' demise was followed by the unthinkable: demolition. From a figure of 4,714 cinemas in 1946, this had been reduced to 4,483 in 1955. Of Derbyshire's main cinemas, only the Derby Hippodrome had closed within that

decade, but the next decade saw a devastating decimation. An astonishing 2,512 cinemas across Britain ceased operations between 1955 and 1965. Derbyshire lost the majority of its cinemas, with Derby alone losing 12.

Basically, the big screen had lost out to the little screen. In 1948, there were only 20,000 television licence holders. In 1949, two-thirds of the people of Britain had never seen a television set working. Yet as early as 1952, a survey's statisticians were attributing three-quarters of the decline in admissions to the cinema to the competition of the television. This was arguably the case in Derbyshire – in 1950, the BBC's first regional transmitter opened at Sutton Coldfield, 'setting off a wave of TV buying', according to Harry Hopkins, author of *The New Look (A Social History of the Forties and Fifties in Britain)*.

The Coronation of 1953 was to intensify that wave. Because of the excitement generated by the live screening on TV of the royal occasion, the nation

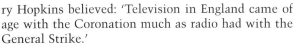

Ilkeston schoolchildren queue outside the New Theatre to see the film of Queen Elizabeth II's Coronation. F.H.Brailsford.

threw itself into the arrangement of 'viewing parties', so that although only 2,700,000 TV receivers were switched on for the two and a half hour ceremony, it was watched by 20,400,000 – almost half the nation. As Harry Hopkins believed: 'Television in England came of age with the Coronation much as radio had with the General Strike.'

Two years later, commercial television had also been introduced. By the end of its first full year, viewers who could choose between the two services were devoting an average of seven hours a week to ITV compared with four for the BBC. Its impact on cinema was crushing, as Harry Hopkins eloquently described:

'At the cinema, where only a year or two ago patient queues had endlessly waited, the gaps in the stalls yawned wider each year. Between 1954 and 1959 more than 800 cinemas were obliged to shut down. Admissions halved. As the neon died and the glittering chandeliers in the foyer gathered dust, the 'Super Cinema', domed and gilded, or chromiumed and tiled, lush carpeted and enveloped in the scented ooze of the Mighty Wurlitzer, joined its predecessor, the Gin Palace, in the vast and curious lumber room of Britain's social history.'

But why, compared with the big, enveloping and occasion-filled sensation of a palatial picture house, did the masses gravitate to the tiny, uninspiring and less magical sensation in the corner of their ordinary, much less palatial sitting rooms? Interestingly, virtually all the lapsed cinema-goers of this era who I have spoken with have not viewed it in those terms. When asked why they stopped going to a place they regularly visited and evidently loved, most replied (some nonchalantly): 'TV came along'. And that was

that, basically. Few offered explanations, seemingly having both embraced the new medium and accepted the passing of the cinema hey-day as inevitable. This may say much about the hypnotic hold television exerted on the population. Even though there were no feature films on TV, access to a wide range of entertainment on a television screen for a family home which had previously only received entertainment stimulus through radio or gramophone records, had a powerful and all-embracing effect. Marion Toft admits deserting her local cinema in Allenton, saying "the cinema lost some of its allure; we began to see the world from a wider perspective and Allenton and the Broadway shrank accordingly." In spite of an evening's cinema comprising a cartoon or comedy short, travelogue, newsreel and feature film, the TV could deliver almost the same range of entertainment on the same night – and more, if one also craved a game show, a play, a classical concert or an art lecture.

Other factors played their part. Whilst cinema could provide the communal experience, some people came to enjoy the quiet privacy of domestic TV viewing. Families were brought closer. Indeed, after surveying 400 TV families, a Dr Belson reported: 'The meeting of a deadline together gives form to the evening, provides a sense of achievement, and creates a feeling of togetherness.'

Even an inveterate cinema-goer admitted to me that television exerted a strong influence on his evening plans simply for providing 'free entertain-

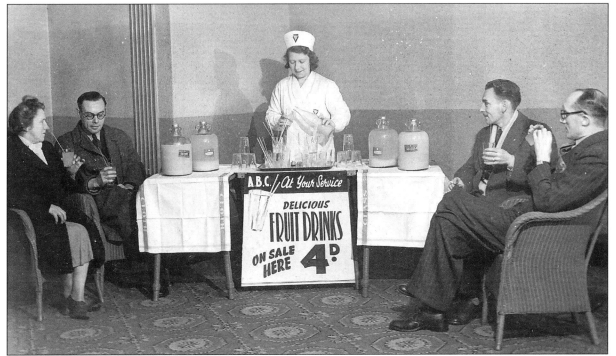

Interval drinks at the Popular in Mill Street, Derby. Compared with today's vibrant scene, this looks almost sad.
Paul Southall.

ment at a switch' (one usually forgets that TV has to be paid for, although it has always been cheaper than the cinema). He also held his hand up when he said: 'we became easily pleased'. This drug-induced drift into docility was more or less complete by the end of the decade. A survey at the turn of 1958 showed that an average Sunday evening found almost half the adult population engaged in viewing TV. Much worse for the cinema, in view of its key audience, was that among working-class viewers, 45 per cent watched television for an average of four hours every night of the week.

However, television's deleterious effect on the cinema-going audience was heightened by other factors. Harry Hopkins observed that in 1954, when the last of the wartime rationing restrictions – that of meat – was finally abolished, 'almost at once, affluence came hurrying on the heels of penury. Boom was in the air'. Britain ushered in the age of 'consumer durables'. At the same time, the concept of 'Hire Purchase' was taking hold. Hire purchase had also spread through all classes, and affected a large slab of the traditional cinema audience. By 1956, half of Britain's TV sets had been bought on HP. Other domestic goods, whose purchase was previously dependent on long years of thrift, were much more easily obtainable, and many of these items – vacuum cleaners, washing machines, power mixers, three-

piece suites – were going into homes; and, in increasing numbers, they were going into new homes, largely on freshly-built estates. There was much work to be done in one's new house. The phrase 'Do-It-Yourself' came into vogue. Harry Hopkins summed up the mood of the times:

"The Common Man had no longer an acute need of one-and-nine-penceworth of vicarious luxury. With the aid of his new house, his car, the HP, his wife's magazines, and his do-it-yourself kit, he could build an only slightly less colourful – and much more satisfying – world for himself at home."

So, although the glittering, plush picture palaces were designed to provide a world away from one's drab domesticity, the ordinary family home was now on the carpeted road to catching up. Indeed, in later years, a vicious circle would be drawn: the more that people drifted away, the less the cinemas could afford to maintain the decor and facilities, never mind improve them. And as successive generations tried the cinema out, the less inclined they would feel about returning, and resuming their parents' social habit. Instead of wrapping themselves in an atmosphere of glamour, comfort and capacity audiences, they would taste a tainted air. They would feel, as described perfectly by Dennis Sharp, author of *Picture Palace*, 'seedy decline and empty, musty vastness'. Sadly, many Derbyshire cinemas descended in this way, which may partly account for the curious lack of protest when so many were waiting for the arrival of the wrecking ball.

A further vicious circle began in the area of the films themselves. Interest in cinema also diminished because there was a shortage of films being produced. That shortage was thus worsened as even fewer audiences came. Film-making was in crisis: most pictures made between 1950 and 1956 cost more to produce than they made at the box office.

Along with improved standards of living at home and the television in that home, were other competitive factors which the cinema could barely counter. Firstly, there was a post-war baby boom. Most of us are aware of the American phrase 'baby boomers' which refers to the result of an inevitable, mass outbreak of serious nookie following the long, uncertain war years. But this trend for baby-making erupted in Britain, too, so that by the turn of the 1950s and through to the middle of the decade, couples were staying in with child (or children) – bearing in mind that babysitting was a largely untried concept – rather than going to the cinema.

More people were going on holiday, both at home and, increasingly, abroad. There was money to be saved for that forthcoming sojourn. For those who frequented the cinema twice a week, there was an easy, obvious form of expense to cut. The 1950s also saw in the five-day week for all, and the encouragement to seek out a widening array of leisure pursuits. As Harry Hopkins observed in his social study of the times:

'The famous English "long weekend" had been an upper middle-class institution with a narrow range of correct class occupations. The weekend of the 1950s was everybody's weekend, a vast, ever-expanding hold-all packed with an immense diversity of interests and pursuits.'

Hopkins reveals that a world of 'small boatery' had grown up, claiming one million adherents. Two million people went fishing. Three times as many people as before the war were learning to ride horses. For more working-class tastes, there was an increase in participatory sports like football. Dancing was on the rise. So was caravanning. Reading too: British adults in the 1950s were averaging 20 books a year; the 'paperback revolution' got underway, with a record 68 million sales in 1958. By 1960, a quarter of the 11 million camera owners also possessed a cine-camera. Some didn't need to go to watch other peoples' films: they were making their own. Children were in the decade when they would become known as 'teenagers', who would increasingly come to own transistor radios, tape recorders, a record collection, and even a scooter. Maybe, after that, a car.

A motor car came the way of around half the people who took out Hire Purchase agreements. The number of cars in use was to double in the 1950s, and most of the new owners were skilled manual and lower-paid white-collar workers. The car increased social as well as physical mobility. Again, sociologist Harry Hopkins had his finger on the starter motor: 'As the Common Man climbed into his new – or more probably second-hand – car, touched the starter, and depressed the accelerator, he rode off not merely from town to suburb or country, but also from one way of life to another.'

Joe Vowles was a case in point. As a 14-year old in 1956, in the same year that his household installed its first television set, Joe became a weekend regular at the Chaddesden Gloria. All of his mates went. He eventually got a girlfriend, Hazel, who was rewarded for her good taste in courting by receiving every Saturday, on the Gloria-bound bus, a 2s 6d box of Meltis Newbury Fruits. Then, in 1960, aged 18, Joe got his first car: "I felt a new-found freedom. Not only with having a car, but also for the fact that I could drive to any pub in Derbyshire." The Saturday cinema visit was supplanted by the pub kerb crawl. But how could a regular weekly cinema visitor suddenly turn complete deserter? "To be honest, the films were almost irrelevant. Hazel and I went for a kiss and a cuddle; it was the one time of the week we were on our own. Yes, sometimes we watched the films, and we enjoyed the spectacle of the big screen, but at the age of 18, you also started to get more discriminating, and we realised that much of what we were seeing week in and week out was, frankly, rubbish. We looked for a better social life, and found it. We still went to the Gloria from time to time, but we became more selective."

Thus we introduce another factor in the decline of cinema debate – the drop in the quality of the product. During the war, the cinema serviced a quantitative need for escape, where qualitative values hardly figured. The cinema was in easy reach, the doors were open every evening, it didn't charge the earth for admission, and three hours screen entertainment was on offer. Barry Norman, in his book *Talking Pictures*, aired one of the suggestions put forward:

'That the quality of the films was poor because Hollywood had misjudged or failed to recognise the audience's more sophisticated taste and carried on believing, as the war years had taught it to do, that any old picture would be good enough.'

Barry doesn't seem to wholly concur with this view, citing it as the first time in history that H.L.Mencken's well-known dictum: 'Nobody ever lost money by underestimating the taste of the public' was to prove false. But he goes on to explain

Site of the Empire/Black Prince, Duckworth Square, Derby. Bill Attenborough.

There Are In Heaven' – released Clark Gable, the so-called 'King of Hollywood', because it could no longer sustain his salary of more than half a million dollars per annum. Eddie Burnham, Somercotes Premier projectionist and avid picture-goer was aware of Hollywood's fall: "By the mid-1950s, the old studio system was starting to crumble. They didn't have real stars anymore. It was the beginning of the end – sex, swearing and violence came in, and I was disillusioned by the fact that Hollywood had gone 50 years without this kind of crap."

Leslie Halliwell summed up the cinema industry's position at this time: "The bread and butter picture no longer made a profit. Only size and sensation sold tickets."

The provincial cinema, reeling in the face of this lifestyle revolution, could come to the fore as an entertainment venue when it could offer something of size and sensation, and that mainly came in the form of the musical. MGM led the way with *Singin' In The Rain*, *Seven Brides For Seven Brothers*, *Easter Parade*, *Annie Get Your Gun*, and *Showboat*, with other studios providing *Guys and Dolls*,

how the Hollywood studio system was eroded by legal sanctions; there is no doubt that the golden age had lost its lustre when, in 1954, MGM – the company which carried the slogan 'More Stars Than *South Pacific* and *The King and I*. Most Derbyshire cinema-goers of the early to mid-1950s will comfortably reel off a succession of musicals they viewed at their local picture house with unquestioned

By the 1960s, Derby cinemas had to put on live concerts to supplement their business.

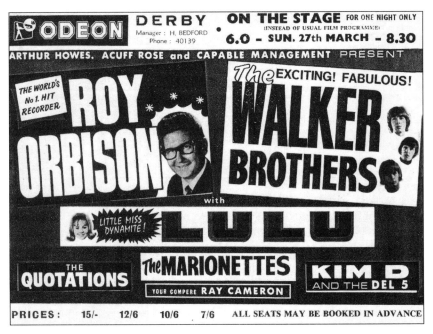

delight. Many will speak of other film delights, like the epic *Quo Vadis* (which received its Midlands première at the Derby Coliseum), *The Greatest Show On Earth* (which produced 15,000 admissions in one week at the Ilkeston Ritz) and *Bridge On The River Kwai* (seen in Cinemascope). The magic still lingered, and the allure of colour was a predominant plus while the masses were huddled in front of monochrome.

If musicals provided the sensation rather than size, CinemaScope supplied both. To show this spectacle, Derbyshire cinemas had to widen their screens, and provide stereo sound. Because of the length and thinness of the projected image, Hollywood director George Stevens dismissed it rather presumptuously as 'only suitable for filming coffins and rattlesnakes'. Movie mogul Sam Goldwyn was equally as cynical: "A wide screen just makes a bad film twice as bad." In spite of their cynicism, CinemaScope was the most successful of the measures introduced to counter ailing audiences, and led to other rival systems like VistaVision, WarnerScope, RegalScope, TechniScope and Technirama. It was to prove a relieving success for some local picture houses, including the Derby Black Prince. This cinema was previously the Empire, which manager Edgar Duckworth welcomingly refurbished in 1948. To salvage its fading reputation, he changed its name to that of the fierce 14th-century Royal warrior, although it is likely the significance would have been largely lost on the lapsed Empire cinema-goers Edgar was trying to win back. But no matter, he did win them back, by closing the cinema for a week in March 1954 to install the new giant screen and necessary technical equipment, and re-opening with *The Robe*, the first picture to be filmed in CinemaScope. Here was a biblical epic promising 'sweeping spectacle, dramatic action and breathtaking colour'. According to Halliwell's Film Guide: 'Photographer Leon Shamroy operated under difficulties with a lens as yet imperfect', but the format found favour. The Black Prince became a mecca for these movies, breaking attendance records for *The King and I*. But although the King reigned

happily for a while, the Black Prince lost his fight, as the CinemaScope films dried up.

Many cinemas experienced problems converting to CinemaScope, anyway. The Derby Cavendish, for example, had a proscenium arch that made it impossible to extend the screen. The Derby Normanton had to take out 100 front row seats in order to accommodate a new screen for Cinema-Scope. The Ilkeston Kings went to considerable expense, removing part of the walls and redesigning the proscenium arch. With a screen area 44ft wide, the Kings took to proclaiming in the press that films could be seen on the 'Giant Screen'. The town's Ritz could not compete with that boast. Like the Derby Cavendish, it was not possible to widen the proscenium, so that any CinemaScope films that were shown on the standard size screen appeared in a pseudo-widescreen, 'letter box' format. In the case of the Ritz, the picture was 26ft wide but only 11ft 3in deep. This was CinemaScope only in name; although the industry gave it its own name – 'Miniscope'.

Other formats quickly dried up after having only dipped their toes in the water. 3D was thought to be a rescuing force for the industry, offering dramatic depth of vision with the odd surprise jumping out of the screen – or so it seemed. The Derby Regal made a serious stab at 3D, and Wilf Holt enjoyed the experience, whatever the film: '*The House of Wax* with its melting skulls, *Battle At Red River* – flaming arrows coming straight at you – or *Kiss me Kate*, with Kathryn Grayson in your lap.' Hollywood was infused with enthusiasm for this new cinema lifesaver. But the quality was poor, it was nowhere near as

The Cavendish Cinema, Derby, in the late 1950s, which experienced difficulties converting to CinemaScope due to its proscenium arch.

The site of the Cavendish Cinema, Derby. A supermarket (out of picture) now occupies the site. John Osborn.

successful as Cinemascope, and as gimmicks go, it soon went. What scuppered its future was the sheer bother of wearing the special spectacles. Many patrons took umbrage at the request to wear the cumbersome glasses; many of those who never minded the specs were never to return them, taking them home either unwittingly, as a souvenir, or with a half-assed idea that they might find some use for them as sunglasses. Worse still, they couldn't use them for many future screenings.

The passing of 3D was welcomed with some relief by the projectionists. As two projectors were in use simultaneously – in order to achieve the 3D effect – there were pauses for reel changes. Furthermore, synchronisation was crucial. The ultimate horror for the operator screening *The House of Wax* would be the sight not of Vincent Price doing his worst, but of the film itself snapping, because the projectionist would have to snip out exactly the same number of frames on the film reel running alongside in order to maintain the 'synch'. (3D was revived briefly in the early 1980s: I remember sitting in the Derby ABC watching a woeful *Jaws 3*. Actually, the 3D effects were well-executed, though they had a tacky, artificial look, and audiences would have been better had the film not suffered such a fusillade of criticism over its dreadful screenplay. *Friday the 13th Part III* fared little better).

Some Derbyshire cinema managers embraced the gimmicks, as they at least provided novelty value. At the Derby Coliseum (which was actually the first Derbyshire cinema to show a film in 3D – *A Day In The Country*), Wilf Holt remembers the gimmicks

"reached the pits" with 'Emergo' a novelty which formed part of the screening of *The House On Haunted Hill*: "a skeleton slid down a wire from the back of the balcony to the side of the screen where it vanished through a hole."

X films were introduced in 1953. This provided a flurry of interest early on, and a welcome burst of fresh publicity, and there was the invariable attraction for those young lads who would have expeditiously sneaked in under age to taste the illicit thrill of scenes they were considered too young to see. Because of its legislative base, the X certificate was not a move designed to arrest cinema's decline. If anything, though, it hastened the decline. Some film-makers viewed the new certification for a picture as good publicity for any that carried it, and thus ensured the contents of their films merited the alluring X. But the X film contributed to the general drop-off in interest in cinema by further excluding the traditional family audience. Cinema became the biggest mass entertainment medium of the century because it attracted both young and old, and families didn't feel the pinch once they had paid the admission price for parents and offspring. Dennis Sharp, author of *Picture Palace*, believes the X films did some damage in a particular way:

'It is not too fanciful to suggest that the nature of these catchpenny films themselves helped to dictate the character of cinemas of the 1950s and 1960s: seedy, deteriorating palaces followed by small, plain, anonymous studios of cut-price construction.'

Dennis also blames the cinema operators of the time for adding to the industry's woes, claiming that,

The old Derby Midland Electric Theatre in its last days, as the Ritz. Derby's first purpose-built cinema went the way of all. Sam Winfield Collection.

for at least a decade, they 'sat back and watched the audiences slip away from them.' This accusation is based on booking policy for films, which effectively eroded the element of choice. Not only had the days of two or three changes of programme disappeared, but also the cinema operators became guilty of block-booking films to whole areas at a time. Many cinema managers lost the freedom to book the films that they knew would suit their audience and, worse still, had the frustration of taking a film that was being screened at the same time as another cinema in the area.

Could life get much worse for local cinemas? Unfortunately, yes: television eventually came to screen films. At first, it was strictly old films, with a condition of sale also stipulating transmission after cinemas had shut. But it was another part of the unstoppable, spiralling descent in the film industry's floundering fight against the small screen menace, exacerbated by a shift of loyalty, as film industry magnates like Bernstein and Rank shuffled off cinema's mortal coil and embraced the new corporate life of TV.

The film industry also realised that the older age groups were the ones who took to TV most. Commercial television, in particular, soon had the effect of creating a majority cinema audience of 10-25 year-olds, and noting that market change, film-makers threw themselves into gearing for that audience age group, particularly young adults.

Derbyshire cinemas did gain a deal of publicity, in 1956, for one such film made for a teenage market – *Rock Around The Clock* – a document of rock'n'roll's emergence, starring Bill Haley and The Comets. The plot was virtually non-existent, but it was stuffed full of good jiving tunes. Young audiences gathered in their numbers, and the gang element occasionally tipped the level of decorum, resulting in over-exuberance, a spot of rowdyism, and a headache for managers. Michael Oxley remembers the film's impact: "I was there in my long coat and drainpipe trousers, dancing in the aisles and taking the ashtrays off the back of seats. I went to see it three times."

Aisle-dancing was a phenomenon cinema manag-

ers had not experienced before, and most took exception to it. Mick Meakin was 14 when he went to the first Derby screening of *Rock Around The Clock* at the Coliseum: "The film was stopped part way through because people were dancing. The manager came on the stage and said the film wouldn't be screened if the dancers didn't sit down and behave. This created a furore, and ice-creams were thrown at him." Realising he wasn't getting through, the manager announced that the film would continue without the sound. He then left the stage, and went out of the auditorium. Shortly after, the audience realised what he had done. A few minutes later, a couple of bobbies appeared. The effect of their walking down the aisles brought a hush. It did no good, though. As soon as the police left, the manager restored the sound from the moment the audience first lost it, and the young crowd resumed their leaping, jumping and cheering, and even dancing in the aisles. 'We're gonna rock, rock, rock till the broad daylight.'

There was a similar disturbance when the Derby Odeon screened *Rock Around The Clock* on 24 September. 'Police Called To Rock'n'Roll Film' was the headline to the following report in the *Derby Evening Telegraph.*

'Police were called last night to the Odeon cinema where the film *Rock Around The Clock* is being shown all this week. Later, after street demonstrations, they arrested two youths. There was storming in the stalls and booing from the balcony at the Odeon, where earlier the manager R.W.G.Bennett said: "we are not expecting any trouble." To forestall any riots, the soundtrack of the first three rock numbers was turned down and the audience of 900 let the manager know that they did not like it. They clapped, slapped, stormed and shouted. As a final resort, they let off two thunderflashes, and that brought the police hurrying to the one and tenpennies'.

After the show, the crowds spilled out of the cinema and demonstrated, danced, clapped and chanted their way down St Peter's Street. Police had to clear the roadway to allow traffic through. The rest of the week's screenings were quieter and trouble-free.

It appears not one first-time screening of *Rock Around The Clock* was unaffected by exuberance. At the Ilkeston Ritz, for example, seats were uprooted, fire extinguishers were let off and light bulbs broken. There was trouble later in the year at the same cinema with the follow-up film *Don't Knock The Rock*. The manager Mr Dresser, appalled at the jiving, shouting and stamping of feet, stopped the film halfway through and threatened to continue the

to diversify. Concerts became commonplace, with other live attractions like variety shows, stage plays and pantomimes. From 1959, the Derby Gaumont utilised its stage for a succession of pop concerts, booking in top-drawer acts such as Little Richard, The Everly Brothers, Cliff Richard, Gene Pitney, Adam Faith, Marty Wilde and The Andrew Sisters (in later years, artists like The Kinks, Roy Orbison, The Hollies, The Yardbirds, and The Walker Brothers appeared, with one evening headlined by The Who, supported by The Merseys and 'their fruit eating bears' and, even more amazingly, Max Wall).

Also in 1959, the Chaddesden Majestic instigated a similar concert policy on Sunday nights. There was a famous kerfuffle that year when Terry Dene made his comeback. It was a controversial return for Terry Dene, because reports were out that he had been ill-treating his wife, the singer Edna Savage (she eventually left him). This coincided with the news that he had spent only two months of his two years national service, and had got a medical discharge. Because of the parallells with Elvis Presley – who was looked on as a selfless hero for serving his time honestly and admirably – this was a well-documented story. He hardly re-emerged smelling of roses. Although a few loyal fans had daubed the words 'We still love you Terry' over the photo display boards, the concert at the Chaddesden Majestic was short-lived and got a mixed reception, as Joe Vowles remembers: "For some reason, there were two or three members of the Military Police standing down each side of the cinema. I assume Terry Dene had hired them to protect him. When it was Dene's time to come on, he wasn't introduced. The curtain rose and there he was. I remember there was applause mixed with booing.

The former Superama, Derby. It succumbed like the others. **Marshall Grey.**

screening without the soundtrack unless the audience behaved. In 1959, the Ripley Hippodrome was so fed up of teenage rowdyism during its rock'n'roll screenings that it decided to ban 'certain elements' as well as reduce the number of films that included rock'n'roll music.

The press headlines about disturbances continued, although some were due not directly to rock'n'roll films but live rock'n'roll concerts. In April 1961, for example, girls rioted during a concert by the Allisons in the Derby Gaumont. In a desperate bid to bring audiences back, many Derbyshire cinemas had begun

He only sang one song, and then the curtain fell. You could tell the audience felt cheated, because all you heard then were boos. After that, he stole away in a car, flanked by those same Military Police. Miki and Griff stole the show. Mind you, there wasn't much of a show to steal. I don't know why Dene bothered coming."

Within a year or two, Terry Dene had dropped out of sight. By that time, so had a number of Derbyshire cinemas. The Ripley Empire closed (and was demolished) in 1956; a year later, the Langley Mill Ritz had gone. In 1958, it was all over for the Somercotes Empire. In the same year, the Derby Popular was shut, the owners blaming its demise on the crippling Entertainment Tax. The Spondon Sitwell also called it a day after 30 years, although this cinema was hit by cruel luck. It was hard enough eking out an existence in the heat of television competition, but to see half of your catchment area rent asunder by a new by-pass was a severe blow. *Bail Out At 43,000 Feet* was its last film.

Other Derbyshire village cinemas were bailing out, having bowed to the inevitable. Betty Alldread, usherette at the Crich Picture House, remembers how the manager tried to keep the cinema going by staging talent contests. "Beauty shows, too. I knew they wouldn't work when I ended up winning my heat. The odd thing was that most people came for the talent contest, but didn't stay for the film! What did work was 'outing' the seats so the manager could run dance evenings. They were popular. But the cinema itself was dying. I can remember the manager Mr Major standing outside the cinema, as people went in, saying: 'if you people don't come, I'm going to have to close it'. And he did. It closed near the end of the 1950s, and turned into Tor Spring factory."

Nellie Mellors remembers the declining years of the Belper Palace: "They never modernised it. It looked rough for quite a few years, and eventually closed in 1960. It went without ceremony, and was quickly forgotten."

At least the Somercotes Premier went with ceremony. In fact, it went with a bang. Not a welcome one, though: on the night of 5 November 1960, after the Premier had closed, a firework exploded inside the cinema. The resultant fire gutted the interior. In more lucrative times, the owner Percy Dennis would have happily redeveloped the place. But having already closed the Pinxton Palace and the Somercotes Empire in the village in the last year, he knew any refurbishment was futile. His cinema in Jacksdale also closed its curtains a month later.

There was a depressing catalogue of countywide closures at this time. Ashbourne lost its Empire. So did Swadlincote and Long Eaton. Heanor said farewell to the Cosy. In Derby, the demise of the Sitwell and Popular cinemas was swiftly followed by the Normanton, Cosmo and Cosy. Most cinemas closed quietly, without fuss, ceremony or protest. The majority of the ardent regulars of yesteryear were long gone, some even unaware of the imminent death of what had once been a slice of their life. A few would have stumbled on the news of their cinema's closure in the local newspaper. Others would have heard the reports of impending shutdown, but what was the point of campaigning against closure? The place had died even before the 'For Sale' notice had been nailed up. Those with fond memories would have heaved a sigh of regret, and gone back to watch the television. Some would even have looked forward to what was coming in its place – a new, popular, prize-winning game called Bingo. This, in fact, occurred at the New Theatre, Ilkeston. David Roddis adds a bitter note in his history of the Erewash Valley cinemas where he refers to the bingo takeover of 1963, which continued until 1982, after which the building fell into disuse. In 1989, there was an application from the current owner to demolish the building and redevelop the site, which led to howls of protest from various Ilkeston organisations. David viewed the outcry over the building's fate as too little, too late, contending that local people 'had sat back for 7 years and done nothing except watch it deteriorate'.

There would have been proportionately more sadness at the passing of the Derby Cavendish, which at least got a proper send off, with a screening on 19 December 1960 of *Sons and Lovers*, followed by a Farewell Dance and Buffet. There was a large sign bearing the words 'Bon Voyage' which straddled the foyer, where the manager Harold Hall was carried shoulder high as the guests sang *For He's A Jolly Good Fellow*. Harold was a fond figurehead, having spent 12 years of unstinting service at the cinema. The closure of the 'Cav' was down to a so-called 'rationalisation policy' by the Rank Organisation. Projectionist David Larkin saw through this executive-speak: "it was a corporate decision based on the fact that Rank didn't want any second-run cinemas." At a time when most cinemas were closing in the face of falling patronage, this seemed a 'rank' decision in the dictionary sense of the word. David Larkin believes the closure was distinctly unfair, as he recalls healthy audiences from the time he arrived in 1955 right up to its end. Early on in his employment, he remembers *Doctor In The House* breaking the cinema's box office record. And only a few weeks before it closed, a screening of *High Society* pulled in considerable audiences. It was a similar picture throughout David's time in the projection box: "During the weekday evenings, we still used to get 400 to 500 people, with Saturdays full down to the front row." Full was 1,600 occupied seats, and every one of them was occupied at the weekly Saturday morning matinées, producing slightly starker memories here for David: "Just imagine the noise of sixteen hundred kids!"

In spite of the great capacity of the Cavendish, 'no matter where you sat, you could see the screen'. But for David, that wasn't the only fine feature of the Cavendish: "It had the personal touch. Harold Hall always wore evening dress, welcomed the patrons in and wished them farewell as they went. He was a great man who won so much devotion. Very few staff left, and we had a lot of regular patrons." The closure hit Harold Hall hard, as David recalls: "It upset him considerably. It had been his life. I remember entering his room when he must have just received the news about the decision to close, because he was sat in his chair, crying. He was a broken man." Harold was eventually re-employed at the Derby Odeon, and then the Burton Odeon.

Worse still, although the Cavendish was put up for sale, with reports that it was due to become either a bingo hall or bowling alley, the demolition men moved in. David Larkin carries the scant consoling knowledge that "the Cavendish was so well built, it was damned hard to knock down."

1960 was a desperately sad year for closures in Derby. Its two longest-serving cinemas shut their doors, having each provided half a century of film entertainment. The Black Prince went out in the Cavendish style with a special charity screening, a souvenir programme, and more cries of *For He's A Jolly Good Fellow* – for the outgoing manager Edgar Duckworth. The Black Prince bowed out, proclaiming in its programme that it had been 'a pioneer of screen entertainment for 50 years'. Certainly, Edgar Duckworth's father Joshua was one of the founding fathers of the cinema industry, and Edgar had continued in the business. He had two spells as the owner of the Empire and, although the boast in the brochure that he was 'one of the first to introduce "Talkies" to Britain 1928' didn't refer to Derby, he did ensure that the Empire (renamed the Black Prince) became only the fourth cinema in Britain to install CinemaScope. However, owing to wrangles in the trade, the Black Prince began to lose many of the most popular releases to the town's Odeon, and audiences shrunk. Mention must be made – as it was in the souvenir programme – of two audience members, Mr J.A.Foulkes and Mr J.C.Shepherd, who patronised the Empire every week – except 1914-18 when war service called – for the 50 years of the cinema's life. 'The Police' were also thanked in the Acknowledgments, 'for their long arm that has

reached inside the Cinema on occasions and been friendly and helpful at all times', although 'drivers of cars parked outside may not agree'. There were also good wishes to the courting couples who had enjoyed the 'secluded hospitality of our back rows', with the added comment that they have been 'the only people, perhaps, who at the end of a performance of one of our less good films, have gone out quite happy.'

Amidst the light-heartedness of the closing brochure, there was the usual air of sad resignation that a fine, long-standing entertainment venue was to disappear, but there was a positive note in the message to the patrons from Edgar Duckworth and son David: 'Almost every Cinema, when it closes, tries to fade away quietly and be forgotten quickly. Happily, in our case the old makes way for the new at once'. The 'new' was the Duckworth Square shopping precinct. Cinema pioneer he may have claimed to be, but Edgar and his son David had both recently returned from America where they had studied in 'real estate' and 'building developments'. It was obvious where their future lay. It wasn't in the cinema business anymore. Derby's first shopping precinct – Duckworth Square – was developed, with a time capsule of the Black Prince history laid under the foundations of the new venture. Commerce has not been kind to Duckworth Square. Indeed, given the sad way the precinct has virtually been abandoned to decay, that time capsule may well be unearthed long before the wishes of that pioneering cinema family.

Derby's first purpose-built cinema – the Midland Electric – disappeared with much less grace and no ceremony, save for a small staff party. Regular attenders at this much-loved picture theatre, with its handsomely-appointed interior (preserved right up to the day of its demise) may still rue the indifference which seemed to greet the announcement of its closure. In 1957, it looked as if the cinema's survival was ensured with new proprietors modernising the frontage, redecorating the interior, and announcing its new name – Ritz – in blue neon. A year later, the cinema screened the Derby première of the MGM musical *Gigi*, but one big film did not a revival make. The cinema then made itself known as the Continental Ritz, and screened foreign films. A bold, but futile and fateful move. The life was draining out of the cinema, and the announcement in the *Derby Evening Telegraph* by the manager that the Ritz was to close 'some time during the next seven weeks' caused hardly a splutter of protest. Many generations held dear memories of the 'Babbo', but no one seemed to cherish its preservation. Unlike today, the local civic society would not have recognised the need to protect this piece of heritage. Almost as a last, cruel campaigning cry by the building itself, a wall of the cinema collapsed during demolition, killing a workman. The ignominy of its end was completed by the sight of items from the interior being offered for sale to the public on the Babington Lane pavement.

There was at least a protest a year later when the Derby Coliseum was forced to close, owing to the widening of the town's new inner ring road – the Coliseum was in the way. A compulsory purchase order was slapped on the cinema, and there was a noted irony to the title of the final film: *Orders Are Orders*. If there be truth in the statement 'out of sight, out of mind', then countless years of entertainment for tens of thousands of locals were bulldozed out of existence. Gladly, that saying doesn't ring true, but the hideous architecture that now squats on the site of this cinema temple is a degrading slight to the many old Coliseum customers who pass it by. Possibly just as insulting is that although in more recent years a modern pub was erected close to the Coliseum site, named itself the Coliseum, and which alluded to the cinema with the fixture of half a dozen photographs of the building, the proprietors sullied the tribute by erecting a pub sign that carried a painting, not of the Coliseum cinema, but the Coliseum in Rome.

Cinema's miserable demise continued apace. With almost each succeeding year through the 1960s, a noted Derbyshire picture house shut its doors. In the same year as the Derby Coliseum, the Heanor Cosy closed. A year later, 1962, the Chaddesden Majestic gave up the struggle, with the manager muttering his despair at the apathy of the locals. In 1963, the Ilkeston New Theatre bowed to bingo, as did the Long Eaton Scala a year later. A year later, another Ilkeston cinema closed – the Kings. It was a sad passing for young Mick Caphill who, even in the late 1950s, found in the local cinema a magical escape from the deprivations of his domestic life: "The Kings was a big, super cinema with a massive screen you could lose yourself in. I used to come home from school, have a quick tea, and nip into the Kings. It smelt good, looked good, had a lovely atmosphere and an air of luxury. At the time, our house didn't have hot water, let alone a bathroom or toilet." But Mick knew the end was nigh, when he would look around him and sometimes see only three or four other faces peering at the screen. For a cinema of over 1,400 seats, the vast emptiness must have been dispiriting.

In the 1960s, cinemas were invariably seen as prime sites for supermarkets. Thus was the fate of the Alfreton Odeon in 1964. The cinema staff, like long-time projectionist Harold Oliver, were crestfallen at having to say farewell to a cinema that had long enjoyed a reputation for its attractive Tudor-style

frontage, palatial auditorium and, of course, its succession of memorable films (as well as variety shows). It must have been a more bitter blow to see all trace of the cinema vanquished in the name of 1960s-style 'progress'.

A similar fate befell the Derby Odeon a year after the Alfreton Odeon, with British Home Stores purchasing the building. Poor Harold Hall, the cinema manager who had shed tears at the passing of the Cavendish only five years previous, had to preside over another closure.

Astonishingly, within two years of the Derby Odeon closing down, a new cinema opened, the first to be built in Derbyshire for almost 30 years. The Compton Group moved in to little ol' Derby to build 'England's newest and most luxurious cinema' – the Superama. According to Carl Chesworth, who became the projectionist at the new cinema on Colyear Street, Compton had beforehand dealt in 'trashy, seedy sex films, even milder than soft porn'. It had decided to clean up its act, and become an exhibitor of quality film in matching surroundings. "The original Compton plan" says Carl, "was to build the perfect cinema, with all the latest technical innovations, and great attention to details like sightlines, seats, drapes and acoustics." Compton had already opened a similar cinema in Birmingham, and the company's strategy involved a year-long study of that operation, with a view to correcting any noticeable faults or flaws, ready for the Derby opening. Similar studies were to continue in Derby, with a view to improving the cinema building yet further in Sheffield. It would appear that here was an arm of the cinema business which had seen picture houses deteriorate, and decided that to return to the pinnacle of luxury and comfort would result in an according return in custom.

But Compton had even more ambitious plans. Its intention was to screen Cinerama films (note the variation on the cinema's title). Cinerama, invented in 1952, introduced an extra-wide screen involving three electronically-synchronized projectors which put the picture on the wall in three sections. The enveloping images thrust the viewer dizzyingly into the action. I remember seeing the first Cinerama story film – *How The West Was Won* – in a special circus-style touring big top. The one exhilarating Cinerama effect I still remember was the ride down the rapids. But I also recall saying to my Mum and Dad – to borrow an Eric Morecambe phrase – 'you can see the joins'. The splits in the screen were noticeably fuzzy. The lines wobbled a bit, too. Soon after, with this imperfection in mind, the single-lens Cinerama was introduced but, by all accounts, the effect was not quite the same. As Leslie Halliwell commented,

Drive-In

I enjoyed a new experience at the end of 1994 – I spent over two hours in the dark of a cinema car park. This sensation might sound akin to watching a plank warp, but as I happened to be attending Derby's first drive-in movie, I can mark it down as a memorable movie-going moment, albeit with reservations. The Derby UCI certainly celebrated its sixth birthday in a novel and properly cinematic way, with screenings of both *The Lion King* and *Jurassic Park*.

Naturally, we couldn't replicate the romantic atmosphere of American drive-ins as depicted in the movies, with wild, willowy youngsters having a snog-fest in open-top Buicks under starlit skies; after all, this was Derby Cattle Market in early December, and in my apology for a Buick, my 'date' for the night – eight-year-old Helena – kept asking her dad for more popcorn and a bigger share of the blanket.

From where we sat, watching *The Lion King* (about 200 yards back), we both agreed the size of the drive-in screen was disappointingly small, with dark images difficult to decipher, but we felt compensated by the quality of sound, piped directly into the car speakers through tuning the radio into a dedicated frequency. Here was one instance where no cinema-going whingers could complain about the volume of the film: it was totally within their control!

I don't think I could become a drive-in addict; cinema is a communal experience, lamentably lost when the audience is cooped up in cars. But if there is a next time, I'll hire a Buick and take my wife.

---

it was "virtually indistinguishable from Cinema-Scope except for the higher definition resulting from using wider film."

The Superama never got around to showing Cinerama films. The screen had yet to be widened sufficiently anyway, and because the concept had all but died by the time the cinema opened, the words 'counter' and 'productive' must have come to mind. Curiously, according to Carl Chesworth, the widening of the screen would have involved the covering of emergency exits.

So was this entire operation all a bit cock-eyed and ill-thought out? Not if you walked into the place. Although the small, modern frontage might have produced a wave of indifference in the picture palace purist, no one could fail to be impressed by the auditorium. In design alone, Derby's Superama would outdo any of today's multiplexes. Its 'oyster-shell' shaped auditorium ensured that none of the ultra-comfortable 650 seats was more than 73 feet from the huge curved screen screen (according to the seat manufacturers Rank Audio Visual, the sheer luxury of the chairs 'makes you feel you could stay all night'), and also made the auditorium acoustically sound and optically superb. As the souvenir opening programme pointed out, there were 'no pillars or other encumbrances'. The decor was 'subdued' to 'emphasise the gentle intimacy', which included attractive gold fibreglass curtains sweeping round the whole of the side walls and proscenium. The whole

effect would be rounded off by a series of coloured lighting and 'manipulated hues'. There was attention also paid to the quality of the projection system. The sound system was a particularly proud feature, attaining 'the highest possible fidelity', and with a dynamic range 'capable of reproducing the extremes of the slightest whisper to the roar of a jet aircraft'. According to Olive Freer, who eventually became manageress: "Ours was the first cinema to have six-track stereo sound. Some people reckoned we had the best sound in the country."

According to Dr Leslie Knopp, the consultant on the Superama's design and equipment, his brief was 'to prepare designs and specifications not only to comply with all the demands of the latest techniques of cinematography, but to anticipate as far as possible the developments likely to take place in the next decade'. However, the Derby Superama didn't see out a whole decade. For all its technical excellence, supreme comfort and lavish decor, the Superama could not sustain its policy of bringing, as it announced, 'the best films in the world'.

The Superama opened with *Khartoum*, and it was obvious the emphasis was to be on quality, as the opening programme announced two forthcoming attractions: *Othello* starring Laurence Olivier, and Fellini's *La Boheme*. "Audiences at first were brilliant" says Carl Chesworth, citing highlights like *Dr Zhivago*, *Ice Station Zebra*, *Anne of A Thousand Days*, *A Man For All Seasons*, and a few James Bond pictures. David Wigley remembers seeing some memorable rock music films – George Harrison's *Concert for Bangla Desh*, Emerson Lake and Palmer's *Pictures At An Exhibition*, the Strawbs *Brave New World*, and *Woodstock*. "Being in stereo and on a wide screen, it was terrific."

The cinema also earnt a reputation for giving long runs to epic dramas and musicals, the most notable being *The Sound Of Music*, which ran for half a year. Audiences turned up in their numbers throughout the six months. One female patron received a bouquet on the occasion of her 100th visit. Spare a thought, though, for projectionist Carl Chesworth, who still does not question the quality of *The Sound Of Music*, but did grow a trifle weary of one screening after another for 26 weeks: "We couldn't even show trailers for forthcoming films. There weren't any. After a while, the highlight of the week was the new commercials arriving." I won't record Carl's reaction when he heard the news that *The Sound Of Music* was returning for another ten weeks.

If a film of the evergreen popularity of *The Sound Of Music* had been released every six months, the Derby Superama could still be around today. But Carl points to 'booking problems'. Basically, as part of a small cinema circuit, premium quality films were not available all the time. The cinema regularly screened re-issues (*Oklahoma, Round The World In 80 Days, Jungle Book*) and little-known films of uncertain worth. "We never showed to an empty audience" says Carl Chesworth, "but we got close to it. We screened *My Fair Lady* to two people. Mind you, it was Christmas Eve." The take-over of Compton by the Rank Organisation (which controlled the Odeon circuit) in 1970 widened the cinema's choice of film releases, but it had actually sounded the death-knell for the newly-renamed Odeon Pennine: four years later, the Gaumont on London Road – which was re-named the Odeon in 1965 – was tripled. In hindsight, in the uncertain climate of the time, Rank had made a choice. In 1975 came a flurry of headlines, starting with:

CINEMA INTO DISCO MOVE CAUSES ROW

Rank had applied for planning permission to convert the Odeon Pennine into a nightspot. However, Derby Borough Council Planning sub-committee refused permission, with Councillor John Christophers declaring that "removal of the cinema would be detrimental to the entertainment communities – it has always shown high quality films." Letters appeared in the local paper: Mrs Stauton of Chaddesden defended the cinema for being the only one in town to offer easy wheelchair access and cited 'another case of the minority having to suffer'; 'Insomnia' of Derby voiced concern about the state of noise that already existed in the Colyear Street area;

Mrs Williamson of Chaddesden agreed, but suggested the provision of an ice rink; R.J.England pointed out that 'The Odeon Pennine is one of the best cinemas in the Midlands', and that it must remain open.

Avid local cinema-goer Doug Hodges went further, describing it as 'the finest cinema in the British Isles – in its acoustics, presentation, courteous staff and projection system'. Doug was the most vigorous campaigner for the retention of the cinema, and won much support in the local press, with a commentator in the *Derby Trader* arguing that 'The Pennine is the only cinema in the town where you still feel you are out for the evening. The surroundings are pleasant, there's a nice bar to use during the interval, and the whole atmosphere is one where you feel they actually want you there. It's like the old days when it was a real treat to go to the pictures of an evening.' However, the columnist's fears were being confirmed: 'As soon as Rank bought the Pennine from the private firm which built it and turned it into such an attractive place, I had the foreboding that it wouldn't remain as it was very long.' However, the argument was made that the Pennine's recent run of repeats, minority-taste movies and sex films wasn't helping the cinema. Doug Hodges' contention was this: if the Pennine reverted to a policy of screening top quality films that he believed the local public wished to see, the cinema would no longer be, as Rank had announced, 'uneconomic'.

Doug Hodges wrote a long series of pleading letters to Rank chairman Sir John Davis. Their contents reveal a desperate, lone voice encountering complete corporate intransigence. Rank's public relations officer Chris Moore made suitably diplomatic noises, claiming he was 'as disturbed as anyone' over the imminent closure, but he also voiced company-speak phrases like 'economic necessity'. Doug Hodges raised the probability of a petition, but Chris Moore pointed out that 'the only way the cinema could have been saved was by people paying their money at the door. They didn't, and the Odeon Pennine has to go'.

It went soon after the Borough Council, in a turnaround, approved the recommendation that permission be granted for the Pennine's conversion into a nightclub. Doug Hodges called the sub-committee members 'barmy', while Councillor Mick Walker claimed there had been only two objections to the cinema closure. He also spoke of 'wide open spaces' when he had visited the cinema on recent occasions. "It is regrettable" he said, "because the facilities at this cinema are excellent." And therein lies the nub of Doug's dismay: that a cinema which could still boast of being the finest in the country was to meet such a woeful, wasteful end after only seven years. The cinema's staff and regular patrons will also have felt sadness for the popular and highly-respected manageress Olive Freer. "A great lady who loved the business" says Carl Chesworth. And it was more than the patrons who appreciated the way she ran the business: "I remember several letters of praise from the Council after officers came to spot check the cinema."

In one of his peremptory letters to Doug, Sir John Davis of Rank said the company's exhibition policy was determined by public requirements and he had little doubt that multi-auditoria would be the way in which the cinema would develop in the future in this country. Notwithstanding his company's cruel elimination of the Pennine, there was a case to be made for so-called 'twinning' and 'tripling'. For example, while the Superama ran *The Sound Of Music* in its one auditorium for six months, the recently-tripled Nottingham Odeon could afford to let it run for as long as there was demand – two and a half years, in fact – happy in the knowledge that other film releases could be shown in its other two auditoria. But, although Sir John's prediction was to prove correct, it so happened that in Derbyshire's case, the 'twinning' and 'tripling' of existing cinemas only delayed their demise (with the sole exception of the Matlock Ritz).

The first cinema to see its auditorium split was the Belper Ritz, in 1971. Ivan Varney, who still works at the Ritz (although it's now a bingo house) believes it was only the second cinema in the country to be twinned (after the Odeon, Nottingham). The Ritz had been struggling as a single auditorium cinema. Successes in the 1960s had been few, although Ivan carries a cherished memory of the incredible night in 1969 when *Jungle Book* opened: "I was told to get to the cinema early. When I arrived, there were so many people on King Street, I thought there had been an evacuation because of fire. Somehow I managed to find a space for my little car in Green Lane, but there was a bigger problem trying to get inside the cinema. There was no way through the front door. Eventually, I had to be squeezed through the window on the ladies' toilet. The cinema then held 555 seats, but we actually accommodated 598 people; as soon as a seat became empty – because some of the smaller children got fed up and were taken out – we filled it, even though the film itself had started running. A the end of the night, the manager was especially delighted with the ice-cream takings of £51, which was remarkable considering an ice-cream was only 9d" (that's the equivalent of 1,360 ice creams, more than two ice-creams per person!).

But come 1971's twinning, 555 seats did not divide down into two roughly equal-sized auditoria. The conversion only allowed for two small studios, each seating only 75. Although there were two larger-size auditoria when Matlock Ritz was twinned – 200 in the 'Major' screen, 100 in the 'Minor' – regular Diane Carnell suddenly turned claustrophobic: "The smallest auditorium was so tiny that with the huge red drapes around you, it felt like you were sitting in a coffin."

I appreciate her point. My experience of sitting in the Belper Ritz auditoria was akin to watching a large television in an overcrowded sitting room. Also, more often than not, that room felt less than crowded. The townsfolk hardly embraced the new cinema, with support sporadic throughout the 1970s. "Sometimes" recalls Ivan Varney, "a film was so poorly attended that we dropped it in the middle of the week to take another one." This happened with the musical *Oliver!* Musicals always performed well in Belper. But not *Oliver!*, even though it arrived only a fortnight after its Derby release. On Monday, two people turned up. It went downhill from there. One person came through the doors on Tuesday. The film was removed on Wednesday when not one solitary cinema-goer showed up.

One account suggests the twinning operation was a crude affair. Bernard Goodwin, who worked at various cinemas in Amber Valley, did some relief projectionist's work at the Ritz and discovered that one screen was running on a 16mm projector: "I remember seeing the *Battle Of Britain* where the grain in the film was so pronounced, it was like watching a home movie. It wasn't even on a proper screen – they used plasterboard, painted white. Even when they got CinemaScope, it was made up of two painted boards suspended from the ceiling. Because they weren't supported at the bottom, they used to wave. It was pathetic."

At the end of 1974, the Derby Odeon on London Road reopened as a triple cinema. Again, the conversion markedly reduced the cinema's original capacity, with 888 seats in the old circle area, and 138 seats occupying sites where the stalls once stood. The fact that the best opening attractions the Odeon could find included *The Island At The Top Of The World*, *That Riviera Touch* and *Confessions of a Window Cleaner* reveals the paucity of product at that time, although at least the element of choice provided the cinema with a lifeline.

There was a similar nondescript line-up of films when, four years later, the ABC (formerly the Regal) in East Street reopened as a triple screen cinema. *Convoy*, *International Velvet* and *Bilitis* were shown in ABC 1, 2 and 3 (553, 382 and 217 seats respectively). By this time, Mike Smith was the manager. He felt the conversion was vital, even though the cinema enjoyed some memorable nights beforehand: "You could sometimes stand there on the steps, with 1,600 people watching a blockbuster, and the place still had that atmosphere of old." But there were simply not enough of those nights: "We just could not go on as a single unit. The building wasn't paying for itself. The fabric of the auditorium had deteriorated. You couldn't heat the cinema adequately. With so few people in the place, you could take the chill off, but that was about it. Even with the heating on, you still needed heat from bodies! Also, the thin audiences were as dispiriting for the staff as well as the audience. So I had no complaints about the tripling. It was the right idea."

Right idea it may have been, but such was the state of the film industry at the time that instead of one sub-standard picture being screened, the cinema got three. There were the odd exceptions: "Blockbusters like *Jaws, Earthquake*, and *Grease* sold themselves, but we struggled with most of the films, and to sell them we had to be publicity conscious the whole time." Mike came a cropper with several publicity stunts, too, all involving the personal appearance of animals to promote certain pictures: "I was jumped on by a tiger, bitten by two lions and kicked by a llama." The tiger incident – connected with a screening of *When The North Wind Blows* – was a close call: "I was next to the Radio Derby reporter who was busy interviewing the tiger when a paper bag floated in the wind. The tiger spotted the bag, and jumped up to catch it. The beast landed on my shoulder. It was frightening for a moment because, basically, you have three types of tigers, ranging from the miniature cub to the grand elder. I got the one in between – the sort of tiger that is big enough to worry about."

Sometimes publicity came much easier. For a screening of *The Exorcist*, usherettes were issued with smelling salts: "It was a gimmick, but it worked" In the end, it proved to be more important than a gimmick, as Mike remembers "bodies fainting everywhere." He also claims to have had the first nationwide casualty of this controversial demonic drama: a man collapsed at the sight of a particularly horrific moment and, on falling, hit his head on the seat. An ambulance was called for, and the wounded patron was rushed to hospital, gaining for the ABC a welcome spread of national newspaper headlines.

Soon after his arrival at the cinema, Mike Smith encouraged the younger element by rejuvenating the Saturday morning ABC Minors shows. Along with the film shows, he supervised a disco session, sing-songs, birthday spots, and various prize-winning contests involving road safety, Easter bonnets, yo-yos, pets and dancing. As part of the publicity for the Saturday shows, the staff and children combined to create a carnival float featuring characters from the various matinée films. The float won a prize, and later, so did Mike, or, as he was referred to then by the children, 'Uncle Mike': he received a certificate and cash award from EMI Cinemas for 'outstanding achievement in the promotion of minors' matinées for 1975'.

That was three years before the cinema was tripled. As soon as the three-screen complex was in place, the matinées were forced to close. Three years after that, Mike Smith left, somewhat disillusioned with the business, claiming it was no longer populated by showmen like him: "The cinema was being run by accountants, not entertainment people." He left to successfully pursue his ambition of running a pub, where he could also spend more time with his wife and family. But Mike Smith had also had enough of the cinema: "I was working long, crazy hours – 9am to 11pm – and I was on call even when I was at home. It became more than a job; it was a way of life. But the problem with that way of life was that the magic was going out of it; I hadn't got the interest I had when I first came in." Certainly, this was not quite the same spirited showman who, on joining the Derby ABC eight years earlier, told the *Derby Evening Telegraph*: "I just get a kick out of entertainment – doesn't everyone?"

By the turn of the 1980s, fewer people were getting a kick out of cinema entertainment. Steven Spielberg had signalled his arrival – with *Jaws* grossing around $400 million worldwide – and George Lucas had broken that box office record with *Star Wars*, but there was a downside to these otherwise accomplished blockbusters: they served to whip up enthusiasm in the industry for more pictures that catered for a new thrill-seeking young audience. The musical had all but died out, along with the epic. A tiresome clutch of sequels appeared – invariably weak, crass, crude cash-ins. From a figure of 327 million in 1965, annual admissions nationwide plummeted to 124 million in 1975, and only two years later had reduced further to 103 million (less than 2 million patrons a week, compared with 31 million in 1946).

Cinemas continued to close. The Chesterfield Odeon seemed buoyant in 1975; it was effectively a multi-purpose complex, with a bar and ballroom, plus exhibition facilities. But the death-knell had been rung by the turn of the 1980s when the Rank owners published a list of 29 'unprofitable' and 'unviable' cinemas. The Odeon, Chesterfield was on that list. It shut down in October 1981.

Projectionist Peter Thompson presided over the last couple of years' screenings at the Ashbourne Elite, which finally gave up the ghost in 1976. By

The Heanor Empire between the wars. The cinema flourished for years but eventually met a sad end in the 1980s. Heanor Local History Society.

Site of the Empire, Heanor. Andy Wilson.

then, the cinema was only showing films three times a week. The final screening – of a western – was a painfully disappointing moment for Peter: "We drew an audience of only ten people. Nobody seemed to care that our one remaining cinema was going."

As manager of the Heanor Empire, Bernard Goodwin felt the same icy blast of indifference, neglect and apathy, not that he blamed the townsfolk totally: "Towards the end of the Empire days, we had to take films that Heanor folk weren't interested in, like *The Lion In Winter* or *Dr Faustus* – that drew half a dozen per night for the entire week. Throughout the 1960s and 1970s, we plodded on, with the odd success, like *Chitty Chitty Bang Bang*, and the *James Bond* and *Carry On* films." But by the end of the 1970s, the Empire was even struggling with apparently big attractions. Val Sisson remembers going to see the first *Star Trek* picture: "I had to wait to see if any other customers showed up; you see, they needed at least six people before they'd run the film. Eventually, we just got enough."

But, clearly, just enough patrons to run a film each night was far from enough to run a cinema for a year. Throughout the early 1980s, the Heanor Empire had only its occasional spurt of patronage, leading some people to comment that the last advertised film *Spasms* was cruelly appropriate. In actual fact, although the film's title was set out on the cinema front – and stayed there for several years afterwards, as if to indicate the involuntary nature of its death –

the film never arrived. Bernard Goodwin was manager at the time: "Our last film was *Legend of Frenchie King*. *Spasms* was supposed to arrive on the Wednesday ready for a Thursday evening screening, so I put up the title last thing on Wednesday. A 'phone call with the renters revealed we wouldn't be getting the programme, because we hadn't paid our bills. It was nothing to do with me. Head Office told me to go and fetch the film from Birmingham. When I refused, saying: 'that's not my job', I was told: 'that's it, you're finished'. I said to him: 'Are you sacking me?' He replied: 'We're sacking everybody'. 'Everybody' also meant the staff of the cinemas at Alfreton, Retford and several others. About 12 in all." The *Spasms* sign was thus even more appropriate in the sense that its end came with – to quote a dictionary definition of 'spasm' – 'a sudden burst of activity', which brought the fall of the Empire.

A few years before, a Southern businessman with cinema in his blood came up to Derbyshire, hunting for old picture houses, with a view to taking one or more over. His name was Sam Lavington. He looked over the Heanor Empire, but the place was so dilapidated, he felt it was uneconomic to run. "I remember recommending we turn on the heating one night, to which the manager replied: 'We can't. There's a hole in the tank'."

Sam was biding his time, running a Derby video store. One day, Harry Greatorex walked in. The two got talking. Harry was known in Ripley as 'Mr Entertainment' (even though, in his early entrepreneurial days, he turned down a pop group called The Beatles because they were too pricey at £150). At the time he met Sam Lavington, Harry was intent on ending his lease on the Ripley Hippodrome. A 'profitable' chat resulted in Sam taking the Hippo off Harry for £1,000.

Why take over a cinema in 1983? Had this man not felt the wind of change with the onset of the video boom? After all, he was part of it. "I felt that unless I owned a cinema, my life would somehow be incomplete, so I took the plunge." Sam was not content to sit back and soak up the profits, because there simply weren't going to be any in this climate. Not unless he made a big effort. "I talked with the audience, listened to what they had to say, told them what I wanted to do with the place, and we made a go of it."

Sam received a vital early fillip: "I will always remember driving into Ripley Market Place and seeing a long queue of people, stretching all the way to the old clock where the Town Hall was. I wondered what was going on, and it was only when I went further round the corner that I realised it was a queue for my old cinema! The film was *Ghostbusters*. That spurred me on for the next seven years."

But Sam Lavington admits he was trying to recreate a lost age. In the course of our meeting, he quoted that beautiful phrase to describe a cinema – 'An Acre of Seats in a Garden of Dreams'. But that referred to a London picture palace; and it was long gone. Sam's starry eyes clouded his vision: "I did the best I could. I put in a new screen, decorated the foyer, and put in new projection equipment and Dolby stereo. I reduced the seating from 500 to 350 so that no one would ever complain of neck cramps again."

Sam was keeping his head above water; enough not to splutter, and just enough to feel buoyant, because in 1986 he took over the recently revamped Screen Long Eaton: "It was a clean, bright , modern place, and popular with the townsfolk because of that. In some ways it was a forerunner of the multiplex ideal – giving audiences comfort and cleanliness."

Sam now saw his own metaphoric omens. "I now thought I was on a rollercoaster, but without realising that what goes up has to come down. At the time, I lived in Heage, and was reminded by someone locally that the Belper Ritz might be worth taking over. I'm afraid that was the start of the demise. I put too much money into a small cinema, and it was simply not going to give me the returns."

Sam reckons that, at the time, the Ripley and Long Eaton cinemas were 'running like racehorses' but with the Belper cinema, he had bought 'a lame duck'. Put more prosaically: "Ripley and Long Eaton were ongoing businesses, but with Belper, I had to make a standing start. I poured most of my revenue into Belper, while draining the revenue of the other two cinemas. I made ground, but it wasn't enough."

To salvage his operation, Sam tried to sell the Belper cinema, with an entrepreneurial dash: "A flat came with the cinema, so I advertised the flat at a cost of £4,500, adding that 'your own personal cinema' came free with the purchase. I got a lot of national press publicity, and coverage on both regional TV news magazines."

He got a buyer, but having left this lame duck behind, his own future was crippled by two unforeseen factors: the new Poll Tax – "the favourable rates I had at Ripley were quadrupled" – and the abstruse politics of leaseholding. In spite of the community charge, Sam Lavington still saw a future for the Ripley Hippodrome. But when he sought to purchase the Ripley Hippodrome following the death of leaseholder Harry Greatorex, a fundamental problem arose: "We couldn't find out who actually owned the place. We never heard from anyone. Time went on. I began to struggle to keep up the rental payments. Eventually, the executors stepped in and took over the building. We couldn't negotiate with them, because they wouldn't let themselves be known."

Having already lost the Screen Long Eaton, Sam drifted out of the business. All he has left is a large album of photos and cuttings, along with remembrances of the small town cinema's 'friendship and warmth'. Sam Lavington prides himself on "making myself known to the customers as often as I could, taking their tickets, selling them sweets. When Mrs Brown brought Johnny to our cinema, the girl selling confectionery already knew that he preferred white chocolate to dark. That's what's missing now – the personal touch."

One could mischievously argue that the personal touch was only achieved because the person count at the cinema was low. The small town cinemas had been engaged in a desperately long, losing fight for patronage. Worse still, patrons had long been engaged in gazing at a deterioration both around the auditoria and up on the screen. For some cinemas, a bingo takeover was a merciful release. The reason the Chaddesden Gloria didn't get the same bulldozer treatment meted out to the Majestic in the same suburb was through receiving the sign of the 'Lucky Seven'. Eventually, though, even bingo foundered here in Chaddesden, before Ladbrokes took it over, installing not only state-of-the-art bingo equipment, but also two mini-cinemas. This refreshing faith in the ailing cinema business was misplaced. Ladbrokes closed it down at the end of 1982, with the low turn out for the last picture show a sorry reflection of its parlous patronage. With only a few dozen seats filled for the two films – including *Herbie Goes Bananas* – the *Derby Evening Telegraph* headlined the story

'Nobody goes Bananas as cinema closes'. Manageress of the previous six years, Delia Cutts, said she had no argument against the decision, but admitted 'an empty feeling'. That empty feeling had affected most Derbyshire cinemas by the turn of the 1980s. Even the Derby ABC: converted into a triple seat cinema in 1978, with only one other cinema in town, its future must have seemed assured. But the bright new manager who breezed in to town – Peter Watkinson – encountered a cinema that was 'rather run down'. Peter has an abiding memory of casting a dreary gaze on "that dreadful ABC purple paint. It was painted dark so it didn't have to be cleaned." He couldn't stand the thought of a future surrounded by purple, so he paid for paint out of petty cash (knowing his bosses wouldn't cough up). However, the job was never finished: "It was like repainting the Forth Bridge." Winning back audiences must have felt equally as onerous. Peter knew he was presiding over a decline. 1983 saw attendances plumb their lowest depths since records began. Peter Watkinson was born into the wrong age; he was a showman who hankered after the golden days. I was in the audience the night Peter revived the days of yore with a special Sunday evening screening of two Marilyn Monroe pictures, a few classic film trailers, a Pathé newsreel and a live organist. ABC Screen 2 was packed. The sign of a revival? Unfortunately not.

On Saturday, 14 July 1984, the cinema screened a further classic film – *That's Entertainment*. But this musical was the ABC's swansong. Like the Coliseum around the corner, the East Street cinema cruelly became a victim of city planners' progress rather than abject audience figures. The Eagle Centre development drive was at full throttle, and the ABC was in the way. However, there is little doubt that if attendances had been a picture of blooming health, the cinema would not have been killed off. As Peter Watkinson said at the time: "The majority of comments we've had (from people who had heard of the closure) are along the lines of 'what a shame it's going – we used to go a lot' but these people have never been since the ABC turned into a triple cinema. No wonder it's going."

Not one part of the old Regal survived. Cinema historian Sam Winfield pleaded for the preservation of the cinema frontage and suggested it be transferred to Crich Tramway Museum, as had happened to the old town Assembly Rooms frontage. Nothing came of it. At the time, a campaign was on to preserve the town's railway station. No similar campaign surfaced before the bulldozer moved in to East Street.

On the morning of Sunday, 15 July 1984, the Derby cinema scene was at its lowest ebb. The ABC's closure had not only cut three commercial screens at a stroke, but also reduced choice by three-quarters. Around the corner – at the London Road site which had, by 1983, become a 'sister' cinema to the East Street ABC – the three-screen complex had lasted less than a decade. The Derby Assembly Rooms enjoyed a brief fling with film, exploiting the emptying provision of big screen entertainment (and doing it rather well, with a massive screen and some well-chosen pictures).

A year before the ABC triple cinema shut, the new ABC Trocadero had been re-converted to the one single auditorium. Peter Watkinson moved in as manager as soon as the ABC East Street closed, and in trying to view the fresh climate in a positive way, he betrayed one of the reasons the climate had dampened, as he announced what the new single auditorium cinema meant: "Derby will now have top quality films because we won't be showing rubbish."

Although there had been a marked drop in the amount of quality product, the nub of the crisis was hidden in Peter's plea to the lapsed cinema-going audience to 'get out of their armchairs' to support Derby's one remaining commercial screen. The armchair had become its own single-seater cinema auditorium, and the audience sat in it was (perfectly) at home watching more films than ever – on video. There seemed to be no future for the British cinema.

However, there was a new kid in town – a town further down the M1, called Milton Keynes. A year after Derby lost its last triple-screen cinema, Milton Keynes gained a ten-screen one. Unbeknown to Derbyshire, it was to signal salvation.

Return From The Ashes
The multiplex, the Metro and the modern age

I stood on the dirt at Milton Keynes and my gut said: 'It's gonna work. And it's gonna work here in Derby too.

Millard Ochs, Chief Executive, AMC 1988

Our experience of the multiplex is that once people try it, they love it, and they come back

Ira Korff, Chief Executive, National Amusements, 1988

And there was popcorn in paradise

Ben M.Hall

THE TV boom produced countless cinema casualties. Two decades on, it was thought the video boom would see off any survivors. By the turn of the 1980s, video stores were sprouting up around Derbyshire in a manner reminiscent of the cinema-building programme of the 1920s. So, the prediction of a revival in cinema-building by the turn of the 1990s would have been viewed as foolish.

The quiet revolution began in 1985. At that time, a look at the US cinema scene would have revealed how such a revolution was possible. Energised by the success of the new multiplex format in the States, which had not simply arrested the cinema decline but actually turned it around, AMC – American Multi Cinemas – planned a UK strategy which started with The Point, Milton Keynes.

For the most part, the twinning and tripling of cinemas in Britain had simply supplied a drip for an ailing patient in intensive care. AMC gave the patient a new injection, but the serum carried with it a risk. "It was a huge gamble" says Steve Knibbs, managing director of the UK's UCI operation (AMC eventually evolved into UCI). "Looking at the cinema attendances of the time, The Point could have been the only multiplex in this country, and that would have been the end of it. We may well have moved inexorably into video, and the theatrical side to cinema presentation could have died. As it turned out, people were getting switched back on to film."

The trigger for that switch was *Ghostbusters*, a comedy blockbuster starring Bill Murray and Dan Ackroyd. Its ground-breaking special effects, irrev-erent humour, and crucial hit song woke up a dormant cinema audience. "*Ghostbusters* was a watershed" claims Steve Knibbs; "it claimed a mass audience interested in going to the cinema again."

So, if The Point was fortunate in its timing – with *Ghostbusters* allied to a general growth in the quality of film product – it can be seen as a stroke of luck which the UK multiplex network deserved (and Derby was to enjoy its own crucial good fortune four years later). After years of disintegrating audiences, it would have been a tragedy if the multi-cinema ideal began and ended in a Buckinghamshire new town, because AMC was offering a fresh start for the flagging cinema scene. The majority cinema-going audience of the time – 15 to 24-year-olds – had spent years sitting in decaying picture houses that effectively belonged to a different age. AMC was ready to exploit that audience by encouraging cinema-going as a habit rather than an occasional pursuit, with the hope that other age-groups would be tempted through the doors. And there lay the crux of AMC's hope: that potential cinema-goers would at least come through the doors, because once they came back out of those doors, they would have forgotten all previous picture house disapprobation.

Here was a brave but bright new world. The fortuitous opening time, coupled with company confidence, brought AMC success. "The place appealed" says Steve Knibbs; "It was comfortable, bright, airy, with wide seats. People were pleasantly surprised, and it was an instant hit." The Point was made.

A year later – 1986 – the Salford Quays complex opened. The following 12 months saw another three multiplex sites spring up. By the end of 1988, there were 14 sites. Numbers 13 and 14 belonged to Derby, the first city in the UK to house two multiplexes. There was no doubt that Derby was a prime potential site. At the start of 1988, the city had been reduced to one commercial screen cinema – the old Gaumont on London Road, now the Cannon – along with one independent film theatre, the Metro. A similar decimation had occurred in the rest of the county. The Chesterfield Regal and the Ilkeston Scala were the only cinemas left in their respective towns, and the only sizeable cinemas outside of Derby. Long Eaton, Matlock, Belper and Ripley had hung on to their more modestly-sized cinemas. With few remaining cinemas over the Staffordshire border, the state of the catchment area for a multiplex would have appeared encouraging.

Almost too encouraging. AMC (Texas) began construction work on 22 February 1988 on a five million pound scheme situated on Mansfield Road. A month later, I was being invited to another 'Ground Breaking' ceremony, for National Amusements (UK) Ltd, another American multi-cinema company (which, incidentally, invented the term 'multiplex'). On 22 March, work began on the Derby Showcase on the corner of Osmaston Park Road and Sinfin Lane

A question often asked is: how did Derby end up with two multiplexes at a time when many cities were still awaiting their first such complex? The simple truth is that neither company knew of each other's plans until it was too late, and even now, neither will admit to being second off the starting block. Steve Knibbs claims "history will show that the AMC site was the first to be signed and announced." National Amusements says 'we had already purchased our property and had begun

construction before AMC announced their plans to build a multiplex', and that the company was 'unaware of any other cinema operator planning to build a multiplex in Derby'.

By the time it was aware, National Amusements was already committed. It had conducted a market study which 'demonstrated that Derby had the demographics to support a modern multiplex'. That study also revealed that 'people in the Derby area had an unusually high per capita, meaning the number of times per year that a person will go to a movie'. National Amusements was also well pleased with its site: it was 'highly visible, had good access and was located within a densely populated area'. National Amusement's commitment was even more concrete in that it had purchased a freehold site: 'If we didn't continue our development we would still own our property; AMC could have terminated at any time'. Undoubtedly, if AMC had pulled out, it might have been viewed as defeatist and have damaged company confidence. One could contend that both companies were anxious not to lose face. As Steve Knibbs admits: "Two heads locked, and neither one would give way."

In the run-up to the respective openings at the end of 1988, I spoke with Millard Ochs, chief executive of AMC, and Ira Korff, chief executive of National Amusements. Both company chiefs boasted to me of their undeniable qualities as a cinema operation. Both spoke of their undying confidence in the future. Both have been proved right in their vision of Derby as a city which would rediscover the pleasure of cinema-going, although not all has turned out as predicted, and neither would have predicted the extraordinarily good fortune they experienced in their first summer of operation.

The former Art College building which houses the Derby Metro Cinema. **Julia Peck.**

Interior of the Metro Cinema showing the fine windows of the former college. **Julia Peck.**

Staff pictured at the opening of the Derby Showcase.

Millard Ochs shrugged off doubts as to the viability of a two-multiplex city by telling me of American cities with a population of only half a million which housed nine multiplexes. "But this is Derby", I cried, "people here now sit at home watching videos." "Yes, and there's a good reason for that" piped up Ira, "the cinemas here are lousy!" He had a point. He emphasised it, too, by revealing that video-viewing had never been very strong in the States, simply because they had good cinemas in place before the video scene tried to take a hold.

My own views on the impending impact of multiplexes were aired before a nation on a December edition of BBC TV's *Film 88*, after Barry Norman had cued in to a special report by asking us to 'turn our attention to the place that currently is the very centre of the cinema world. No, not New York, but Derby, where cinemas multiply at a rate to leave rabbits breathless with admiration. If the same sort of thing were to happen in similar towns around the country, it would revolutionise people's cinema-going habits'.

In other words, Derby had become a testing ground. Would it work in Derby? The 'Film Critic, BBC Radio Derby' came into vision. A personable fellow, if there ever looked one, but he was not about to endear himself to the local population tuned in, when he declared: "Somebody told me when I first arrived in this city that the people of Derby were 'none-bothered'. And there is just a little bit of apathy about everything. I can't put my finger on exactly what it is, but I do get that feeling." I ought to say that the 'somebody' was a respected local historian, so I felt qualified to make that comment, although under the glare of the TV camera, I wasn't able to phrase my statement in the more definite, desired way, namely by pointing in particular to the recent neglect of local cinema. I genuinely felt anxious about the future, as I went on to state that "too many people in this city have drifted away from the cinema, and they're sat at home, as we speak, watching their videos." But I did introduce a note of optimism: "If they (the multiplexes) can get people – particularly families – through the doors to see a film like *Who Framed Roger Rabbit?* (the AMC's opening film), then maybe both cinemas can make a go of it."

My terse closing statement was maybe not so optimistic. In answering the final big question: is Derby big enough for two multiplexes? I answered: "I doubt it." I need to point out that the rest of my sentence – "but I'd be happy to eat those words" – was left on the cutting-room floor. Nonetheless, my response was still not as definite as either Jeff Schnabel, director of operations, AMC, who said, albeit without a tone of enthusiasm: "In my opinion, it is", or Ira Korff, chief executive, National Amusements, who went the other way and said, quite forcibly: "Absolutely not."

Ira Korff was suffused with misplaced over-confidence in his own operation to the extent of arrogance, which led him to further state that "if one (Derby multiplex) closes, it certainly won't be us." For an experienced cinema businessman, Ira Korff had missed two factors which were more likely to sustain the viability of both multiplex operations. Firstly, and most crucially, although the multiplex sites were less than five miles apart, both occupied separate catchment areas. Secondly, encouraged by this realisation, both cinema giants were positioned to more effectively target their potential audience, with the Showcase looking to the southern side of the city, and the UCI to the north. One could toss in a third factor, and argue that the sheer prospect of the two giants lining up to do battle acted as a rallying call in the bid to outdo each other.

Where Ira Korff showed his acumen was the belief that 'Once a multiplex visitor, always a multiplex visitor'. This belief also stimulated the rival AMC operation pre-Point. As Steve Knibbs stated simply: "We knew people would come back if they tried us." To achieve this aim, the multiplex policy-makers

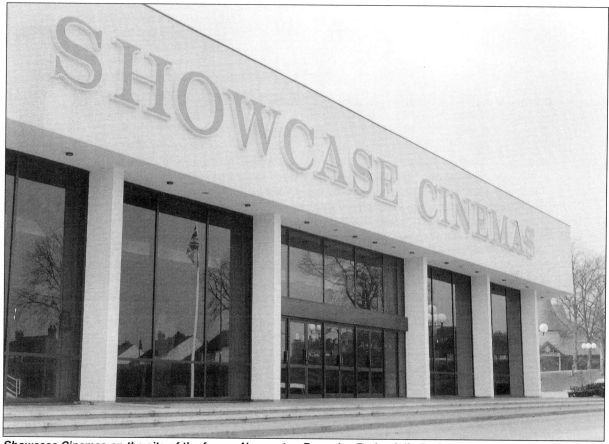

Showcase Cinemas on the site of the former Normanton Barracks, Derby. **Julia Peck.**

Take your pick. One of the two corridors leading to screens at the Showcase. **Julia Peck.**

decided they must spare no expense on comfort and convenience. They knew how vital it was to secure both the lapsed cinema-goers (who had largely joined the video-viewing generation), and the coming generation of potential picture-goers. Once inside, drawn by curiosity and/or a particular film, all had to be encouraged to return, having been made palpably aware that these new-fangled cinemas were a good deal more welcoming than the run-down picture houses that had long operated on a flea-pittance.

The convenience factor was immediately made evident outside – in the car park. Although the video boom saw off many an ailing cinema, it was largely the pull of TV that caused our cinemas to go to seed in the first place. But, as the last chapter indicated, the increase in car ownership also had its effect and, ironically, this is a factor that has enabled the modern multi-cinema to thrive. Up to the 1950s, the long-standing local cinema was – naturally or by design – easily accessible by bus. But as the years progressed, with increasingly less reliance on public transport as car travel rose, most existing cinemas became less favourably situated. The end-of-the-decade trend for out-of-town shopping parks was one also followed by the multiplexes, who looked to large conurbation sites where car space mattered more than bus routes. Ira Korff saw the 1,000 capacity Showcase car park as a vital factor: "It makes a real difference if there's no hassle involved in finding a parking space." The UCI was equally aware of the importance. As Steve Knibbs stated it: "People like things on their doorsteps these days; they don't want to travel far." And that includes the bother of walking to a cinema having parked the car several streets away. The 'drive' towards cinema as a family pursuit would also be enhanced by the ease of car parking.

Appearance and atmosphere were also vitally important. Although the standard Showcase exterior would have proved unexciting, the allure began just past the glass entrance doors. Visitors then beheld a vast, airy and impressive foyer (or 'lobby' as the company would term it). The 10,000 square feet would certainly have made an indelible impression on anyone who had visited any other cinema in the area and in any previous era. The marked modernity and comfortable ambience would have continued into the auditoria which, although plain and functional, had the added attraction of the cinema's renowned 'showcase': its custom-built 'rocking chair loungers'.

The attraction of the UCI (United Cinemas International took over from AMC only two weeks into the Derby operation) began outside. Any visitors approaching from the Derby end of Mansfield Road would have gazed initially on an uninspiring, square-boxed building. But as they swept down into the cinema's driveway, their eye would invariably have been caught by the laser light shooting across the prominent angled-glass, inverted 'V' frontage. The greater glitz of the UCI would also be mirrored in the foyer, considerably less cavernous than the Showcase, but a good deal more showy and, in the daylight hours, equally as airy, courtesy of the canopy of glass, with bright illuminated light taking over in the evenings. (Interestingly, the Showcase reception area, in spite of its colossal dimensions, has a quiet, subdued air, while the UCI's more compact space has more life and razzmatazz). Once into a UCI screen, customers would have occupied seats not quite as comfy as the Showcase rockers, although Millard Ochs described them to me as 'ergonomically-designed – like sitting in a Mercedes as compared with a Ford' (with cupholders on the arm), and the seating would have been similarly wide-spaced, in an auditorium providing the same air-conditioned, if spartan, splendour.

Both cinemas would have impressed with their automotive, state-of-the-art sound and projection systems. The quality of customer service was also out to be noticed straightaway, with bright, youthful staff on incentive schemes, groomed to smile and utter corporate phrases (at Showcase Cinemas I have glimpsed a poster on the staff side of the door leading to the foyer which carries a notice along the lines of: 'You are entering a customer area. Smile'. There are similar such guidelines posted up inside the UCI offices).

The Derby Showcase – 11 screens, 2,650 seats – opened on 18 November 1988. The Derby UCI – 10 screens, 2,000 seats – opened on 2 December 1988.

"It's a cinema revolution – with some risky financial aspects to it." So said Ira.

"It will determine the future of the multiplex age – if Derby is viable." Thus spoke Ochs.

Indeed, Derby was to become an important bench mark of the British multi-cinema scene. From here on, such was the cruciality of the situation that Derby even became the subject of constant discussion in Hollywood itself (at least according to British Film Institute chief Wilf Stevenson, who I spoke with during Derby's initial multiplex year).

Derby didn't let the multiplex scene down. A year on, an estimated one million customers had come through the doors. The American ideal had arrived. So had the American language: Millard Ochs translated the fact that first-year attendances had showed equal success for Showcase and UCI in announcing 'we're splitting the gross'. National Amusements then declared a policy whereby its official audience figures were never published, but promotions executive Elisa Lefer made public the

Barbara Windsor helps Councillor Les Shepley, the Mayor of Derby, open the UCI in 1988. Derek Wales.

company's pleasure and, to equal extent, relief: "We've injected a shot of life into the cinema blood here."

However, there seemed little apparent spillage of blood as the two giants had slugged it out in that first, fateful year. I was expecting at least a spot of mud-slinging, especially as Millard Ochs had professed to me that 'the competition will get dirty'. It appeared not. "No, it was never dirty" says Steve Knibbs. And it never will be: "We simply put ourselves on display for the public, and let the public choose. We work hard on promotion and our good service policy. We spend a lot of time on training, and listening to the public, asking them what they want and acting on it."

Where UCI and Showcase differed most noticeably was in the area of extra provision. Basically, the UCI laid on extras; the Showcase didn't. UCI believed that to make the cinema visit more of an evening out, they should provide a bar and fast food restaurant. Showcase, however, viewed these not as attractions but as 'detractions', adding: "We will focus on what we know best – how to run a cinema." Ira Korff must have spotted my doubting gaze over this issue as he then announced, with a twinkle in his eye: "we don't need to lay on a fast food restaurant because McDonalds follow us everywhere. You watch them open on a site close by." He was right.

However, neither multiplex operation has been proved right in everything, unless its foresight is long-term. To quote Millard Ochs: "The more the screens, the less the delay between releases in the USA and the UK." One is still left wondering, at the time of going to print, how much longer it will take. Millard also believed back in '88 that as more youngsters are exposed to film, Britain would turn into a major film-making centre in the world. Ok, we'll give that one more time.

Ira Korff boasted of the Showcase policy that decreed 'No adverts'. Admirable policy, too. A pity it's no longer in force. Ira also foresaw a cinema boom that would force film companies to delay their films' availability on video. No change there, Ira. Well, not yet. Astonishingly, though, in the first 12 months of the Derby operations, the video 'sell-thru' phenomenon suddenly appeared (which meant video tapes were now available to buy rather than simply rent). This industry was worth £250 million by the end of its first year.

In the face of this competition, and with Derby's apparently languid interest in cinema, how did the Showcase and the UCI not only survive but thrive? In spite of their clear, confident business heads, neither Korff nor Ochs could have envisioned the extraordinarily good fortune they experienced in their first summer of operations. Behind the seemingly optimistic, unflustered executive-speak would be two anxious men in a brave new world, hoping for some luck. They got it. In giant dollops. Precisely, in big films.

The Showcase Cinema line-up in its opening week hardly augured well. Of the new films, only *A Fish Called Wanda, Good Morning Vietnam* and *Big* could be termed 'major attractions'. Let's face it, what do you remember of the other opening films – *Kansas, Man In Love, Switching Channels, The Light Horseman, Big Business* and *The Seventh Sign*?

However, within a fortnight – when the UCI opened – the film line-up was more attractive. Added to *Vietnam, Wanda* and *Big* were *Beetlejuice, Coming To America, Buster, Scrooged* and the cinema's ground-breaking opening feature *Who Framed Roger Rabbit?* Naturally, these same top attractions were being screened at the Showcase. However, at this early stage, it was not a case of competition but self-sufficiency.

By the close of the following summer, 1989, both cinemas had sweltered, but not under the tense, excessive, perspirant heat of survival. The heat was genuine. Locally, we were basking in the warmth of the sun. Hardly the weather to encourage people into the dark of a cinema auditorium. Yet, in cinematic terms, the summer of 1989 was a *Field of Dreams*, and to quote the famous, haunting line from the film: 'If you build it, he will come'.

And he came. So did many others. In spite of the mid-year heatwave, which might have presaged the harbingers of doom, the multitudinous multiplex attendances bucked the trend. This fervent and fantastic revolution in cinema-going habits, following a dormant era of domesticity and a drive towards alternative pleasures, was down to the plain and simple fact that at a traditionally thin time for ticket sales, Derby was swamped by an extraordinary burst of blockbusters and other alluring film attractions.

The hottest films of that summer were *Batman*, *Rainman* and *Indiana Jones and The Temple of Doom*. Other big attractions during that year included *Lethal Weapon 2*, *Back To The Future II*, *Shirley Valentine*, *When Harry Met Sally*, *Dead Poets Society*, *Naked Gun*, *Mississippi Burning*, *Twins*, *The Accused*, *Field of Dreams*, *Working Girl*, *A*

The UCI at Derby's Meteor Centre. **Julia Peck.**

Cry In The Dark, *Gorillas In The Mist*, *Licence To Kill*, *Cocktail*, *Scandal*, *The Abyss*, *Three Fugitives*, *Dirty Rotten Scoundrels*, *Oliver and Co*, *Karate Kid III* and *Star Trek V* – there has never been a year like it, and Derby got it at the most crucial time in its cinema history. Thus, the future of both the Derby Showcase and Derby UCI was assured. People had come.

If truth be known, the people had been coming back for some time. Attendances for the year 1989 had shown the fifth annual increase nationally. Significantly, the first year of a rise rather than another fall was 1985, the year The Point opened. Admission figures have risen ever since; not surprisingly, with a further 15 multiplexes opening in 1989, another 12 in 1990, and 16 in 1991, bringing the total to 57, and the number of multiplex screens to 510.

It might also be unsurprising to know that Derby's one remaining commercial cinema – the Cannon – didn't survive for very long. But it was not for the reason one might suppose. Through a cruel and massive irony, the cinema was closed down only a month after the multiplex openings because of a ceiling collapse. A large slab of plaster fell down, only ten minutes before a children's show. A few days later, I was shown the damage, and felt a chill. I thought of the time I sat in The Tavern In The Town, a Birmingham pub, exactly a week to the time and date before it was blown apart by the IRA. I also now think of the time I sat to watch a private preview film screening at the Derby Cannon, exactly one week to the time and date before that plaster would have

fallen down precisely on the spot where I liked to sit.

For a short while, my excitement over the multiplex invasion was deadened by the Cannon closure. Here was an auditorium regarded as the most attractive outside of London's West End. Like the Superama shut-down, it seemed such a woeful waste. However, commerce had been kicking its teeth in, and the ceiling collapse was the equivalent of a final blow to the head. In a happier commercial climate, the roof would surely have been repaired. But the ceiling of success for the city cinema had been raised higher by the out-of-town competition, and it is doubtful the Cannon would have seen out 1989 had it reached 1988 intact. The place was now a ruin. Thank heavens it still stands, as it may still have a future – as the new site for the Derby Metro.

The Derby Metro emerged unscathed from the multiplex incursion. Indeed, it more than survived; it thrived. As we massed at the doors of doubt soon after the foundation stones were laid at both the Showcase and UCI, the Doubting Thomases were ruminating not only on the future of the Cannon, but also on the small independent cinema on Green Lane – a mini Metro compared with the Greyhound bus of its American rivals. With its small, single-screen, 126-seat cinema (plus considerable parking problems unless you arrived spectacularly early), it seemed only a matter of time before the Metro was devoured by the multiplex monster. Not so. Indeed, it has prospered with its policy of screening films at the more 'serious' end of the spectrum.

The first local stirrings of interest in more serious film began after World War Two, with the formation of the Derby Film Society (originally the Derby Cameo Society). The small membership, which varied between 80 and 120, enjoyed a programme of films from around the world. Its record attendance came in 1956 with *The Wild One* starring Marlon Brando, which was only available to film clubs and societies as it had been refused a certificate.

The Derby Film Society lasted until 1973. Two years later, a British Film Institute grant supported the start of a similarly-minded society – at the Derby Playhouse – which opened at its new Theatre Walk

The foyer of the UCI at Derby. Julia Peck.

venue with complete film projection facilities. The Playhouse film operation lasted a variable four years. I remember sitting in the well-raked auditorium enjoying unequalled screen size and superb sound reproduction. But I also recall the empty spaces. In 1979, the theatre screened its last two pictures, both with patently appropriate titles – *Goodbye Girl* and *Don't Look Now*.

But the journey of cultural cinema was to continue on the Metro which was, to all intents and purposes, a replacement for the Playhouse film theatre. Indeed, the Playhouse projection equipment found its way to the Green Lane cinema, and in 1981, with a £50,000 grant from the British Film Institute and Derby City Council, the Metro was born, an attractive refurbishment of the old Victorian Lecture Theatre in what was then the Derby College of Art and Design.

One man who came with the former Playhouse projectors was Brian Shaw, a life-long devotee of the business, who began work at the Alvaston Rex at the age of 12, staying for 20 years until it closed. He is still at the Metro to this day. Also there from the first day is Doug Hodges, the leading figure in the bitter campaign for the retention of the Derby Odeon Pennine. He was the first member of the public to pay for Metro membership (his number is M2; he could have been M1, 'but they thought I wouldn't like to be

a motorway'), and recently became the cinema's first Life Member.

The Metro's first film officer (later its director) Laurie Heyward was a bright, thrusting, articulate and committed film enthusiast who embedded the Metro on the consciousness of kindred cineaste souls. He was to instigate the Derby Film Festival, which now runs in cahoots with the two multiplexes (and currently under the chairmanship of someone not a million molecules away from the keyboard that pressed these words into action) and, more crucially, established the Metro's firm identity as a purveyor of quality cinema.

I remember special nights when film figures put in personal appearances: Terry Jones of *Monty Python's Flying Circus* introduced a Japanese version of *Monty Python and The Holy Grail* (even for me as a card-carrying Pythonite, that was very hard going!); Nicholas Roeg, one of the great British film-makers, brought his latest picture *Insignificance*; another leading independent director Ken Loach arrived for a special screening of his new film *Hidden Agenda* (which, unfortunately, had a hidden reel: the last one was missing, so the director had to explain to the audience what occurred at the end!); and I recall a personal audience with an aging but still charismatic James Mason.

With its wide cross-section of foreign language/cult/classic/'arthouse' screenings, the Metro enjoyed a healthy, if occasionally variable, few opening years, cocooned to some extent by its grant-aid status but not giving its funding bodies any concern that they were propping up an empty enterprise. Indeed, less than a decade into its life, the Metro was to realise its particular value. Ironically, but significantly, it took a multiplex invasion to show its worth.

A year into the Showcase and UCI operation, Laurie Heyward announced that the Derby Metro had 'more or less' returned its box office figure to the pre-multiplex level, 'which is very exciting, as it does suggest that the relationship between cultural cinema and commercial cinema can be a productive one, largely because the multiplexes free cinemas like the Metro to show the wider diversity of films that still doesn't get the chance to get on the commercial circuit'. In simple, sweeping terms, the Showcase and UCI chains have pursued a play-safe policy, screening movies for a mass audience, pointing up the Metro even more as a genuine alternative. Indeed, from 1984, when the Derby ABC triple-screen cinema closed, leaving only one commercial screen in the city (the Cannon), the Metro had pursued a more populist policy. "We've now returned to our roots" said Laurie in 1989, "when we were one of nine screens."

So, ironic as it may seem, the Metro has become more distinctive even though it provides one of 22 screens. The Metro itself has looked to increase its screens, and become its own cinema complex (albeit on a smaller scale), but with no expansion offered within the building it occupies, it has had to look elsewhere in the city. It is currently looking under the directorship of Tony Whitehead (at the turn of 1994, Laurie Heyward took up the post of Visual Arts Officer with West Midlands Arts).

On his arrival, Tony Whitehead was surprised to find a city the size of Derby with two multiplexes, but he has never allowed their dominance of the local film market to concern him. On the contrary, from the outset he felt buoyant about it: "I thought: if a city can support two multiplexes, it's a city whose population likes its cinema, and I also feel that the multiplexes are competing against each other rather than against us. We would see ourselves as complimentary rather than competitive." Indeed, Tony wants the multi-cinemas to increase in popularity, aware as he is of the 'knock-on' effect: "The more that people in the city go to the movies, the better it is for the Metro." He also wants the Showcase and UCI to continue with their commercial-minded policy, even though he admits a certain ambivalence about this: "In the best possible world, the multiplexes would be offering a wider range of films, but I'm happy they don't because we get all those films they reject." However, Tony is quick to point out that the Metro is not a dumping ground for films that cannot get a screening elsewhere: "In fact, we have people who, given a choice, will choose us", a point borne out by the example of the film *The Piano*, one of the few Metro-bound movies to also gain an audience at the mainstream multiplexes, but which still played to packed houses when it arrived at the Green Lane cinema more than a month later.

Tony also welcomes the success of films like *The Piano* in helping to deflate the highfalutin image of the so-called 'arthouse' film, and the film theatres that screen them. Tony signalled this change of climate with the issue of a press release to mark his first year at the Metro:

'The Metro Cinema? Isn't that the place up on Green Lane where arty types and film students go to see weird movies, usually with subtitles that you can't read properly?'

Well, no it isn't actually. Certainly not according to Tony Whitehead. "We're offering people genuine choice" he says. "It would be very sad if, with 20-odd cinema screens in Derby, not one of them was showing *Ed Wood* or *La Reine Margot*. Yet both of these played to packed houses at the Metro this year, so they're hardly obscure minority films."

"The weird, arty films? Well, yes, our proud boast is that we genuinely present the widest range of possible movies to the people of Derby: you don't necessarily need ten screens to offer people variety. But don't forget that today's experimental film-maker often ends up as tomorrow's great."

It is not just the range of films shown that sees the Metro outstripping the multiplexes. It's the number of them, too: even though it is a one-screen cinema, the Metro's annual figure of around 250 screenings betters the 11 screen Showcase, with films from 30 different countries also far out-distancing the multiplexes' global reach.

Tony cites the Metro as the cinema equivalent of a small, dedicated specialist shop in comparison with the multiplex's equivalent role of a supermarket: "The supermarket has anything you want as long as it sells above a certain level. If it doesn't, it won't be on the shelves. We're the place you go to when the bigger store doesn't have that item you're looking for, and where you expect to get friendly, enthusiastic and informed service. They get a response from us, rather than the blank look they might get from someone who's just there to tear tickets."

But the other attraction of the Metro is the place itself. The Green Lane building provides a charm of its own, with an attractive staircase sweeping you up to the small reception area, liberally festooned with bright film posters. The auditorium – the old Victorian Lecture Theatre – is a small, simple but still impressive area with a warm ambience, and distinguished by four large spherical lights on tall poles which lend a 1930s-style art deco appeal.

The Metro audience – ranging from students to middle-aged and older core enthusiasts – is made up of many regular faces, encouraged further by the recent 'Metro Movie-goers' scheme which gives frequent attenders discounts on tickets every time they visit. The Metro has thus manifested a true 'club' (as opposed to 'clique') atmosphere. "Many people feel it's their cinema" says Tony, "and they also like the fact that they don't have to sit with people chomping sweets, chewing popcorn and talking through movies. I know that doesn't happen all the time at the multiplexes, but you only have to have that happen once to turn off a serious film enthusiast for life."

If the Metro audience has a complaint, it is increasingly that the cinema doesn't show films for long enough. This is a measure of the cinema's growing popularity: "Its size was fine when it first opened" says Tony, "but it's now a wider market place." A feasibility study into the suitability of the city's Railway Institute building created another flurry of excitement over a possible move to a site that would incorporate a permanent home for Derby's cajun music club The Swamp, but the report revealed inadequacies in the acoustic properties of the building, which would have involved a considerable outlay, and the building carried with it a high valuation anyway, plus an imponderable parking problem. It was back to the drawing board.

Since then, the National Lottery has energised plans for a move, and the Metro is now looking seriously at a Lottery-backed move to an even more central and suitable site, which would give life again to Derby's first super-cinema: the Derby Gaumont Palace on London Road, one of only three remaining city cinema sites where the building is virtually intact and untouched both outside and in (the other two being the Gloria and the Hippodrome; both the Popular and the Superama would require a massive amount of refurbishment to return each of them to a cinema auditorium).

It is highly appropriate that news of a prospective move to the Gaumont has surfaced in cinema's centenary year when memories of the heartfelt halcyon days of the dream palaces have been revived. And Tony Whitehead is determined to see this particular dream move occur: "It's a slow process, but we are pursuing it rigorously and conscientiously."

At the time of going to the print, a feasibility study is in progress. The findings look promising. The shell of the Gaumont's cinema auditorium is still there, even though the fixtures and fittings are gone. Can Tony and the Metro possibly duplicate the Gaumont's much vaunted decor and atmosphere? "We hope to revive the ambience and romance to match that with the forward thinking, and the imaginative approach to cinema that the Metro has always stood for."

There is every possibility, then, that the Metro could find a new life in an old, well-loved picture palace as cinema begins its second centenary. This new life, as Tony Whitehead sees it, could also see a change in the fiscal set up at the Metro. "It's not possible to be confident of public subsidy in the current climate, so we want to relocate to control our own financial destiny."

What of the destiny of the independent town cinemas out in the county? Prior to the opening of the Derby Showcase, I asked Ira Korff if the multiplexes would consign the small provincial cinemas to the scrap heap. "Not so" predicted the Showcase chief, "wherever we have opened a multiplex, Showcase has renewed interest in movie-going and actually increased other cinemas' business." A curious comment from a man who believed Derby was not big enough to support two multiplexes, and who performed a *volte-face* two years later when he responded to a *Derby Evening Telegraph* article

headlined 'Closure threat to cinemas': "I have always felt there would be too many screens in Derby. We are doing fine, but I can understand how, given the two new complexes, some of the independents are being affected."

The newspaper story (19 November 1990) was prompted by the issuing of 'a desperate SOS to Derbyshire film fans – Save Our Screens!' At the time, three independent cinemas – at Belper, Ripley and Long Eaton – were feeling the pinch, the pinch of their regular clientele by the Showcase and UCI. The main problem was being caused by the multiplexes screening box office hits before the independents could receive them. Peter and Maureen Moss, who were running Belper's Ritz cinema at the time, called the situation 'bleak', and spoke of their anger at the way they had been treated in the matter of film distribution, to the extent that they were considering an appeal to the Office of Fair Trading.

A similar predicament was being voiced by the Ripley Hippodrome. Co-owner Lorraine Godkin said: "There is a chance we might have to close if it doesn't pick up. We haven't put a time limit on it – we are just trying to see if we can get one or two films that will help pick up audiences. It is since the two multiplexes opened that I have noticed the downturn." The cinema actually hung on for another year, closing in December 1991.

Time also ran out on the Belper Ritz. And so did the last owner. An unhappy Peter and Maureen Moss sold the lease and moved on to run a cinema in Mablethorpe. The new owner was to be the last; behind with the rent and failing to improve on audience figures, he performed a 'moonlight flit' in October 1991, taking with him a few fixtures and fittings and, inevitably, any future the cinema might have had.

Chesterfield's remaining cinema, the Regal, struggled on before closing in April 1993, as much a victim of competition from the Sheffield Meadowhall multiplex as the two in Derby. However, the Ilkeston Scala, although adjacent to a multiplex in both Derby and Nottingham, has survived. "There has never been any talk of closure" says manager Jim Jerram. Two factors have contributed to this. The first refers back to the comment from Steve Knibbs of the UCI chain that people today are not predisposed to travelling a distance to obtain their leisure pleasure, preferring it on their doorstep. Another reason the Scala enjoys good local patronage is borne out by Jim Jerram's comment that "it is now a two-bus trip to Nottingham." This speaks of a cinema audience which does not fit into the multiplex schemata: those people who have no car transport.

Also, for the bus or car users who prefer the short

trip to their local Scala, the Ilkeston cinema has happily built on the cinema-going habit stimulated by the multiplex invasion by managing to acquire what the Belper Ritz could never have: big box office films on the same release date as the Derby Showcase and UCI. Its future as a building is assured: it is Grade II Listed, which has brought concomitant difficulties in attempts by the owners to twin the cinema. So, it continues as a single-screen 500-seater cinema, standing almost like a quaint museum piece in the corner of the town market place, as a fond memento of another age.

Only two other Derbyshire town cinemas stand along with it: the Screen, Long Eaton and the Matlock Ritz, even though, unlike the Ilkeston Scala, both have to wait for the first-run blockbusters. At the same time as Peter and Maureen Moss were experiencing the death throes of the Belper Ritz (two years after the Derby multiplex openings), the Long Eaton Screen manager John Francis was also contemplating closure: "I am fighting for survival. We haven't got a fair crack at the top films." He further told the *Derby Evening Telegraph*: "We need to take over £900 per week to break even, but one night last week we took about £12.50. We will fight to get people back in but come April we will have to see how things stand. My son and I bought the cinema about 12 months ago and put everything we had into it. I love this town and just hope people will support us."

As it turns out, people have supported them. Through the support of a regular, loyal clientele, and 'hard work and the help and support of my family,' John Francis' Screen cinema has managed to survive, even though 'it's just keeping its head above water'. Brenda Meakin is one of those regular supporters: "Convenience is one thing; in the summer we can have a pleasant walk there and back. It's also very friendly, the owner is always around to either welcome you or wish you goodnight, and it still provides an interval, which in a long film is very nice to have." On the downside, Brenda points to the building itself – "it's getting old, and some seating needs replacing" – and to less choice of films: "It doesn't always manage to have some of the top-selling films." However, John Francis has found that a regular supply of family-orientated films has been an important factor, with particular highlights being *Jurassic Park*, *Aladdin*, *The Lion King* and *The Addams Family*.

Film selection has been all-important to the two men who together run the Matlock Ritz, Chris White and Matthew Latimer: "We've managed to survive by selecting only quality films that we think will appeal to a majority of the local people, and by getting these

films as quickly as possible." So, as well as doing the expected sound business with blockbusters, the Ritz has attracted welcomingly high audiences for traditional English period films (recent examples include *The Madness of King George* and *Carrington*), and its Monday night screenings of 'Classics'. Any particular highlights? "We regard it as a highlight every time a film plays to a full house." According to Steve Knibbs of the UCI, the Matlock Ritz provides a good example of how 'a small independent exhibitor can do well, by applying the personal touch and working on the local audience and their needs'.

Chris and Matthew are also in a fortunate location. The drive to Derby or Sheffield is long enough to make Matlock residents think twice about the trip and thus consider the Ritz screenings. Also, its position as the only cinema in the Peak District draws in a number of tourists. Either way, the co-proprietors look forward to the future "with some optimism, as long as good quality films are regularly released and available."

The quality of film product looks certain to continue, although not every quality film that is released finds its way to the two Derby multiplexes. This has proved to be the biggest disappointment for the local cinema-goers I have spoken with. Steve Knibbs shamelessly admits to 'serving a mass audience.' That was evident virtually from the start. Expectations of single screens being set aside for less commercial fare or classic oldies quickly faded. My expectations were low, anyway: when I questioned the original UCI chief Millard Ochs over the provision of classic/cult/arthouse/foreign movies, he responded: "If there's a demand, write to us, let us know, and we'll put it together. If there's a community out there who wants it, we'll do it. But I have to say that in other sites, we haven't had much interest." However, one could contend that the UCI could have acted from a different standpoint, in being bold enough to try and create interest itself rather than wait for it to be created by the audience.

However, within the first year of the multiplex operation in Derby, there did surface a demand for alternative films, and the UCI created the Screen 11 club (although only possessing ten screens, the term Screen 11 was used to indicate that once a week an auditorium would be set aside for a screening of a classic film). Although only short-lived, it was a venture which may well have had an influence on the UCI head office, as shortly after, the multiplex chain gave birth to the Director's Chair, special one-off screenings at all UCI cinemas of, largely, 'critically acclaimed movies'. This was a welcome move as so many films applauded by critics and screened in London (and even in neighbouring

Nottingham) were failing to open at both the Derby multiplexes.

In 1991, the Derby UCI showed remarkable taste, perspicacity and wisdom in allowing me to take over the selections for the Director's Chair. Fond memories since include packed or near-capacity houses for myriad movies, notably *Casablanca*, *Howard's End*, *Field of Dreams*, *Blade Runner – The Director's Cut*, *Gone With The Wind*, *Lorenzo's Oil*, *The Big Sleep*, *Il Postino*, *Dune*, plus excitingly unexpected sell-outs for Kenneth Branagh's *Much Ado About Nothing*, the 1992 version of *Wuthering Heights* and the rapturously romantic *Somewhere In Time*, a 1980 film starring Christopher Reeve and Jane Seymour. To sell out the screening of a forgotten 14-year-old love story and, above all, to feel an audience discovering for the first time a rare cinematic gem, made this Director's Chair event the most moving and memorable of the last five years.

Even more extraordinarily, big audiences have assembled for screenings of quality films that had already enjoyed a run at the UCI and were felt worth bringing back. Mostly, these have included films that received only a limited run, and yet cinema-goers have turned up in their numbers to see a Director's Chair screening, for example, of *Four Weddings and A Funeral*, even though it had been screened at the UCI over a period of at least three months and was available on video! An interesting market research study is waiting here for the UCI, to determine many cinema-goers' viewing habits and patterns.

What makes the Director's Chair even more vital in Derby is the fact that the city has, paradoxically, become a victim of its two-multiplex status. Although the combined audiences of the Showcase and UCI give Derby one of the highest attendance figures in the country (at one stage, there were more people per head of population going to the cinema in the area than any other), it is not regarded in the distribution trade as a 'key city'. Put simply, because of limited prints of non-mainstream pictures, the distributors of these pictures are reluctant to give two prints of a film to one city. Derby is not regarded as a key city because the audience is, effectively, split. So, when such a film becomes available, the distributors feel obliged to offer it to both Derby multiplexes. If both cinemas request it, the film invariably doesn't show. If the one cinema requests that specialised audience picture, only then does it usually get a screening. This is cited as a frustration by the Derby Showcase: 'We try to exclusively play less mainstream releases, based on the fact that we have one additional screen than the UCI. We have been unsuccessful in booking some of these films because the UCI insists on playing whatever we play, and the film distributors have been reluctant to show favouritism to either multiplex.'

The Showcase further states that it has 'played numerous titles that the UCI has not.' However, out of that long list, I only considered a handful worthy of a later screening at the UCI Director's Chair, and there is a list equally as long of titles that have not been played at the Derby Showcase. This includes a large body of quality foreign language films. Also, some of these films receive a screening at the nearby Nottingham Showcase. But Showcase insist that there is no blanket ban on sub-titled pictures at Derby: 'Showcase Derby will play any film that the distributors have on offer to us, including foreign films. However, it has proven to be difficult to obtain these films in Derby, since distributors often release a limited number of prints, and they prefer to utilise them in larger markets where they have the potential to gain the highest grosses. Showcase Nottingham has 14 screens, three more than Derby, which makes it easier to schedule less mainstream or foreign product. The distributors are also more willing to release these films at Showcase Nottingham since it has been extremely successful in showing up-market product, due to the fact that one print of a film is usually the only one serving the entire population.'

As to the provision of a Director's Chair-style set-up, whereby the Showcase could give one-off screenings to classic films along with recent foreign releases, the Showcase argues that 'given the fact that UCI is already running a successful Director's Chair series, it makes no sense for us to duplicate their effort'. One could argue that this town is big enough for the both of them to run this once-a-week film club, but the Showcase defends any accusations of playing safe: 'It may appear that Showcase Derby plays nothing but commercial films, but we will play any rated film that is on offer to us from the film distributors. We are known nationally as the biggest supporter of independent film in the UK.'

Given that the Derby Showcase screens more films than the Derby UCI, and gives every film at least a week's run, while the UCI devotes only one screening each week to its Director's Chair choices – many of which are not shown at the Showcase – the two cinemas are just about equal in their provision of choice. But even given the constraints, it is still dispiriting to note a lack of quality in that choice.

As a sign that the UCI is firmly driven by profit, the Director's Chair series at Derby was suspended for about two months in the summer of 1995 to maximise the screenings of a welter of blockbusters which all came at once, even though the Director's Chair only ties up one screen for two hours on a Wednesday night.

The provision of the Director's Chair itself may be viewed as paltry – given that small amount of screen time – but Steve Knibbs of the UCI defends the cinema chain's policy in cities like Derby by not only, like the Showcase, pointing to the lack of wide print distribution of quality films, but also claiming a thin market for many non-mainstream pictures or, in Steve's terminology, 'more esoteric product'. He cites the problem whereby "you can tie up one auditorium with more esoteric product for a whole week and play to audiences of only ten or 20 people at a time. That market is student-driven, and served well by the regional film theatres. Outside of London, there is a small market for arthouse, foreign films etc. It's very difficult and expensive to track down that audience and get them to come to you on a regular basis. We know from experience that we would play to empty houses. It's a shame." Steve contends that the single screening per week for the Director's Chair is ideal because "there's more chance of filling the auditorium, and it makes for a better atmosphere."

On balance, it would be churlish to dwell on the specific area of choice when weighed against a large body of outstanding commercial films that have been screened since the Derby multiplexes opened, and which has led to the pleasing, unprecedented, and largely unexpected, success of the Derby multiplex operation itself, which Steve Knibbs believes has paved the way for the rest of the country: "What Derby has proved is that if you build carefully, places like Derby can stand more screens, and there are other cities where you can repeat the Derby experience, and do good business."

Although the Derby Showcase has not been as successful as it hoped, pointing out that it "did not anticipate another multiplex within our catchment area", it does agree that "it is successful for the film distributors, since the combined grossing potential of the Showcase and the UCI is better than that of the majority of multiplexes located in larger markets."

Steve Knibbs concurs: "We would be doing better business in Derby if we were the only cinema, but looked at neutrally and for the good of cinema, there are more people overall going to the cinema now than there would have been had there just been the one multiplex"

The multiplex still has its detractors, particularly those whose film-going fervour remains in the rosy-tinted past. Sadly, many avid two-or-three-times-a-week cinema-goers of the 1940s, 1950s and 1960s have dismissed the multiplexes without giving them a try. One can accept the thorny problem presented by contemporary film: there are sweeping accusations that modern pictures are thick with fornication, four-letter words and foul violence. It is certainly true that

the uppermost concerns of the film-makers of the Golden Age were to provide glamour, melodrama, dignity, decency and innocence. However, a pleasing aspect of 1990s cinema is that more movie-makers are producing films 'like they used to make 'em'.

The problem for some people, though, is that the cinemas are nothing like they used to make 'em. Former Somercotes Premier projectionist Eddie Burnham wants nothing to do with the multiplex ideal: "They've turned film entertainment into a slot machine; there's no romance to the cinema anymore." Peter Thompson, former projectionist at the Ashbourne Elite, feels a similar coldness, claiming that the multiplexes are "too clinical, too organised. In Ashbourne, you felt a greater sense of occasion going to the cinema. There was a friendly, family atmosphere; everyone knew the staff." Swadlincote cinema historian Graham Nutt says "going to the cinema doesn't do anything for me now. The new cinemas don't have the same atmosphere, because I feel as if I'm sitting in someone's lounge. The cinemas we went to were always big, open and palatial."

To former Derby ABC manager Mike Smith, a visit to a Derby multiplex was a disappointment: "It doesn't have the magic of a single screen cinema. It wasn't cinema as I knew it, or would want to know it. To me as a showman, it was more like a business."

It is a business, by necessity. A return to single screen cinemas, magical as that might be, would be financial suicide in a climate where cinema audiences are still low in comparison even with the 1960s. Steve Knibbs admits that the serving of a mass audience is "not to everyone's tastes, particularly for older people." Also, older people like Eddie Burnham cite a 'lack of romance' at the multiplexes as an indication of both the more lavish make-up of the older cinemas and the nature of the films screened. Those factors would also form part of the 'sense of occasion' that Peter Thompson feels is missing. Naturally, the modern cinemas cannot change the make-up of the films they receive. As for the decor? Building and operating costs in the multiplex age could never run to duplication of the dream palaces of the bygone age. Expense further rules out the provision of large auditoria, as Graham Nutt would like to see.

What's more, the multiplex can still cope with the massively popular new film releases that call for more seats than even its largest auditorium can provide, by opening up two, three, sometimes four auditoria for that same film simply by automotive 'interlocking'. Thus, heavy demand can be met. Ideally, viewing a film like *Toy Story* in a giant 1,000-seater auditorium would provide that greater atmosphere, but the multiplex operators have been astute in their assumption that with demand for such films proving variable rather than constant, the building of big auditoria would be less cost-effective, and the use of the interlocking system highly productive.

Further multiplex detractors rail against the architecture, which can obviously have its effect on the overall ambience. Writing in the *Sunday Times*, Hugh Pearman highlights an oddity of the cinema revival: 'One of the strangest things about the revival of the cinema during the past ten years… is that the late flowering of this art should have gone hand in hand with the worst architecture of its 100-year history. The edge-of-town multiplex may have a dozen films showing, easy parking and great big buckets of popcorn to hand round, but architecturally it is about as interesting as the distribution warehouse it is so often placed next to.'

Would it be scurrilous to suggest that the average multiplex looks like a warehouse because it could slyly turn into one if the cinema scene should collapse? I came to carry this belief as soon as I cast eyes on the second multiplex site to be built in Britain – Salford Quays – boring and boxy to an almost brazen degree. Although the architecture of the Derby Showcase and UCI is not quite so despairingly dull, both buildings are part of a not-so-grand design symptomatic of the unimaginative, cost-cutting procedures of a typical multiplex, as delineated by Hugh Pearman:

'The poverty of design of most multiplexes is linked directly to the budget seat prices. Per square foot, they have to be very, very cheap buildings, and quick to put up. Accountancy-led picture-house conglomerates can see no further than this. The notion that an interesting new building might attract paying customers appears not to occur to them, even though that was precisely the point of the great over-the-top movie theatres of the 1920s and 1930s.'

This brings us back to both Peter Thompson's disillusionment over the cinema's lost sense of occasion, and Mike Smith's belief that he now views a strictly commercial concern as opposed to a showman's paradise. As Hugh Pearman further contends, even the earliest picture houses 'recognised that there was an experience to cinema-going that was more than just the seeing of the film, and that this required some design input. The architecture of the cinemas imparted the required sense of occasion to movie-going. Today's multiplexes clearly regard the activity as little different from visiting a discount superstore.'

The point of Hugh Pearman's article (and argument) was that a newly-designed cinema in Southampton – Harbour Lights – broke the mould by being brave in its design, one of 'immense flair'. Its glass façade certainly looks bold, attractive and tasteful. Perhaps it also feels British. Herein dwells another common complaint about the multiplex. Former Matlock Ritz projectionist Michael Oxley abhors the modern cinema complexes as 'too Americanised… all this razzmatazz, popcorn and stuff'. Gilbert Adair, in a *Sunday Times* article headlined 'Cinema thrives on a complex' complained of being 'plunged into a totally American ambience'. For Gilbert, the preponderance of popcorn gives a British multiplex an American smell. He also hankers after the Kia-Oras and choc-ices that have been replaced by Hershey Bars and tortilla chips.

However, Gilbert Adair concedes that multiplexes have 'made the whole experience fun again', and refers back to his film-going days of the 1960s when cinemas 'tended to be moth-eaten dumps, peeling and unappealing, their usherettes surly, their carpets frayed, their screens filthy'.

Gilbert then turns back on the offensive, declaring that British multiplexes 'condition us to assume that going to the cinema is, of necessity, by definition, an American experience'. This is even experienced when one makes a simple telephone call to a multiplex: American know-how dictates that you must sound out your first name and ask how you may help the caller (to be fair, this has spread to British industry as a whole).

Steve Knibbs is vigorous in his defence of the Americanisation of the UCI: "What is wrong with a clean, bright environment with staff that don't actually say 'have a nice day' but serve the customers well? Look at our sound system, the comfort, the quality of our projection… if these are American values, then I would say we have lost our way as Britons somewhere along the way in not wanting these things. There is this aura about British cinemas, which produce statements along the lines of 'cinemas should be art deco, with curtains etc'. If our service is American, then it means that America got it right, before us. If people didn't like Milton Keynes in the first place, they wouldn't have come."

Certainly, none of the aura of old British cinema is employed in a multiplex: the manager is young, to accord with the majority cinema-going audience. He dresses smartly, but is a long sartorial distance from the evening-suited splendour of the benign, more elderly and experienced manager of the picture palace who would both greet the incoming patrons and see them out. Young staff are everywhere, at the pay desk and in projection booth. Not only that, but the confectionery even has the sweet taste of youth – the corn pops in tune with its main audience. The food also chimes with Americana, yet another aspect that attracts, encourages and props up the multiplexes' main clientele (14 to 24-year-olds) while arguably distancing the older age groups. I have myself felt the paradox of walking into a screening of a mature-audience attraction like *A River Runs Through It* or *Lorenzo's Oil* and witnessing an auditorium of patrons sitting uncomfortably amidst a rock soundtrack issuing from the speakers.

However, be thankful for the Derby Showcase and UCI. I certainly am, having walked into a Warners. A visit to the Leicester Warner Bros multiplex had me grasping for a word beyond 'garish'. It was not so much the sickly, over-powering smell of popcorn, more the oppressive, disco-laden atmosphere of the foyer with its neon-clad bank of TV sets and flashing lights which would be a haven for the young, and Hades for all other age groups. By the time you reach the red, gaudy, six-foot high screen number indicators, you feel a sign of welcome to the majority minors, but a fiery warning to anyone older. Could one then thank the heavens that Derby got its multiplexes before this brash operator began its UK assault? Not Paul Usher...

Paul Usher is a man with many gripes about the multiplex, and the Derby Showcase in particular. He claims, firstly, that the sound quality 'is not as they would have you believe. Yes, it can be loud, but a poorly set frequency response makes harsh, piercing tones.' He also claims that the screen has 'ripples and bulges causing areas of focus to be poor; I even saw a large mark on one screen'. At one screening – which turned out to be his last – Paul contends that 'the focus was so poor, the credits were unreadable'. His complaint caused the focus to only 'improve slightly'. He eventually got a refund, after claiming 'my eyes could take no more'. His eyes were also offended by

the fact that 'I could not sit where I wished to unless I moved piles of rubbish'.

Paul now views films at home, lamenting the days when 'you could be shown to your seat, ice-cream was cheap, so were the films (not merely one film in the programme either), and you could view the films all day'. Paul also claims that modern VCR stereo systems can be 'superior' to multiplex sound systems (which is highly contentious), but he does admit he misses one part of the cinema experience he cannot reproduce at home: the big screen effect.

There are many charges here to contend with, although Paul Usher's list of grievances constitutes the only letter of its type I received. Also, on enquiring to the Showcase about the nature of complaints it has received about its Derby cinema, there is no mention of the kind of the grumbles aired by Paul. Furthermore, Showcase says it has 'instituted numerous changes at Showcase Derby in response to input from patrons, and we take this input very seriously'. As a result, the cinema has introduced advanced booking, provided film synopses and performance schedules to its movie guides, with the biggest category of feedback centred on its concession stand, bringing Showcase to introduce a wide variety of new foods and drink.

The Derby UCI has installed a 'Suggestion Box' and has also acted on demands from its audience for both seats and a clock in the foyer, less litter, more car park lighting and more provision for children, who felt the UCI was 'an adult palace'.

In both cinema cases, there is more an air of constructive criticism than clangorous complaint. Derbyshire people have voted with their feet. The multiplexes are here to stay.

Showcase Cinema, Derby, interior

Showcase Cinema, Derby, interior

Metro Cinema, Derby, interior

UCI Cinema, Derby, interior
All photos © Julia Peck, 1996

And Now Tomorrow

A Postscript

Dad, will you take us to see Toy Story *again?*
Claire and Helena Franklin

You have probably noticed by now that each of the chapters (and the choice 'snippets' dotted throughout the book) bear headings that are actual film titles. Happily, the chapter *Decline and Fall* was followed by *Return From The Ashes*. The way it looked in the mid-1980s, the final chapter of this book could have been titled after a Rene Clair picture from 1945: *And Then There Were None*.

As it is, I can take my daughters to see *Toy Story* again. And again. More film treats await us in the future. Quality has joined hands with quantity: for the last decade, we have seen a fortuitous combination of a growth in quality films and an increase in the quantity of screens available to show them. Indeed, one seems to have fed on the other. Whatever the factors, these are now exciting times.

Toy Story is an exhilarating example of the *Thrill Of It All*. The drive of digital technology is said to be forming the biggest revolution in cinema since the Talkies. One has the feeling that even now, we ain't heard nothing yet.

A little revolution in the actual cinema-going habit locally has surprised and delighted me. It goes even beyond the statement from Steve Knibbs of the UCI that 'cinema has got back on to peoples' leisure agenda'. Both the original chief executives of the two Derby multiplexes – Ira Korff and Millard Ochs – assured me that people would come not only to choose a day in the week to visit the cinema but also to choose the film once they turned up. I concede to their sagacity. Only recently, on a Wednesday evening, a couple loitering in the Derby UCI foyer spotted the Radio Derby film critic and asked after my Director's Chair choice for that night, as they had surveyed the bill of fare and were still trying to make up their minds.

Based on this assumption, the cinema near you has almost become the equivalent of the favourite local restaurant. You know there is quality in the bill of fare, so you go as often as you can, and decide on the menu when you get there – and you have heard that there is a fresh dish your friends have discovered to be delicious. One could eat at home, but there's a tastier world waiting out there. Likewise, at home, one has a

film on TV at the instant flick of a switch. But up on a screen a few miles down the road is size, sensation... and something new, which you have heard about maybe not just from your friends but also from your radio, newspaper, magazine or television.

Significantly this book's title *A Cinema Near You* was suggested by my daughter Helena after hearing the phrase so often while watching film commercials on television. There is an obvious irony in the film industry advertising the big screen on the small. The fact that it is selling the better viewing experience is proven, for one, by the complete lack of ads for TV at the cinema.

But the reason why the cinema will always have a future as a more satisfying and superior entertainment extends beyond the obvious screen size. Yes, the sheer size of the images makes a movie a more enveloping experience, and let us not forget the obvious point that movies have always been made for the cinema screen (and those that are not deserve to go straight to video hell). But, there are more subtle and significant pointers to the greater glory of going to the Pictures.

Ironically, a TV critic supplies the best argument I know against the watching of films on television. Craig Brown, writing in the *Sunday Times*, opened one of his reviews by expressing the point: 'Television is such a casual medium – flickering away in the corner, surrounded by furniture, interrupted by life – that it rarely holds your complete attention... even one's favourite programmes are hardly ever so compelling that the 'phone is left unanswered, the bottle unpoured, the conversation silenced.'

At the cinema, however, distractions are set at an absolute minimum. We can devote our minds totally to the movie on screen, and with modern projection systems providing superb quality of sound and vision, enjoyment is thus more total. Is it any wonder I hear people forever saying how disappointed they were by a film on TV?

Watching films on video can be worse, if you don't happen to get hold of the latest rental title in the first few weeks. You can usually recognise a regularly rented movie by the fuzzy picture and mushy sound (particularly bad news if Sylvester Stallone is in the lead). I remember that one evening at home watching *The Fugitive* was ruined by having to turn up the volume to a point of audibility that also brought on high levels of hiss and a certain wife consistently calling for clarification – "WHAT did he say?" (and Harrison Ford does not mumble). Fortunately, I had already seen it at the cinema.

Now, I love my wife's company, but watching a movie with her alone in our room bears no comparison with a full cinema house. This is possibly the most persuasive argument for seeing a movie at the cinema: the sheer thrill of seeing it with an audience. I am forever frustrated at having to watch most movies with nothing other than a notebook to accompany me. So, I always look forward to my Guild of Regional Film Writers' Cinema Days events (an opportunity to view over a dozen forthcoming films over three and a half days) as one can feel the tingle of pleasure at the certain knowledge that a certain film is either as good as you have heard, or better. Or, better still, you feel a surge of excitement that the film you knew nothing about turns out to be a rare treat, and approval is signalled by applause at the close.

I still cherish the time when, having missed the preview screening of *True Lies* owing to a holiday, I went with my brother-in-law, Tim, to a normal evening screening. The auditorium was packed, the atmosphere was electric, and every astounding stunt-filled slice of action was greeted with gasps, whoops and wails. A welcome pint up the road where we mulled over the main points of action, and the evening was complete. It is an altogether different and equally as satisfying an occasion when you see a great comedy. At a recent public screening of *The Birdcage*, one could palpably feel that the chuckles, giggles and side-splitting laughter had become infectious. Whoever said that 'laughter is a communal experience' must be a cinema-goer.

This is why cinema has endured and will continue to prosper. Even now, when promoting cinema on the radio or in the local paper, (or even in conversation about the subject), I find myself quoting the simple yet salient slogan of British Film Year: 'Cinema – the best place to see a film'. There is a definite irony here. British Film Year was launched in 1984, with the aim of increasing domestic cinema attendances. It worked, to a small extent. But, arguably, as in the last two World Wars, Britain watched as the Americans moved in to complete the job. In 1985, Britain saw its first multiplex and, from there on, audience figures were set to spiral.

More than a decade on, we can celebrate cinema's centenary with considerable cheer. Expansion is the order of the day. Steve Knibbs of the UCI states that: "The next phase of building will also see the now traditional multiplex move on to its next stage of development. As our customers become more demanding and as competition increases, it will no longer be enough to just offer multiple screens and a concession stand." Steve is referring to cinemas being an integral part of an 'entertainment and retail evolution'.

Will the UCI expand its own site in Derby? Will National Amusements develop its Derby operation in some way? Could Derbyshire even see another multiplex being built as part of a new out-of-town retail/leisure park? After all, Virgin Cinemas is now out there, having taken over MGM. By 1997, Warner Bros Theatres is set to become the leading multiplex circuit in the UK. There are rumblings of a cinema complex sprouting up in the Matlock area, as part of a giant shopping park. The expectations of a Derby Metro move to the site of Derbyshire's first super-cinema (the Gaumont) are tremendously exciting, particularly for the way it would merge cinema's historical heritage with its contemporary values and its future prospects.

National Amusements (who run Showcase Cinemas), is confident that this country has become just that – a national amusement. I share its optimism:

'Cinema has always faced an onslaught of new entertainment technologies that have been positioned as poised to replace the Silver Screen. But as we celebrate 100 years of cinema, we see that attendance is up, the number of films in production worldwide is up, the number of cinemas under construction worldwide is up. There is every indication that 100 years from now, the Silver Screen will still be the only satisfying, and most popular, way to enjoy a motion picture.'

Hear, hear... See you at the movies...

Fade Out

There is nothing in my opinion that can ever match the compulsive magic of that big screen in a darkened auditorium. No interactive game, however demanding, no virtual reality, however absorbing, will ever surpass the heightened and unique pleasure we derive from experiencing laughter, love, fear – and all of the emotions of which we are capable – in the company of other human beings.

Lord Attenborough, from a speech commemorating the launch of 'Cinema 100'

AS with any book of social history, which relies on research and reminiscence (and the author having all the time in the world), I cannot guarantee that every memory is strictly accurate. Because of the passage of time and the vicissitudes of the mind, some recollections may be slightly erroneous, exaggerated or romanticised, and I have not been able to confirm every single fact, story and account. Some have been impossible to verify. I would be happy to hear from you if you feel an entry here needs correcting.

I would be even happier if you feel you can add some weft to the tapestry. In fact, I am sure there are scores of stories that could further enrich what is already here. I have decided not to feel frustration at the letters that may arrive after the publication of this book which contain a wealth of new, untold and wondrous stories. Indeed, I am excited by the prospect of including them in a further, more expansive edition, which could appropriately be published when the multiplexes celebrate a decade in Derby, in 1998. So, bombard me with more.

Here's looking at you, kid... I think this is just the beginning of a beautiful friendship.

Bibliography

Atwell, David: *Cathedrals Of The Movies, A History of British Cinemas and Their Audiences*, London Architectural Press, 1980.

Betts, Ernest: *The Film Business*, George Allen & Unwin, 1973.

Box, Kathleen: *The Cinema And The Public – An Enquiry into Cinema-Going Habits and Expenditure Made in 1946*, HMSO, 1947.

Christian, Roy & Heath John: *Yesterday's Town*, Barracuda Books, 1985.

Dewe, Tom: *Censored – What They Didn't Allow You To See, And Why: The Story of Film Censorship in Britain*, Chatto & Windus, 1994.

Field, Audrey: *Picture Palace*, Gentry Books, 1974.

Halliwell, Leslie: *Seats In All Parts*, Grafton Books, 1985.

Hopkins, Harry: *The New Look – Social History of the Forties and Fifties in Britain*, Secker & Warburg, 1963.

Lawrence, D.H.: *The Lost Girl*, Penguin, 1950.

Lewis, C.Day: *Newsreel*, 1938.

Low, Rachael (and Manvell, Roger): *The History Of British Film Vol I 1896-1906*, Allen & Unwin, 1948; *Vol II 1906-1914*, Allen & Unwin, 1949; *Vol III 1914-1918*, Allen & Unwin 1950; *Vol IV 1918-1929*, Allen & Unwin, 1971.

Mayer, J.P.: *Sociology Of The Film*, Faber, 1946.

Mayer, J.P.: *British Cinemas And Their Audiences*, Dobson, 1948.

Morton Shand, P.: *Modern Theatres and Cinemas – The Architecture of Pleasure*, Ideal Kinema, 1931.

Norman, Barry: *Talking Pictures – The Story of Hollywood*, BBC Hodder & Stoughton, 1987. Extracts reprinted by permission of Curtis Brown Ltd on behalf of Barry Norman. Copyright: Barry Norman 1987.

Nutt, Graham: *Tuppenny Rush – The Arrival of Cinemas And Film-Making In Swadlincote*, Trent Valley Publications, 1992.

O'Brien, Margaret, & Eyles, Allen (Eds): *Enter The Dreamhouse – Memories of Cinemas in South London from the Twenties to the Sixties*, Museum of The Moving Image/British Film Institute, 1993.

Perry, George: *The Great British Picture Show*, Michael Joseph, 1985.

Robertson, Patrick: *The Guinness Book of Movies Facts and Feats*, Guinness, 1993.

Roddis, David: *The Thrill of It All – The Story of the Cinema in Ilkeston and the Erewash Valley*, 1993.

Sexton, R. & Betts, B.F.: *American Theaters Today*, 1927.

Sharp, Dennis: *Picture Palaces*, Evelyn, 1969.

Stead, Peter: *Film and the Working Class*, Routledge, 1989.

Williamson, James: (Unpublished) *Notebooks*, 1926.

Winfield, Sam: *Dream Palaces of Derby*, 1995 (published by author).

Periodicals and Newspapers
Ashbourne News Telegraph; *Bioscope*; Braithwaite, P: *The Cinema Industry 1950-1970 And Its Customers*, thesis submitted for a CNAA Degree in Business Studies, 1970; *Derby Evening Telegraph* (formerly the *Derby Daily Telegraph*); *Derby Express*; *Derby Mercury*; *Derby Trader*; *Derbyshire Advertiser*; *Design and Construction*; England, Leonard: *What The Cinema Means To The British Public*, 1949; Horne, Mary: *The Cinema In The Village*, *Home & Country*, 1919; *Ilkeston Advertiser*; *Kine Weekly*; *Kinematograph & Lantern Weekly* (now *Kine Weekly*); *Sunday Times*; *The Times*; *Visual Education*; Wilkinson, F.: *The Cinema as a Social Force*, October 1958.

Index